SEARS

MODERN HOMES

MARTINO FINE BOOKS

EASTFORD, CT

2021

Bibliographical Note

This edition is an unabridged republication of *Modem Homes*, originally published by Sears, Roebuck and Co., Chicago, Illinois, 1913. In the present volume, the color illustrations in the original edition have been reproduced in black-and-white, and the inside cover illustrations have been moved to pp. 125 and 126.

Martino Fine Books
P.O. Box 913,
Eastford, CT 06242 USA

ISBN   978-1-68422-532-3

Copyright 2021
Martino Fine Books

Cover Design Tiziana Matarazzo

Printed in the United States of America On 100% Acid-Free Paper

Are You Looking for a Home?

THIS book has solved the home building problem for thousands of people. No matter whether you are looking for an imposing residence, a modern bungalow or a cozy cottage you will surely be able to make a suitable choice from the 112 designs illustrated, described and priced in the following pages. If you have made up your mind to break away from the rent paying class this year and join the independent army of home owners, you could not possibly have made a better beginning than by getting this Book of Modern Homes. You do not have to pay a penny for architectural services. We give you free, plans, specifications and an itemized bill of materials of the kind that would cost you about $100.00 from a local architect. For our offer of free plans see page 3. We furnish materials for the house of your choice, from the foundation to the roof, with the exception of cement, brick and plaster, which we do not furnish. Our materials are guaranteed to be the best of their kind on the market, insuring a permanent building.

The pictures shown above were copied from actual photographs of houses built according to our plans and with our materials. The owners will tell you that we saved them from 25 to 50 per cent and gave them grades of material that they could not possibly duplicate in the local market. (See pages 124 and 125 for letters from our customers and pictures of their houses.)

Stop Paying Rent.　　Quit Building "Castles in the Air."　　Build a Real Castle — A Home of Your Own.

If you keep on paying rent for another year you will not be any better equipped to start building than you are at this moment. On the other hand, you will have wasted the whole year's rent, which you ought to have applied on the cost of your own building. Why look around for a new flat or a temporary cottage from which you will very probably move in six or twelve months' time? Why not have a place where you will have plenty of room for the children to play, where there will be no embarrassing protests from your neighbors in the flat below? You have seen the signs on buildings reading "Tenants with children not desired." Does not this condition of affairs make it necessary for you to make up your own mind NOW that you will build your own home? Don't waste your time dreaming of the home you are going to have "sometime." Build it this year.

Build Now.　We Have the House You Want at the Price You Want to Pay.

If you really want a home, if you want to construct it of first class materials and wish to save at least $500.00 on the job, sit down today and write us for full particulars regarding our building proposition. Remember that money alone never built anything, whereas Resolution, Grit and Co-operation have improved entire sections and created big cities. We will show you how to secure the house of your choice if you will simply take the trouble to consult us. First make your selection of a house from this book, then send for plans, specifications and bill of materials (see page 3), and when you have studied them thoroughly we will be at your service for any particular information you may desire. We have helped thousands of people to become home owners. Let Us Help You.

96N.3.10.28.13.15

—1—

SEARS, ROEBUCK AND CO., CHICAGO, ILLINOIS

Your Choice of Over One Hundred Modern Homes

Plans Drawn by Licensed Architects of Wide Experience, Embodying All the Very Newest Ideas in Convenient and Artistic Arrangement

HUNDREDS of our customers during the past year selected homes from former editions of this book, built them or had them built by contract according to our plans and with our materials, and they saved from $500.00 to $1,500.00 each. These big savings have made them our best advertisers. Read the letters from customers on page 124 and see the pictures of their homes on page 125.

We satisfy our customers by furnishing the highest grades of material at lower prices than are asked anywhere else. They all endorse our methods and recommend them to others. While our estimates, including labor, on the houses in this book are considered very low, many of our customers have built according to our plans for even less than our figure. Furthermore, our proposition is different from any other, because we guarantee every dollar's worth of building material we sell. Should we fail to please you, you take no risk; you are at liberty to return all or any part of the material purchased from us which proves unsatisfactory and we will cheerfully return your money and any freight charges you have paid.

Consider carefully the houses shown in this book, study the floor plans of each, and when you find a house that appeals to you write for the plans, specifications and itemized bill of materials in accordance with our offers on page 3. Our plans or blue prints are much more carefully drawn than the plans provided by the average architect who charges from $100.00 to $200.00 for his services, ours being accurate and correct in detail. They are the work of architects of wide experience; the typewritten specifications thoroughly cover the method of constructing the house, insuring a first-class job. The bill of materials, which is a part of our plans, but which is never supplied by the average architect, carefully describes every item of building material of every description; in fact, this bill of materials is our bid. We will agree to furnish all materials for the amount specified in our bill of materials, which we guarantee against advance for sixty days after you receive the plans.

The cost of the original tracings, the writing of the original specifications and bill of materials for each of the houses in this book is from $100.00 to $200.00, varying according to size and style of the house. From the original tracing sheets we have reproduced a large number of plans and have printed a supply of bills of materials. We are offering them to our customers on a very liberal plan, enabling you to get plans of the very highest class, with specifications and bills of materials which originally cost $100.00 to $200.00, for $1.00 in cash or free of charge, as per our offers on page 3.

Our object in making such a liberal offer to the public is to quickly convince prospective builders that we can make them big savings in building material. While one might possibly overlook the fact that we can make him a saving of a few dollars on any one item, he cannot overlook the fact that we can save him $500.00 to $1,500.00 or more on a building. This Book of Modern Homes puts the matter of our money saving prices so forcibly before the prospective builder that he cannot overlook the great advantages in buying mill work and all building materials from us. You can tell at once just what the building material will cost you. It furnishes convincing proof that we can make you a very large saving.

There is no mystery in our prices; they are simply the natural result of our well known policy of merchandising, selling goods at prices based on the actual cost to produce with but one profit added. The application of this principle to mill work, lumber, lath, shingles and other building material—a line on which everybody has been obliged to pay big prices heretofore because of market conditions, monopolies, manufacturers' agreements or local associations made for the purpose of keeping up prices—enables us to make you a large saving, while at the same time we are able to give you absolutely the finest quality throughout. Every item of building material we handle is backed by our unlimited guarantee of satisfaction or money returned.

On pages 112 to 116 we show designs for barn plans.

We Want to Explain Our Object in Making the Two Above Liberal Offers

Considering the original cost of these blue prints, specifications and bills of materials, even though they were duplicated in vast quantities, they could not be disposed of profitably according to our offers. Our only object is to convince you that we can save you from $150.00 on a house usually costing $600.00 to build to $1,500.00 on a house usually costing $6,000.00 to build. We want nothing more than the opportunity to place these plans, specifications and bill of materials in the hands of anyone intending to build, or in the hands of any contractor, builder or carpenter, because we know that as they furnish a basis of comparison for qualities and prices with the qualities and prices of material furnished by dealers elsewhere, we will get the orders. Take advantage of either of these liberal offers. You cannot fully appreciate the great saving we are able to make you on building materials until you receive a complete set of our plans, specifications and bill of materials, for **they are the proof.** They will convince anyone.

All prices quoted in this book are F. O. B. the cars at our factories or yards.

Lumber is quoted F. O. B. the cars at our yards in Southern Illinois.

Mill work and finish are quoted F. O. B. the cars at our mills in Eastern Iowa or Southern Ohio.

Hardware, paints and other accessories are quoted F. O. B. the cars at Chicago, Ill.

On request we will gladly quote you prices delivered to your station.

IMPORTANT

Unless otherwise instructed we will ship lumber, nails and outside frames first, allowing sufficient time for these items to reach you so that you can get the building enclosed and the roof on, thus giving you some place to protect the inside finish, doors, etc., from the weather when they reach you.

To Find the House You Are Going to Build

When you have finally decided upon the design of house best suited for your requirements, you will, no doubt, have occasion very frequently to refer to the page on which it is illustrated and described. The following table has been compiled for your convenience.

MODERN HOME No. 187

**SEE THIS HOUSE IN COLORS
ON FRONT COVER PAGE.**

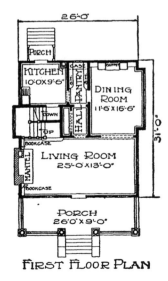

FIRST FLOOR PLAN

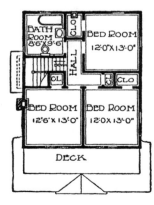

SECOND FLOOR PLAN

—4—

$1,273.00

For $1,273.00 we will furnish all the material to build this Seven-Room House, consisting of Lumber, Lath, Shingles, Mill Work, Ceiling, Flooring, Finishing Lumber, Mantel, Sideboard, Building Paper, Pipe, Gutter, Sash Weights, Hardware and Painting Material. NO EXTRAS, as we guarantee enough material at the above price to build this house according to our plans.

By allowing a fair price for labor, cement, stone and plaster, which we do not furnish, this house can be built for $3,120.00, including all material and labor.

For Our Offer of Free Plans See Page 3.

THIS house has been pronounced by building experts to be an architectural triumph. When built on a lot of proper size and painted in refined contrasting colors its effect is strikingly attractive. The cobblestone foundation and chimney, the unique arrangement of the shingles used for siding and the stonekote panels, make this house stand out with an air of distinction among high class buildings. The arrangement of the rooms leaves nothing to be desired from the standpoint of light and ventilation. The living room extends the entire width of the house, measuring 25x13 feet. Note the balcony or deck on the second floor and the double bay window over the side entrance.

First Floor.

The large living room is lighted by four windows in the front and two on the right hand side. A cased opening leads to the dining room, in which a spacious and graceful buffet with seats on each side is the principal attraction. Floors and trim in both rooms are of clear oak. An oak stairway leads from the living room to the second floor, the circular landing and handsome newels adding considerably to its appearance. In the kitchen the floor is maple with yellow pine trim. A good size pantry, approached both from the kitchen and dining room, is provided with shelves and pantry case.

Second Floor.

All bedrooms and bathroom have maple flooring with yellow pine trim. Bedrooms have good size closets and are well lighted. An 18x24-inch opening leads to the attic.

For size of rooms see floor plans.

Built on a stone foundation and excavated under the entire house. We furnish *A* cedar shingles for the roof and sides of the second story; framing timbers of the best quality yellow pine. All windows glazed with "A" quality glass.

Height of Ceilings.

Basement, 7 feet from floor to joists with cement floor.
First floor, 9 feet from floor to ceiling.
Second floor, 8 feet 6 inches from floor to ceiling.

Painted with two coats of the best paint outside, one coat of shingle stain for shingle siding, varnish and wood filler for interior finish.

This house can be built on a lot 32 feet wide.

Complete Warm Air Heating Plant, for soft coal, extra	$ 88.26
Complete Warm Air Heating Plant for hard coal, extra	90.42
Complete Steam Heating Plant, extra	191.90
Complete Hot Water Heating Plant, extra	243.39
Complete Plumbing Outfit, extra	120.45
Acetylene Lighting Plant, extra	48.70

**SEARS, ROEBUCK
AND CO.**   **CHICAGO,
ILLINOIS**

MODERN HOME No. 167

This house has been built at Seymour, Conn., Bloomington, Ill., Germania, Iowa, Indianapolis, Ind., Bay City, Mich., Lake View, N. Y., Geneva, Ohio, Rennerdale, Penn., Crosby, Texas, Roanoke, Va., and several other cities.

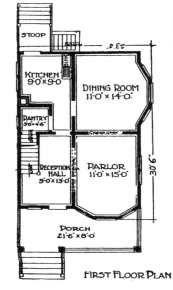

FIRST FLOOR PLAN

KITCHEN 9'0"x9'0"
DINING ROOM 11'0" x 14'0"
PANTRY 5'0"x4'6"
RECEPTION HALL 9'0"x13'0"
PARLOR 11'0" x 15'0"
PORCH 21'-6"x8'-0"
STOOP
23'-0"
30'-0"

SAVED $250.00.

Pittsfield, Mass.

Sears, Roebuck and Co.,
Chicago, Ill.

Gentlemen:—I am now living in my new house built from your plan No. 167 and I can safely say that by my buying all my lumber from you for finishing I have saved $250.00. I bought a complete hot air outfit from you and not counting my work it cost me only $10.00 to have it installed. I cheerfully recommend your fair dealings and good quality of goods to those wishing to build.   Yours truly,

WALTER H. SMITH.

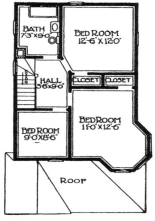

BATH 7'3"x9'6"
BED ROOM 12'-6" X 12'0"
HALL 5'6"x9'0"
CLOSET CLOSET
BED ROOM 11'0"x12'-6"
BED ROOM 9'0"X8'6"
ROOF

SECOND FLOOR PLAN
—5—

$823.00

For $823.00 we will furnish all the material to build this Eight-Room House, consisting of Mill Work, Flooring, Ceiling, Siding, Finishing Lumber, Building Paper, Pipe, Gutter, Sash Weights, Hardware, Painting Material, Lumber, Lath and Shingles. NO EXTRAS, as we guarantee enough material at the above price to build this house according to our plans.

By allowing a fair price for labor, cement, brick and plaster, which we do not furnish, this house can be built for about $1,584.00, including all material and labor.

For Our Offer of Free Plans See Page 3.

THIS is a well proportioned house which affords a great deal of room at a low cost. It is very popular in all sections of the country. Our price for all of the material required in its construction will enable you to make a substantial saving. Read Mr. Walter H. Smith's letter printed on this page, proving a saving of $250.00 on an $800.00 order.

First Floor.

A bevel plate glass front door, 3x7 feet, opens from the porch into the reception hall. In this hall there is an open yellow pine stairway leading to the second floor. A cased opening leads from the hall into the parlor and another cased opening from the parlor into the dining room. The kitchen has a good size pantry. Please note that we furnish colored leaded art glass sash for the hall. We also furnish a crystal leaded front window for the parlor. Interior doors are made of clear yellow pine with clear grade yellow pine trim, such as casing, baseboard and molding. Inside cellar stairs directly under the main stairs lead to the basement.

Second Floor.

All doors and trim on this floor are of yellow pine. The three bedrooms and bathroom can be entered direct from the hall, and all rooms have an abundance of light and air.

Painted two coats outside; color to suit. Varnish and wood filler for two coats of interior finish. Cost of paint, varnish and wood filler is included in above price. If you have a house of this size that needs repainting, we will sell the outside paint (two coats) and shingle stain in the color combination shown for only $26.16.

Built on a concrete block foundation, frame construction, sided with cypress narrow bevel edge siding and has a cedar shingle roof.

Excavated basement under the entire house, 7 feet from floor to joists, with cement floor. First floor, 9 feet from floor to ceiling; second floor, 8 feet from floor to ceiling.

This house can be built on a lot 28 feet wide.

Complete Warm Air Heating Plant, for soft coal, extra	$ 75.28
Complete Warm Air Heating Plant, for hard coal, extra	78.52
Complete Steam Heating Plant, extra	179.95
Complete Hot Water Heating Plant, extra	205.72
Complete Plumbing Outfit, extra	122.81
Acetylene Lighting Plant, extra	48.70

SEARS, ROEBUCK AND CO.   **CHICAGO, ILLINOIS**

MODERN HOME No. 145

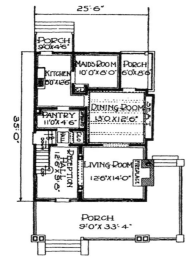

FIRST FLOOR PLAN

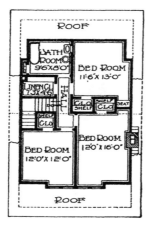

SECOND FLOOR PLAN

—6—

$1,294.00

For $1,294.00 we will furnish all of the material to build this Eight-Room House, consisting of Lumber, Lath, Shingles, Mill Work, Ceiling, Flooring, Finishing Lumber, Brick Mantel, Building Paper, Pipe, Gutter, Sash Weights, Hardware and Painting Material. NO EXTRAS, as we guarantee enough material at the above price to build this house according to our plans.

By allowing a fair price for labor, cement, brick and plaster, which we do not furnish, this house can be built complete for about $3,050.00, including all material and labor.

For Our Offer of Free Plans See Page 3.

MODERN HOME No. 145 is a Colonial house with bungalow effect. Note the arrangement by which the monotony of the long sloping roof is broken, permitting four Colonial windows, providing the two front bedrooms of the second floor with an abundance of light. The cobblestone outside chimney and the clusters of columns on the front porch with a bay window in the dining room, are features that will be sure to please. The porch extends across the entire width of the house and along the right side past the exposed cobblestone chimney. We recommend applying the shingles on the sides in alternate rows 2 inches and 6 inches to the weather, as shown in the illustration.

First Floor.

The front door opens into a large reception hall, 12 feet 6 inches by 9 feet 8 inches, in which there is an open stairway leading to the second floor. A brick mantel is specified for the living room and a beamed ceiling for the dining room. Floors and Craftsman trim in the living room, dining room and hall are of clear oak; maple floor in the kitchen, pantry and maid's room, with yellow pine Craftsman trim. A rear porch, 6 feet by 8 feet 6 inches, is approached from the dining room. By this arrangement the dining room is lighted from the rear, as well as by means of the bay window on the right.

Second Floor.

Floors and trim for the three bedrooms and bathroom are No. 1 grade yellow pine. All three bedrooms are of good size, well lighted and thoroughly ventilated. A feature of the second floor which will commend itself to the housewife is the linen closet, 7 feet 3 inches by 4 feet 6 inches.

For size of rooms see floor plans.

Built on a concrete foundation and excavated under the entire house. We furnish *A* cedar shingles for roof and shingle siding; framing timbers of the best quality yellow pine. All windows glazed with "A" quality glass.

Height of Ceilings.

Basement, 7 feet from floor to joists, with cement floor.
First floor, 9 feet from floor to ceiling.
Second floor, 8 feet 6 inches from floor to ceiling.
Painted with two coats of best paint outside; one coat of shingle stain for shingle siding; varnish and wood filler for interior finish. Cost of paint, varnish, wood filler and shingle stain is included in above price. If you have a house of this size that needs repainting, we will sell the outside paint (two coats) and shingle stain in the color combination shown for only $40.82.

This house can be built on a lot 37 feet wide.

Complete Warm Air Heating Plant, for soft coal, extra	$ 88.33
Complete Warm Air Heating Plant, for hard coal, extra	90.49
Complete Steam Heating Plant, extra	210.70
Complete Hot Water Heating Plant, extra	251.13
Complete Plumbing Outfit, extra	137.07
Acetylene Lighting Plant, extra	49.50

SEARS, ROEBUCK AND CO. **CHICAGO, ILLINOIS**

MODERN HOME No. 202

$1,389.00

For $1,389.00 we will furnish all of the material to build this Eight-Room House, consisting of Mill Work, Flooring, Ceiling, Finishing Lumber, Building Paper, Pipe, Gutter, Sash Weights, Hardware, Medicine Case, Painting Material, Lumber, Lath and Shingles. NO EXTRAS, as we guarantee enough material at the above price to build this house according to our plans.

By allowing a fair price for labor, stone, cement and plaster, which we do not furnish, this house can be built for about $2,990.00, including all material and labor.

For Our Free Offer of Plans See Page 3.

IF YOU are looking for a Colonial house with twentieth century improvements our Modern Home No. 202 will be an excellent selection. The combination porch and pergola is a feature that will at once attract your attention. The quadruple Colonial windows on the second story afford an abundance of light for the two front bedrooms. The massive Colonial columns lend an air of strength and durability to the whole building, while the Colonial effect is further strengthened by the use of shingles for siding.

First Floor.

The entrance to the living room is from the porch on the left. This living room has a beamed ceiling; oak floor and Craftsman trim. A partly open stairway leads from the living room to the second floor. To the right of the living room a den or library is approached by a cased opening with heavy colonnades. A feature of the den is the bay, lighted by a triple window. Floor and trim in this room are of clear oak. The dining room has oak floor. Craftsman trim, plate rail and beamed ceiling, with a bay window and a seat extending clear across the bay, similar to the arrangement of the bay window in the den. In the kitchen the floor is of maple with oak trim. The floors for the pergola, side and rear porches are of solid weather resisting fir.

Second Floor.

The floors and Craftsman trim for the entire second floor are of clear yellow pine. Each bedroom is of good size and well lighted and all are provided with closets. A medicine case is specified for the bathroom. Between the two front bedrooms there is a convenient dressing room with mirror door.
For size of rooms see floor plans.

Built on a concrete foundation and excavated under the entire house. We furnish *A* cedar shingles for roof and sides; framing timbers of the best quality of yellow pine. All windows glazed with "A" quality glass.

Height of Ceiling.

Basement, 7 feet from floor to joist, with cement floor.
First floor, 9 feet from floor to ceiling.
Second floor, 8 feet 6 inches from floor to ceiling.
Painted with two coats of best paint outside, one coat of shingle stain for shingle siding, varnish and wood filler for interior finish. Cost of paint, varnish, wood filler and shingle stain is included in above price. If you have a house of this size that needs repainting, we will sell the outside paint (two coats) and shingle stain in the color combination shown for only $36.09.

This house can be built on a lot 48 feet wide.

Complete Warm Air Heating Plant, for soft coal, extra	$ 93.31
Complete Warm Air Heating Plant, for hard coal, extra	95.47
Complete Steam Henting Plant, extra	218.65
Complete Hot Water Heating Plant, extra	274.30
Complete Plumbing Outfit, extra	119.00
Acetylene Lighting Plant, extra	51.90

SEARS, ROEBUCK AND CO. **CHICAGO, ILLINOIS**

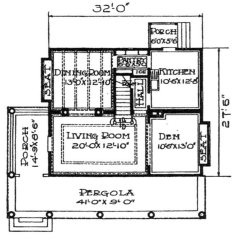

FIRST FLOOR PLAN

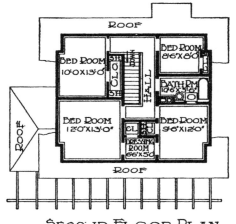

SECOND FLOOR PLAN

MODERN HOME No. 181

$757⁰⁰

For $757.00 we will furnish all the material to build this Six-Room House, consisting of Lumber, Lath, Shingles, Mill Work, Flooring, Ceiling, Siding, Finishing Lumber, Building Paper, Pipe, Gutter, Sash Weights, Hardware and Painting Material. NO EXTRAS, as we guarantee enough material at the above price to build this house according to our plans.

By allowing a fair price for labor, cement, brick and plaster, which we do not furnish, this house can be built for about $1,257.00, including all material and labor.

For Our Offer of Free Plans See Page 3.

A NEAT and roomy house at a very low price. Was designed with two objects in view, economy of floor space and low cost. Contains six good rooms and bathroom. Porch is 22 feet by 8 feet. Front door opens into the living room which is 16 feet 1 inch long by 11 feet 6 inches wide. A door in the living room opens onto the closed stairway leading to the second floor. The dining room is separated from the living room by a large cased opening which makes practically one large room of these two rooms. Has kitchen and good size pantry. Entrance to the basement is through this pantry.

First Floor.

The front door is made of white pine, 1¾ inches thick. Inside doors are made of the best grade yellow pine and are of the five-cross panel design with yellow pine trim to match. Floors in living room and dining room are made of clear oak; the kitchen and pantry floors are maple. All floors on the first floor are laid over yellow pine floor lining.

Second Floor.

The stairway from the first floor opens into a hall on the second floor from which any one of the three bedrooms or bathroom may be entered. All three bedrooms are well lighted and each has a good size clothes closet.

All doors on the second floor are the best quality yellow pine of the four-panel design with yellow pine trim to match. Floors are of the best quality yellow pine.

Built on a concrete foundation and excavated under entire house. We furnish clear cypress siding and cedar shingles; framing timbers of the best quality yellow pine. All windows glazed with "A" quality glass.

Height of Ceilings.

Basement, 7 feet floor to joists, with cement floor.
First floor, 9 feet from floor to ceiling.
Second floor, 8 feet 6 inches from floor to ceiling.

Painted with two coats of best paint outside, varnish and wood filler for interior finish. Cost of paint, varnish, wood filler and shingle stain is included in above price. If you have a house of this size that needs repainting, we will sell the outside paint (two coats) and shingle stain in the color combination shown for only $23.88.

This house can be built on a lot 28 feet wide.

Complete Warm Air Heating Plant, for soft coal, extra	$ 69.12
Complete Warm Air Heating Plant, for hard coal, extra	72.76
Complete Steam Heating Plant, extra	153.80
Complete Hot Water Heating Plant, extra	184.20
Complete Plumbing Outfit, extra	120.40
Acetylene Lighting Plant, extra	47.90

SEARS, ROEBUCK AND CO.　　　　　**CHICAGO, ILLINOIS**

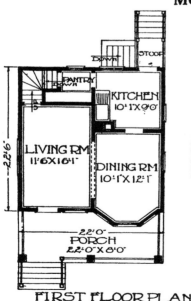

FIRST FLOOR PLAN

This house has been built at Gary, Ind., Hammond, Ind., Laporte, Ind., Morristown, N. J., Richmond Hill, N. Y., Hempstead, N. Y., Galeton, Penn., New Castle, Penn., and West Point, Va.

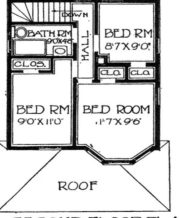

SECOND FLOOR PLAN

$1,057 00

For $1,057.00 we will furnish all the material to build this Eight-Room House, consisting of Mill Work, Ceiling, Siding, Flooring, Finishing Lumber, Building Paper, Pipe, Gutter, Sash Weights, Hardware, Painting Material, Lumber, Lath and Shingles. NO EXTRAS, as we guarantee enough material at the above price to build this house according to our plans.

By allowing a fair price for labor, cement, brick and plaster, which we do not furnish, this house can be built for about $2,000.00, including all material and labor.

For Our Offer of Free Plans See Page 3.

THIS modern type of residence can be built at a surprisingly low cost. Read Mr. Johnson's letter printed on this page, showing a saving of about $800.00. Modern Home No. 114 is a high class house in every sense of the word. It has a large front porch, 24 feet long. The combination of hip and gable roof and Colonial porch columns give it a massive and refined appearance.

First Floor.

The door from the vestibule opens into the large sitting room. Between this room and the dining room we specify a pair of double sliding doors. There is a large cased opening between parlor and sitting room. Stairs from the dining room lead to the second floor and directly under the main stairs is a cellar stairway to the basement. Note that the kitchen is lighted by windows on two sides. The chamber on this floor can be converted into a library or sewing room if desired. Clear yellow pine five-cross panel doors for all rooms on this floor with clear yellow pine casing, baseboard and molding to match. Clear grade yellow pine flooring.

Second Floor.

There are three large bedrooms with closets, closet off the hall, bathroom and stair hall on this floor. All doors, flooring and trim are of clear yellow pine.

Built on a concrete block foundation, frame construction, sided with narrow bevel edge cypress siding and has Oriental Asphalt Shingle roof, guaranteed for fifteen years.

Painted two coats outside; your choice of color. Varnish and wood filler for interior finish. Cost of paint, varnish and wood filler is included in above price. If you have a house of this size that needs repainting, we will sell the outside paint (two coats) in the color combination shown for only $19.22.

Excavated basement under the entire house, 7 feet from floor to joists. First floor, 9 feet 2 inches from floor to ceiling; second floor, 8 feet from floor to ceiling.

This house measures 26x46 feet and can be built on a lot 30 feet wide.

Complete Warm Air Heating Plant, for soft coal, extra.................$ 93.34
Complete Warm Air Heating Plant, for hard coal, extra.............. 95.39
Complete Steam Heating Plant, extra............................ 179.65
Complete Hot Water Heating Plant, extra........................ 232.98
Complete Plumbing Outfit, extra............................... 119.54
Acetylene Lighting Plant, extra............................... 51.10

SEARS, ROEBUCK AND CO.	CHICAGO, ILLINOIS

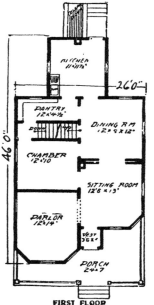

FIRST FLOOR

MODERN HOME No. 114

This house has been built at Norwalk, Conn., Joliet, Ill., Richvalley, Ind., Bedford, Iowa, Coldwater, Kan., Maple City, Mich., Sweet Springs, Mo., Weyerts, Neb., Elizabeth, N. J., Addison, N. Y., Sandusky, Ohio, Wooster, Ohio, Monongahela, Penn., Bennington, Vt., Racine, Wis., and other cities.

SAVED $800.00 ON MODERN HOME No. 114.

Roselle Park, N. J.
Sears, Roebuck and Co., Chicago, Ill.
Gentlemen:—I enclose herewith photograph of my house, the same which I built according to the general layout of plans No. 114. Am very glad to say that whatever I purchased from you for my house, which I think amounted to $800.00 or $900.00, has been found to be very satisfactory. I know that I could not have obtained the same material here for less than about twice the amount, considering quality. All transactions between you and me have been attended to promptly and fairly in every respect.
Your customer,
JOHN C. JOHNSON.

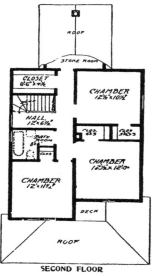

SECOND FLOOR

—9—

MODERN HOME No. 162.   Yellow Pine Finish.   Price, $883.00.
MODERN HOME No. 153.   Oak Finish, First Floor; Birch, Second Floor.   Price, $1,031.00.

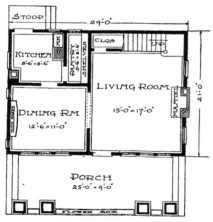

FIRST FLOOR

This house has been built at Washington, D. C., Caldwell, Idaho, Bloomington, Ill., Crystal Lake, Ill., Gary, Ind., New Haven, Ind., Pratt, Kan., Harrods Creek, Ky., Rochester, Minn., Pass Christian, Miss., New York, N. Y., Fargo, N. Dak., Siam, O., Sioux Falls, S. Dak., Madison, Wis., and other cities.

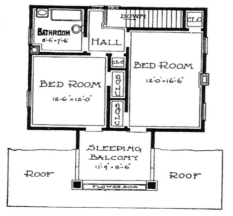

SECOND FLOOR

—10—

$883.00

For $883.00 we will furnish all the material to build this Five-Room Bungalow, consisting of Mill Work, Flooring, Ceiling, Siding, Finishing Lumber, Sideboard, Building Paper, Pipe, Gutter, Sash Weights, Hardware, Mantel, Painting Material, Lumber, Lath and Shingles and Best-of-all Felt Roofing for roof over Sleeping Balcony. NO EXTRAS, as we guarantee enough material at the above price to build this house according to our plans.

By allowing a fair price for labor, cement, brick and plaster, which we do not furnish, this house can be built for about $1,643.00, including all material and labor.

For Our Offer of Free Plans See Page 3.

A FIVE-ROOM bungalow of Craftsman style with front porch 25 feet long by 9 feet wide, and open air sleeping balcony 11 feet 9 inches by 8 feet 6 inches.

Front door opens into a large living room 17x15 feet, which has a quarter sawed oak mantel, staircase, closet under stairs. Living room has three front windows, also one window on each side of fireplace. Cased opening leads from living room to dining room. Dining room has sideboard facing the cased opening with leaded glass sash on each side, also three windows in the front. Plate rail around the entire room.

Double swinging door leads to kitchen, which has one window directly over the sink, another on the side. Pantry is convenient to kitchen or dining room.

For No. 162, first and second floor trimmed in yellow pine, we furnish front door 3x7 feet, 1¾ inches thick, with a long bevel plate glass. Inside doors are five-cross panel yellow pine. Clear yellow pine trim and flooring.

First Floor.

For No. 153 we furnish front door, also inside doors and moldings of clear red oak in the latest Craftsman design. Clear red oak flooring for the living room and dining room. Maple flooring for kitchen and pantry.

Second Floor.

No. 153 is trimmed in birch. We furnish front door leading to the balcony and inside doors and trim of birch, Craftsman design, and clear maple flooring.

Stairs on second floor are within arm's reach of either bedrooms or bathroom. One bedroom, 12 feet by 16 feet 6 inches, has two closets and door leading to sleeping balcony, also two windows on the side. Other bedroom, 12 feet 6 inches by 12 feet, has one closet and door leading to sleeping balcony, and window on the side.

Bathroom is 7 feet 6 inches by 8 feet 6 inches. Walls up to height of 4 feet 6 inches finished in cement and cut to imitate tile and white enamel. A linen closet in hall.

Built on a concrete block foundation, excavated basement under entire building. Frame construction and sided with clear red wood bevel siding. Shingled with *A* shingles. All framing lumber is No. 1 yellow pine.

Paint furnished for two coats outside, your choice of color. Varnish and wood filler for two coats, interior hard oil finish. Cost of paint, varnish, wood filler and shingle stain is included in above price. **If you have a house of this size that needs repainting, we will sell the outside paint (two coats) and shingle stain in the color combination shown for only $22.95.**

Basement has cement floor. Basement, 7 feet high from floor to joists.

First floor, 9 feet from floor to ceiling.

Second floor, 8 feet 6 inches from floor to ceiling.

We furnish our No. 153, which is the same as No. 162, with the exception that it is trimmed with clear Craftsman (oak first floor, birch second floor) and hardwood flooring as specified above. If you want this house trimmed in oak and birch send for plan No. 153.

This house can be built on a lot 35 feet wide.

Complete Warm Air Heating Plant, for soft coal, extra	$ 79.23
Complete Warm Air Heating Plant, for hard coal, extra	81.39
Complete Steam Heating Plant, extra	162.21
Complete Hot Water Heating Plant, extra	203.87
Complete Plumbing Outfit, extra	107.93
Acetylene Lighting Plant, extra	48.70

SEARS, ROEBUCK AND CO.   **CHICAGO, ILLINOIS**

MODERN HOME No. 172

This house has been built at Washington, D. C., Clinton, Ill., Evanston, Ill., Gary, Ind., Indianapolis, Ind., Whiteford, Md., New Bedford, Mass., Port Monmouth, N. J., Rochester, N. Y., McKeesport, Penn., Dallas, Texas, Pecos, Texas, Arlington, Va., Richmond, Va., Kenosha, Wis., and other cities.

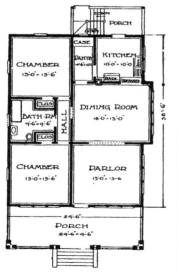

FLOOR PLAN

HERE IS A MAN WHO SAVED $775.00. READ HIS LETTER.

Pisgah, Iowa.

Sears, Roebuck and Co., Chicago, Ill.

Gentlemen:—I am sending a photograph of the house I bought of you. The house I bought last season is now completed and I am more than satisfied with the material you sent me. The house cost me $1,410.00 and I am satisfied it would have cost me $2,000.00 if I had bought the material in my own town. I also bought of you a car of lumber to build a barn in 1910, which cost me $315.00, but which would have cost me $500.00 if I bought the lumber here. A great many men have said it was the best lumber they had ever seen for the money.

Yours truly, JOHN S. BRYAN.

$975.00

For $975.00 we will furnish all the material to build this Five-Room Bungalow, consisting of Lumber, Lath, Shingles, Mill Work, Flooring, Ceiling, Siding, China Closet, Finishing Lumber, Building Paper, Pipe, Gutter, Sash Weights, Hardware and Painting Material. NO EXTRAS, as we guarantee enough material at the above price to build this house according to our plans.

By allowing a fair price for labor, stone, concrete, brick and plaster, which we do not furnish, this bungalow can be built for about $1,615.00, including all material and labor.

For Our Offer of Free Plans See Page 3.

A MODERN bungalow of frame construction. Considered the best five-room bungalow ever built at anywhere near this low price. The extra wide siding, the visible rafters over porches and eaves give a pleasing rustic effect. The roof is ornamented by an attractive dormer with three windows. The front and side of the bungalow are beautified by many triple and double windows, making every room light and airy. The porch extends across the front of the house and is 29 feet 6 inches wide by 9 feet 6 inches deep, making a cool and shady retreat. Porch columns are arranged in clusters, supported by a base which is sided with the same material as used on the rest of the house.

First Floor.

The front entrance leads directly into a large parlor, size 15 feet by 13 feet 6 inches. Directly to the rear is located a large dining room, separated from the parlor by cased opening. Dining room is 18 feet long by 13 feet wide and has a sideboard or china closet and is trimmed with plate rail. Directly to the rear of this room is the kitchen, size 10 feet by 10 feet, with a door leading to the rear porch. The pantry being located between the kitchen and dining room makes it possible to use this room as a butler's serving pantry and pantry combined. On the left side of the house are located two large and airy chambers, size 13 feet by 13 feet 6 inches, with closets, and conveniently located between the two chambers is a bathroom, size 9 feet 6 inches by 9 feet 6 inches.

For the front door we furnish a heavy bevel glass door. Interior doors are five-cross panel yellow pine with clear yellow pine casings and trim throughout. Interior can be finished either light or dark finish, dark finish preferred. Clear yellow pine for the floor for the entire house and porches.

Built on concrete foundation, basement excavated and has cement floors. It is frame construction sided with 10-inch No. 1 boards and has a cedar shingle roof.

Height of Ceiling.

Basement, 7 feet from floor to joists.
First floor, 9 feet from floor to ceiling.
A very pleasing effect can be had by painting siding brown, and shingles a moss green, all trimmings to be painted pure white, as shown in illustration.
Cost of paint, varnish, filler and shingle stain is included in above price. If you have a house of this size that needs repainting, we will sell the outside paint (two coats) and shingle stain in the color combination shown for only $32.44.

This house can be built on a lot 40 feet wide.

Complete Warm Air Heating Plant, for soft coal, extra	$ 60.44
Complete Warm Air Heating Plant, for hard coal, extra	63.35
Complete Steam Heating Plant, extra	156.51
Complete Hot Water Heating Plant, extra	206.28
Complete Plumbing Outfit, extra	117.83
Acetylene Lighting Plant, extra	47.25

SEARS, ROEBUCK AND CO.　　　　**CHICAGO, ILLINOIS**

MODERN HOME No. 217

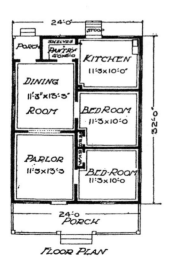

FLOOR PLAN

Over one hundred homes of this design built from our plans and with our materials, several of which can be found at La Porte, Ind. Also built at Gary, Ind., Aurora, Ill., Joliet, Ill., Middletown, N. Y., Boston, Mass., Sioux Falls, S. Dak., Newark, N. J., Alton, Texas, Bay Shore, N. Y., Delmar, Del., Jackson, Mich., and several other cities.

$543.00

For $543.00 we will furnish all the material to build this Five-Room Bungalow, consisting of Mill Work, Lumber, Lath, Shingles, Ceiling, Siding, Flooring, Finishing Lumber, Building Paper, Pipe, Gutter, Sash Weights, Hardware and Painting Material. NO EXTRAS, as we guarantee enough material at the above price to build this house according to our plans.

By allowing a fair price for labor, brick, cement and plaster, which we do not furnish, this house can be built for about $960.00, including all material and labor.

For Our Offer of Free Plans See Page 3.

THIS tasty design of bungalow is a winner for the price which we ask for all the materials required in its construction. As stated elsewhere on this page, over one hundred of these houses have been built. As will be seen by the floor plan, the porch extends over the entire front of the house. Five rooms with pantry and rear porch, all of good size, make this house quite convenient for the average family desiring to own a home for the smallest possible outlay.

First Floor.

The front door is of veneered oak 1¾ inches thick, glazed with sand blast design glass. The parlor and dining room are divided by a large cased opening. Each bedroom has a wardrobe or closet. All interior doors except wardrobe doors are of the five-panel design, made of the best quality yellow pine, with clear yellow pine trim. Floors are clear yellow pine. All rooms are well lighted by good size windows. Colonial windows for the front.

Built on a concrete block foundation; frame construction. Sided with narrow beveled clear cypress siding. Cedar shingles furnished for the roof. 8 feet 4 inches from floor to ceiling.

Paint furnished for two coats outside, varnish and wood filler for two coats of interior finish. Cost of paint, varnish, wood filler and shingle stain is included in above price. **If you have a house of this size that needs repainting, we will sell the outside paint (two coats) and shingle stain in the color combination shown for only $26.34.**

This house can be built on a lot 30 feet wide.

Complete Warm Air Heating Plant, for soft coal, extra	$ 49.58
Complete Warm Air Heating Plant, for hard coal, extra	52.64
Complete Steam Heating Plant, extra	111.05
Complete Hot Water Heating Plant, extra	139.80
Acetylene Lighting Plant, extra	46.75

SEARS, ROEBUCK AND CO.   **CHICAGO, ILLINOIS**

MODERN HOME No. 203

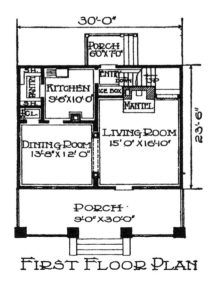

FIRST FLOOR PLAN

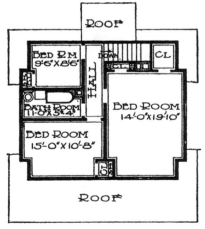

SECOND FLOOR PLAN

—13—

$1,089.00

For $1,089.00 we will furnish all of the material to build this Seven-Room House, consisting of Lumber, Lath, Shingles, Mill Work, Ceiling, Flooring, Finishing Lumber, Brick Mantel, Medicine Case, Building Paper, Pipe, Gutter, Sash Weights, Hardware and Painting Material. NO EXTRAS, as we guarantee enough material at the above price to build this house according to our plans.

By allowing a fair price for labor, cement, brick and plaster, which we do not furnish, this house can be built complete for about $2,200.00, including all material and labor.

For Our Offer of Free Plans See Page 3.

IN MODERN HOME No. 203 we have the Colonial design prevailing, massiveness and durability brought out very strongly by the cobblestone foundation and posts. The triple and double Colonial windows in the first and second stories not only insure an abundance of light, but add very much to the appearance of the house itself. The double roof effect is another unique arrangement, while the manner in which the shingles are applied to take the place of siding allows a pleasing contrast in paint and shingle stain.

First Floor.

A massive front door glazed with bevel plate glass leads from the front porch into the living room. This is an extra large room with an imposing brick mantel in the rear. The living room is separated from the dining room by a cased opening with two heavy colonnades. Floors and trim in both rooms are of clear oak. The front porch has a fir floor; maple floor and yellow pine trim in the kitchen. In addition to the triple window which lights the dining room, there are also two twelve-light Colonial windows on the left side. Two windows of similar design and size light the living room on the right side, so that both rooms are always well lighted and ventilated.

Second Floor.

The three bedrooms on this floor have yellow pine floors and trim; maple floor and yellow pine trim in the bathroom. The bedroom on the right is an extra large room, measuring 19 feet 10 inches by 14 feet, lighted by a double Colonial window on the front and by a twelve-light Colonial window on the right.

For size of other rooms see floor plans.

Built on a cobblestone foundation and excavated under the entire house. We furnish "A" cedar shingles for roof and sides; framing timbers of the best quality yellow pine. All windows glazed with "A" quality glass.

Height of Ceilings.

Basement, 7 feet from floor to joists, with cement floor.
First floor, 9 feet from floor to ceiling.
Second floor, 8 feet 6 inches from floor to ceiling.

Painted with two coats of best paint outside, one coat of shingle stain for shingle siding, varnish and wood filler for interior finish.

This house can be built on a lot 35 feet wide.

Complete Warm Air Heating Plant, for soft coal, extra	$ 94.61
Complete Warm Air Heating Plant, for hard coal, extra	96.77
Complete Steam Heating Plant, extra	182.80
Complete Hot Water Heating Plant, extra	232.26
Complete Plumbing Outfit, extra	117.73
Acetylene Lighting Plant, extra	48.70

SEARS, ROEBUCK AND CO.　　　**CHICAGO, ILLINOIS**

MODERN HOME No. 138

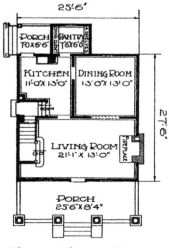

FIRST FLOOR PLAN

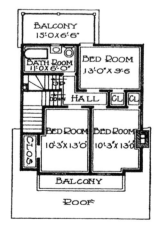

SECOND FLOOR PLAN

$1,047.00

For $1,047.00 we will furnish all the material to build this Six-Room House, consisting of Mill Work, Flooring, Ceiling, Finishing Lumber, Building Paper, Pipe, Gutter, Sash Weights, Hardware, Medicine Case, Painting Material, Lumber, Lath and Shingles. NO EXTRAS, as we guarantee enough material at the above price to build this house according to our plans.

By allowing a fair price for labor, stone, cement and plaster, which we do not furnish, this house can be built for about $2,825.90, including all material and labor.

For Our Offer of Free Plans See Page 3.

HOUSES like this with cobblestone foundation, porch, piers and chimney are becoming quite popular. In many sections of the East and West cobblestone of various tints can be procured at a nominal price (very often can be procured free of charge), and when used in a design such as our Modern Home No. 138 they add a beautiful effect to the building. The manner in which the shingles are applied to take the place of siding on this house lends an additional charm to its appearance. Each alternate row of shingles is laid 2 and 6 inches to the weather. When stained a suitable color they look very beautiful. Note the graceful columns on the spacious front porch and the open balcony overhead.

First Floor.

A veneered oak front door 1¾ inches thick, glazed with bevel plate glass, leads from the large porch into the living room, in which there is an open stairway to the second floor. A cased opening leads from the living room into the dining room. The floor in this room is clear oak, which is also specified for the trim. A massive brick mantel is seen to the right on entering the living room, on each side of which are leaded crystal glass windows. The dining room has oak floor and trim throughout, is well lighted and of generous size. A double swinging door leads from the dining room into the kitchen, which can also be entered from the grade entrance and the living room. The kitchen has maple floor and yellow pine trim. A good size pantry with 6-foot shelves is provided in the rear of the kitchen, also a china closet.

Second Floor.

Clear yellow pine flooring and trim are specified for the second floor, which contains three bedrooms and a bathroom. There is a front and a rear balcony on this floor. Each bedroom has a good size closet. There is a medicine case in the bathroom. Plenty of light and air in all rooms.

For size of rooms see floor plans.

Built on a stone foundation and excavated under the entire house. We furnish *A* cedar shingles for the roof and sides; framing timbers of the best quality yellow pine. All windows glazed with "A" quality glass.

Height of Ceilings.

Basement, 7 feet from floor to joist, with cement floor.
First floor, 9 feet from floor to ceiling.
Second floor, 8 feet 6 inches from floor to ceiling.

Painted with two coats of best paint outside, one coat of shingle stain for shingle siding, varnish and wood filler for interior finish.

This house can be built on a lot 30 feet wide.

Complete Warm Air Heating Plant, for soft coal, extra	$ 88.53
Complete Warm Air Heating Plant, for hard coal, extra	90.69
Complete Steam Heating Plant, extra	182.25
Complete Hot Water Heating Plant, extra	288.50
Complete Plumbing Outfit, extra	116.56
Acetylene Lighting Plant, extra	48.70

SEARS, ROEBUCK AND CO.   **CHICAGO, ILLINOIS**

$1,080⁰⁰

For $1,080.00 we will furnish all the material to build this Seven-Room House, consisting of Mill Work, Buffet, Medicine Case, Pantry Case, Ceiling, Siding, Flooring, Finishing Lumber, Building Paper, Pipe, Gutter, Sash Weights, Hardware, Painting Material, Lumber, Lath and Shingles. NO EXTRAS, as we guarantee enough material at the above price to build this house according to our plans.

By allowing a fair price for labor, cement, brick and plaster, which we do not furnish, this house can be built for about $2,450.00, including all material and labor.

For Our Offer of Free Plans See Page 3.

IN MODERN HOME No. 155 we have a two-story house with bungalow effect. Note the large sloping roof and the spacious screened in front porch. An abundance of light and ventilation is provided for in this house, as can be seen by the number of windows specified. Ventilation is further provided for by two sleeping balconies on the second floor, one in the front and one in the rear. The illustration shows the front sleeping balcony closed in with French windows which can be folded back when the screens are in place. Casement sash can be used on the front porch and will fold back in the same way, affording complete protection in cold weather. This arrangement by which either windows or screens can be exchanged in a few minutes at any time is a very convenient one and will be fully appreciated.

First Floor.
A beautiful Craftsman oak door leads from the front porch into the large living room. This room has oak trim and floor. Two French doors lead into the dining room which also has oak trim and floor with a massive oak buffet at the rear end, over which is placed a one-light sash. The pantry and kitchen have maple floors, with clear grade yellow pine trim. A grade entrance is provided on the right side leading into the living room and basement.

Second Floor.
Solid pine doors lead from the balcony into the two front bedrooms. There is a solid pine door glazed with double strength glass leading from the rear bedroom to the sleeping porch. The bathroom is located on this floor, back of which there is a large closet or storeroom. Plenty of light and air in all rooms. Clear yellow pine trim throughout. For size of rooms see floor plans.

Built on a concrete foundation and excavated under entire house. We furnish clear cypress siding and cedar shingles; framing timbers of the best quality yellow pine. All windows glazed with "A" quality glass.

Height of Ceilings.
Basement, 7 feet from floor to joist, with cement floor.
First floor, 8 feet 6 inches from floor to ceiling.
Second floor, 8 feet from floor to ceiling.
Painted with two coats of best paint outside, varnish and wood filler for interior finish.

This house can be built on a lot 35 feet wide.

Comlete Warm Air Heating Plant, for soft coal, extra	$ 80.04
Complete Warm Air Heating Plant, for hard coal, extra	82.20
Complete Steam Heating Plant, extra	162.55
Complete Hot Water Heating Plant, extra	205.75
Complete Plumbing Outfit, extra	115.48
Acetylene Lighting Plant, extra	51.10

SEARS, ROEBUCK AND CO.   **CHICAGO, ILLINOIS**

MODERN HOME No. 155

FIRST FLOOR PLAN

PORCH

KITCHEN 9'0"x12'6"

BUFFET

DINING ROOM 11'6"x12'6"

PANTRY

ENTRY

SHELVES

CUPBOARD

LIVING ROOM 17'6"x12'6"

PORCH 21'0"x9'6"

44'6"

22'0"

SAVED $450.00.
Salina, Kan.
Sears, Roebuck and Co.,
Chicago, Ill.
Gentlemen:—I am sending you a photo of my new house built with material ordered from you, and after your plans. I saved $450.00 and the material is better than I could buy here. Respectfully yours,
JNO. HOLZENBERG.

SAVED AT LEAST ONE-THIRD.
Terrell, Texas.
Sears, Roebuck and Co.,
Chicago, Ill.
Gentlemen:—I am mailing to you photograph of home built by me at Terrell, Texas, from plans furnished by you. Amount saved by buying mill work, hardware and plumbing of you was about 35 per cent or at least one-third.
Yours truly,
JOSEPHUS AUTREY.

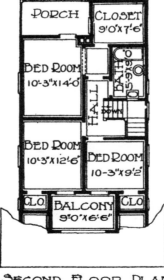

SECOND FLOOR PLAN

PORCH

CLOSET 9'0"x7'6"

BED ROOM 10'3"x14'0"

BATH 5'x9'0"

HALL

DOWN

BED ROOM 10'3"x12'6"

BED ROOM 10'3"x9'2"

CLO.

BALCONY 9'0"x6'6"

CLO.

MODERN HOME No. 204

$1,318⁰⁰

For $1,318.00 we will furnish all of the material to build this Nine-Room House, consisting of Lumber, Lath, Shingles, Mill Work, Ceiling, Flooring, Finishing Lumber, Mantel, Building Paper, Pipe, Gutter, Sash Weights, Hardware and Painting Material. NO EXTRAS, as we guarantee enough material at the above price to build this house according to our plans.

By allowing a fair price for labor, cement, brick and plaster, which we do not furnish, this house can be built complete for about $2,900.00, including all material and labor.

For Our Offer of Free Plans See Page 3.

THERE is an individuality about this house that will please the man who is looking for something really different from the general run of buildings in any vicinity. Two unique features are apparent on the first glance at the illustration, namely, the wing for the dining room affording light from three sides, and the screened sleeping porch on the second floor. The dining room measures 14x13 feet, and while it appears to be isolated or apart from the main building, it is still within easy access from the kitchen and the hall. In addition to the sleeping porch on the second story, measuring 7x16 feet, there is also a screened porch measuring 10 feet 3 inches by 11 feet in the rear of the first floor.

First Floor.

A Craftsman veneered oak door with side lights, glazed Colonial design, leads from the porch into the hall. Here an open stairway leads to the second floor. A cased opening leads from the hall into the living room, which measures 18x14 feet. In this room a massive brick mantel with a bookcase on each side at once commands attention. The living room and screened porch in the rear are connected by a Craftsman oak door. Another Craftsman door leads from the bedroom to the screened porch. Oak trim and oak floors in the living room, dining room, main hall and bedroom off the hall. Yellow pine trim and maple floors in the maid's room, kitchen, pantry and rear hall. All windows glazed Colonial design.

Second Floor.

Yellow pine floor and trim specified for the two bedrooms on this floor, sleeping porch, hall and bathroom. Windows on four sides give plenty of light to all rooms.

For size of rooms see floor plans.

Built on a concrete foundation and excavated under the entire house. We furnish *A* cedar shingles for roof and sides; framing timbers of the best quality yellow pine. All windows glazed with "A" quality glass.

Height of Ceilings.

Basement, 7 feet from floor to joist, with cement floor.
First floor, 9 feet from floor to ceiling.
Second floor, 8 feet 6 inches from floor to ceiling.
Painted with two coats of best paint outside, one coat of shingle stain for siding, varnish and wood filler for interior finish.

This house can be built on a lot 50 feet wide.

Complete Warm Air Heating Plant, for soft coal, extra	$ 87.89
Complete Warm Air Heating Plant, for hard coal, extra	90.05
Complete Steam Heating Plant, extra	261.80
Complete Hot Water Heating Plant, extra	282.97
Complete Plumbing Outfit, extra	119.27
Acetylene Lighting Plant, extra	51.10

SEARS, ROEBUCK AND CO. **CHICAGO, ILLINOIS**

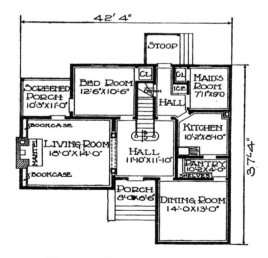

FIRST FLOOR PLAN

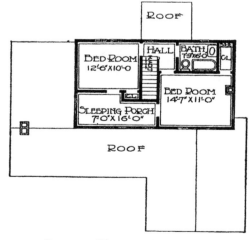

SECOND FLOOR PLAN

—16—

MODERN HOME No. 164

This house has been built at Miami, Fla., Closter, N. J., Beach Haven, N. J., Dunkirk, N. Y., New York, N. Y., and Rochester, N. Y.

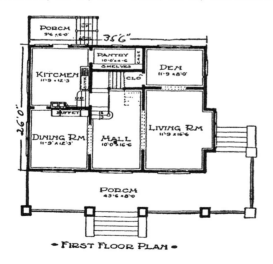

• FIRST FLOOR PLAN •

— SECOND FLOOR PLAN —

$1,569.00

For $1,569.00 we will furnish all the material to build this Nine-Room House, consisting of Lumber, Lath, Shingles, Mill Work, Ceiling, Flooring, Finishing Lumber, Buffet, Medicine Case, Building Paper, Pipe, Gutter, Sash Weights, Hardware and Painting Material. NO EXTRAS, as we guarantee enough material at the above price to build this house according to our plans.

By allowing a fair price for labor, cement, brick and plaster, which we do not furnish, this house can be built for about $2,800.00, including all material and labor.

For Our Offer of Free Plans See Page 3.

A COLONIAL two-story house with a gambrel roof, having a large front porch, 8 feet wide by 45 feet 6 inches long. On the same level with this porch there is an open terrace on the left elevation, 12x10 feet. The entire house, including the porch columns, is sided with shingles. Paneled lattice work is provided under the porch, constructed with square porch balusters.

First Floor.

Our Beauty oak veneered front door, 3x7 feet, 1¾ inches thick, glazed with bevel plate glass, having side lights on each side also glazed with bevel plate glass, opens from the front porch into the hall. In this hall there is an open oak staircase leading to the second floor. Large cased openings from the hall to the dining room and living room. Another cased opening from the living room to the den, which can be used as a library. The dining room is provided with a large oak buffet. A bay window in the living room and a good size pantry off the kitchen. We furnish two-panel veneered doors for the first floor with Craftsman design clear oak trim. Clear oak flooring for the hall and main rooms on the first floor. Clear maple flooring for the kitchen and pantry.

Second Floor.

On this floor are two large and two medium size bedrooms with hall and bathroom. Each bedroom is provided with a suitable closet. Clear solid yellow pine five-cross panel doors and yellow pine trim. Each room has yellow pine flooring and is well lighted on two sides.

Built on a concrete foundation, frame construction, sided and roofed with cedar shingles.

Painted two coats on all outside work except shingles, which are stained with creosote stain, color to suit owner. Varnish and wood filler for two coats of interior finish.

Excavated basement under the entire house, 7 feet from floor to joists, with cement floor. First floor, 9 feet from floor to ceiling; second floor, 8 feet 6 inches from floor to ceiling.

This house can be built on a lot 50 feet wide.

Complete Warm Air Heating Plant, for soft coal, extra	$ 97.48
Complete Warm Air Heating Plant, for hard coal, extra	99.64
Complete Steam Heating Plant, extra	283.20
Complete Hot Water Heating Plant, extra	288.64
Complete Plumbing Outfit, extra	115.86
Acetylene Lighting Plant, extra	51.10

SEARS, ROEBUCK AND CO.　　　　**CHICAGO, ILLINOIS**

MODERN HOME No. 151

$1,332⁰⁰

For $1,332.00 we will furnish all the material to build this Six-Room Bungalow, consisting of Mill Work, Ceiling, Siding, Flooring, Finishing Lumber, Building Paper, Pipe, Gutter, Sash Weights, Buffet, Medicine Case, Pantry Case, Hardware, Painting Material, Lumber, Lath and Shingles. NO EXTRAS, as we guarantee enough material at the above price to build this house according to our plans.

By allowing a fair price for labor, cement, brick and plaster, which we do not furnish, this house can be built for about $2,885.00, including all material and labor.

For Our Offer of Free Plans See Page 3.

Main Floor

A Craftsman oak door leads from the spacious porch into the large living room which has a paneled beam ceiling. A massive brick fireplace with seats on both sides enchances the bungalow effect. Colored leaded art glass sash over each seat. An arch opening with four massive Colonial columns and balustrades connects this room with the dining room. For this room we specify a Craftsman oak buffet with plate glass mirror, Craftsman oak doors, Craftsman trim and beamed ceiling. Note the large front bedroom with bay window. Closets provided for each bedroom, and linen closet for the bathroom. Oak flooring for all rooms except the kitchen, back bedroom, bathroom and pantry which have maple flooring. Rooms on the main floor are 9 feet 4 inches from floor to ceiling.

Basement

The excavated basement under the entire house has a cement floor and measures 7 feet from floor to joists.

Built on cement block foundation. Sided with narrow bevel edge clear cypress siding and shingled with cedar shingles.

Built at Ithaca, N. Y., Wichita, Kan., Dunkirk, N. Y., Greeley, Colo., Alliance, Neb., Culver, Ind., Breckenridge, Mich., Boston, Mass., and other cities.

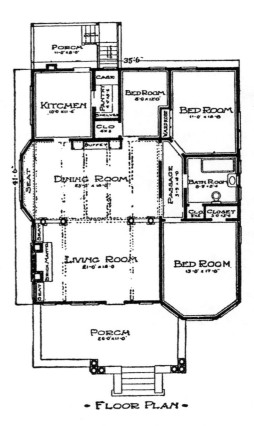

- FLOOR PLAN -

A FINE example of a modern bungalow, conveniently arranged, perfectly lighted and ventilated with a great many large windows. Pronounced a success by practical builders. For interior view see opposite page. Painted two coats outside; your choice of color. Varnish and wood filler for interior finish.

This bungalow can be built on a lot 50 feet wide.

Complete Warm Air Heating Plant, for soft coal, extra	$ 77.72
Complete Warm Air Heating Plant, for hard coal, extra	80.47
Complete Steam Heating Plant, extra	183.10
Complete Hot Water Heating Plant, extra	229.00
Complete Plumbing Outfit, extra	116.55
Acetylene Lighting Plant, extra	47.90

SEARS, ROEBUCK AND CO.   **CHICAGO, ILLINOIS**

—18—

Living and Dining Room of Our Bungalow No. 151

This illustration is an exact reproduction of the interior of our Bungalow No. 151, looking through the living room into the dining room, and is a perfect picture of simple elegance and homelike comfort.

Note the large rustic brick fireplace with a leaded art glass sash and a seat on each side. The Colonial columns and balustrade work are new and up to date features which are being used only in high priced houses. From the first impression you would think this house would cost over $4,000.00, but we make it possible for you to build it for less than $2,900.00.

Compare this house with similar houses already built in your neighborhood at a cost of from $4,000.00 to $5,000.00. There are many reasons why such homes are usually very expensive. Architects charge all the way from $100.00 to $150.00 for a set of plans and specifications. This is the amount we save you to start with, and our competent, practical and expert architects specify stock sizes and patterns of doors, windows, trim, etc., which enables you to buy your materials for several hundred dollars less than you could buy them if they were furnished according to ordinary architects' specifications, which in most cases are odd sizes and patterns and have to be made to order.

We own our own saw mill and ship lumber direct from our mill to you. We also own and operate one of the biggest mill work factories in the country and ship all doors, windows, moldings, in fact, a complete line of mill work and building materials, direct to you. In this way we save you several hundred dollars which is usually paid for profits to jobbers and retail dealers.

Don't build until you have had our quotations on materials.

Our plans are so complete in every detail that any ordinary workman can build any one of the houses shown in this book, with no lost time whatever to figure out how the different parts are to be put together.

SEARS, ROEBUCK AND CO.

—19—

CHICAGO, ILLINOIS

MODERN HOME No. 178

$1,611<u>00</u>

For $1,611.00 we will furnish all the material to build this Nine-Room House, consisting of Lumber, Lath, Shingles, Mill Work, Flooring, Siding, Ceiling, Finishing Lumber, Building Paper, Pipe, Gutter, Sash Weights, Hardware, Brick Mantel, Buffet, Medicine Case and Painting Material. NO EXTRAS, as we guarantee enough material at the above price to build this house according to our plans.

By allowing a fair price for labor, cement, brick and plaster, which we do not furnish, this house can be built for about $3,200.00, including all material and labor.

For Our Offer of Free Plans See Page 3.

A CRAFTSMAN style two-story house with a bungalow style roof. Top lights of windows are divided in square designs to harmonize with this style of architecture. The arches between the porch columns are raised high enough to give good light in the rooms on the second floor. The wide porch extends across the entire front of house and is sided from the rail down to the grade line with wide boards. Same house is furnished with Colonial exterior without extra charge. See Modern Home No. 210 below.

First Floor.

An oak Craftsman front door opens into the large reception hall. At the rear end of the reception hall is a unique design oak open stairway and under the stairway is a door that opens to the basement stairs. At each side of the entrance in the reception hall is a large cased opening, one leading to the dining room, the other leading to the living room. The living room presents a very attractive appearance, having a rustic fireplace with combination bookcases and seats at each side, extending across the entire length of the room, which is 22 feet, with casement sash over the bookcases. Living room and dining room have beamed ceilings and wide oak cornices. In the dining room is a handsome buffet facing the reception hall and a casement sash on each side of it. The dining room has a large bay window extending across the end of the room. A door opens from the dining room into the large kitchen, and from the kitchen is a door which opens to a large pantry. Another door opens to the inside stairway leading to the basement. The entire first floor, excepting the kitchen and pantry, is trimmed with clear red oak woodwork and clear oak flooring. Kitchen and pantry flooring is of clear maple.

Second Floor.

The head of the main stairway opens into a large well lighted hall, and from this hall there is a door opening into each of the four large bedrooms and bathroom. Each bedroom is equipped with a closet, and all have windows on two sides, which affords an ample amount of light and ventilation. The doors and trim are of clear yellow pine. Flooring is clear maple.

MODERN HOME No. 210

Built on a concrete block foundation. Sided with clear beveled cypress siding and the roof is shingled with cedar shingles. Porch floor is clear fir, 1⅛ inches thick. Has an excavated basement under the entire house, 7 feet high from floor to joists. Rooms on first floor, 9 feet to ceilings; on the second floor, 8 feet 6 inches to ceilings. Cement floor in basement.

We furnish paint for two coats on outside work, but a very desirable effect may be had by staining the siding with a brown stain and painting the finishing lumber and outside trim, door frames and window frames with pure white.

We also furnish sufficient filler and varnish to finish interior.

This house can be built on a lot 50 feet wide.

Complete Warm Air Heating Plant, for soft coal, extra...	$104.38
Complete Warm Air Heating Plant, for hard coal, extra...	106.76
Complete Steam Heating Plant, extra...	298.40
Complete Hot Water Heating Plant, extra...	346.55
Complete Plumbing Outfit, extra...	116.48
Acetylene Lighting Plant, extra.	51.10

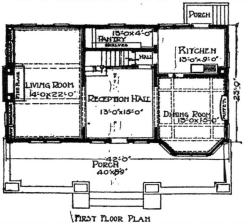

FIRST FLOOR PLAN

SECOND FLOOR PLAN

SEARS, ROEBUCK AND CO., CHICAGO

MODERN HOME No. 124

This house has been built at Texarkana, Ark., Washington, D. C., Clayton, Ga., Lombard, Ill., Taylorville, Ill., Grand Rapids, Mich., Brooklyn, N. Y., Dunkirk, N. Y., New York, N. Y., Montvale, N. J., Akin, N. Y., and Du Bois, Penn.

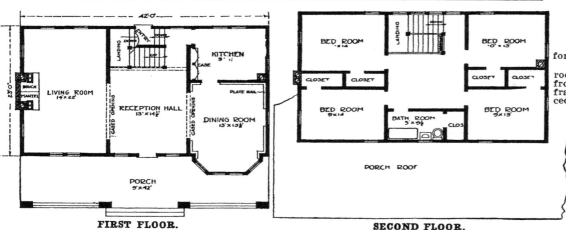

FIRST FLOOR.

SECOND FLOOR.

—21—

$1,185.00

For $1,185.00 we will furnish all the material to build this Nine-Room Two-Story Bungalow, consisting of Mill Work, Ceiling, Siding, Flooring, Finishing Lumber, Building Paper, Pipe, Gutter, Sash Weights, Hardware, Painting Material, Mantel, Lumber, Lath and Shingles. NO EXTRAS, as we guarantee enough material at the above price to build this bungalow according to our plans.

By allowing a fair price for labor, cement, brick and plaster, which we do not furnish, this house can be built for about $2,156.00 including all material and labor.

For Our Offer of Free Plans See Page 3.

THIS two-story bungalow is fast becoming a great favorite in the Central, Eastern and Western states. You will note that it has been built in several cities in Illinois, Michigan, New York, New Jersey and Pennsylvania as well as Arkansas and Georgia. Everyone who has built it is pleased with the fine quality of the materials furnished and the big saving made on the order. This bungalow can be finished with Craftsman hardwood trim at a small advance in price.

First Floor.

A large porch 9x42 feet extends across the entire front of the house. We furnish a Victoria front door, glazed with leaded glass which leads from the spacious porch into a large reception hall. Cased openings lead from this hall into the living room and dining room. It will be seen that this bungalow is so arranged that the large reception hall, dining room and extra large living room practically make one big room extending the entire length of the house. We furnish a brick mantel for the living room. A very unique arrangement is the open stairway in the rear of the reception hall, which leads to the second floor. Doors are five-cross panel yellow pine with clear yellow pine trim, such as casing, baseboard and molding. The windows are divided into eight and twelve lights, which are in perfect harmony with bungalow architecture.

Second Floor.

This floor has four bedrooms, a large hall and a bathroom. All doors are clear solid five-cross panel yellow pine with clear yellow pine trim to match. Bedrooms have an abundance of light, each room having two windows, one on each side so that perfect ventilation can be secured.

Painted two coats outside; your choice of color. Wood filler and varnish for two coats of interior finish.

There is an excavated cellar, 10x14 feet, 7 feet from floor to joists. The rooms on the first floor are 9 feet from floor to ceiling; second floor, 8 feet from floor to ceiling. This bungalow is built on a concrete block foundation, frame construction, sided with narrow bevel edge cypress siding and has cedar shingle roof.

This bungalow can be built on a lot 48 feet wide.

Complete Warm Air Heating Plant, for soft coal, extra	$ 90.49
Complete Warm Air Heating Plant, for hard coal, extra	93.50
Complete Steam Heating Plant, extra	293.30
Complete Hot Water Heating Plant, extra	346.00
Complete Plumbing Outfit, extra	120.84
Acetylene Lighting Plant, extra	51.10

SEARS, ROEBUCK AND CO.

CHICAGO, ILLINOIS

MODERN HOME No. 225

$1,465.00

For $1,465.00 we will furnish all the material to build this Seven-Room Bungalow, consisting of Lumber, Lath, Shingles, Mill Work, Flooring, Ceiling, Siding, Finishing Lumber, Building Paper, Pipe, Gutter, Sash Weights, Hardware and Painting Material. **NO EXTRAS**, as we guarantee enough material at the above price to build this house according to our plans.

By allowing a fair price for labor, cement, brick and plaster, which we do not furnish, this house can be built for about $2,800.00, including all material and labor.

For Our Offer of Free Plans See Page 3.

THIS charming bungalow will appeal to the discriminating home builder. The exterior is very attractive and has many good features. The long sloping roof relieved by the wide dormer, the grouping of columns at the corners of the porch, and the brick chimney showing on the outside walls. The wide porch extending entirely across the front of the house, together with the open air dining room at the back of the house, afford plenty of room for outdoor living. The large living room is 17 feet wide by 27 feet long, has a beamed ceiling, a nicely planned stairway and a very attractive fireplace of molded brick. A large cased opening divides the living room from the dining room. A large Craftsman buffet of oak is built in across one end of the dining room. The kitchen has a good size pantry, in which is built a handy pantry case.

First Floor.

The front door is 1¾ inches thick, made of oak in the Craftsman style, glazed with rich plate glass. Inside doors are made in the Craftsman style, 1⅜ inches thick, of veneered oak, with Craftsman oak trim to match. Rear door is of white pine 1¾ inches thick, glazed with "A" quality double strength glass. Beamed ceiling in the living room, plate rail entirely around the dining room. Oak floor in the living room and dining room. Maple floor in the kitchen and pantry.

Second Floor.

An elegant oak stairway leads to the second floor. Doors are made of birch in the two-panel design, with birch trim to match. Good size clothes closet in each of the three bedrooms. Maple floor for the entire second floor, except in the bathroom, which has a mosaic tile floor.

Built on a concrete foundation. Framing timbers of the best No. 1 quality, and cedar shingles. Basement has cement floor and is 7 feet from floor to joists.
First floor is 9 feet from floor to ceiling.
Second floor, 7 feet 6 inches from floor to ceiling. Stain and paint for exterior, varnish and wood filler for interior.

This house requires a lot at least 50 feet wide to set it off properly.

Complete Warm Air Heating Plant, for soft coal, extra:	$ 90.70
Complete Warm Air Heating Plant, for hard coal, extra	92.69
Complete Steam Heating Plant, extra	186.65
Complete Hot Water Heating Plant, extra	233.49
Complete Plumbing Outfit, extra	121.06
Acetylene Lighting Plant, extra	49.50

SEARS, ROEBUCK AND CO.   **CHICAGO, ILLINOIS**

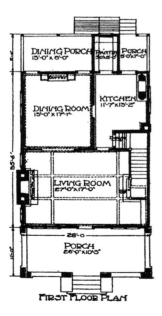

FIRST FLOOR PLAN

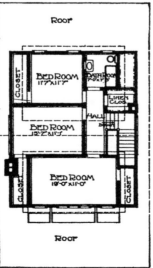

SECOND FLOOR PLAN

—22—

MODERN HOME No. 228

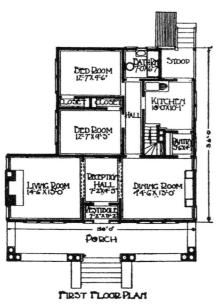

FIRST FLOOR PLAN

$1,280.00

For $1,280.00 we will furnish all the material to build this Six-Room Bungalow, consisting of Lumber, Lath, Shingles, Mill Work, Flooring, Ceiling, Siding, China Closet, Fireplace, Finishing Lumber, Building Paper, Pipe, Gutter, Sash Weights, Hardware and Painting Material. NO EXTRAS, as we guarantee enough material at the above price to build this house according to our plans.

By allowing a fair price for labor, stone, concrete and plaster, which we do not furnish, this bungalow can be built for about $2,200.00, including all material and labor.

For Our Offer of Free Plans See Page 3.

A WELL designed bungalow is the most attractive of all styles of houses. With this in mind, our architect has designed what may truly be termed a perfect bungalow. One is impressed with the exterior appearance, the wide projecting eaves, the low lines suggesting room and comfort.

On entering this house one passes through the vestibule into the reception hall, which has a large cased opening on both sides, making practically one large room out of the reception hall, living room and dining room. The living room has a massive brick fireplace, on either side of which is a large colored art glass window. The dining room has a large Craftsman oak buffet built in, with a leaded art glass sash on each side. The kitchen is just a convenient size, being 10 feet by 10 feet 1 inch. The entrance to the dining room from the kitchen is through the pantry. There are two nice bedrooms, each having a good size clothes closet.

First Floor.

The front and vestibule doors are 1¾ inches thick, made of oak in the Craftsman style, each door having eight small lights of bevel plate glass. All interior doors are of the Craftsman style with Craftsman trim in oak to match. The rear door is of soft pine, 1¾ inches thick, glazed with plain "A" quality double strength glass. Oak floors in every room, with the exception of the kitchen and bathroom; these two rooms have maple flooring.

Basement.

Basement under entire house, 7 feet from floor to joists; cement floor. Both outside and inside stairways.

Built on a concrete foundation. Excavated under entire house. This house is roofed with cedar shingles and all framing timbers are of the best quality. Windows are of Colonial pattern and glazed with "A" quality glass. First floor is 9 feet from floor to ceiling. Basement 7 feet from floor to joists.

Stain and paint furnished for the outside, varnish and wood filler for interior finish.

This bungalow can be built on a lot 40 feet wide.

Complete Warm Air Heating Plant, for soft coal, extra	$ 57.61
Complete Warm Air Heating Plant, for hard coal, extra	61.09
Complete Steam Heating Plant, extra	145.30
Complete Hot Water Heating Plant, extra	180.65
Complete Plumbing Outfit, extra	112.86
Acetylene Lighting Plant, extra	47.90

SEARS, ROEBUCK AND CO.　　　　**CHICAGO, ILLINOIS**

MODERN HOME No. 126

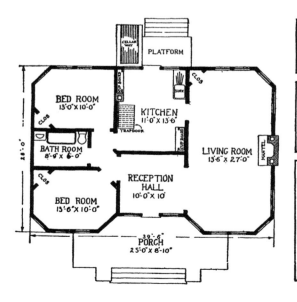

Paint for two coats outside. Varnish and wood filler for two coats of interior finish.

Built at Des Moines, Iowa, Glencoe, Ky., Houston, Texas, Chicago, Ill., Merchantville, N. J., Aurora, Ill., Maysville, Okla., Adrian, Mich., Laporte, Ind., and other cities.

HE SAVED 25 PER CENT ON MODERN HOME No. 126.
2736 Meredith Ave., Omaha, Neb.
Sears, Roebuck and Co., Chicago, Ill.
Gentlemen:—I am sending photo of my new house, built according to your plans and with material purchased from you. I could not have been better satisfied as to the quality of the material, the promptness of the shipments and the way I was treated. I saved about 25 per cent on the material as compared with local prices. My carpenter said it was **the best grade of lumber he had ever used.** Yours truly,
R. L. GILCHRIST.

—24—

$814⁰⁰

For $814.00 we will furnish all the material to build this Six-Room Bungalow, consisting of Mill Work, Flooring, Ceiling, Finishing Lumber, Building Paper, Pipe, Gutter, Sash Weights, Mantel, Hardware, Painting Material, Lumber, Lath and Shingles. NO EXTRAS, as we guarantee enough material at the above price to build this house according to our plans.

By allowing a fair price for labor, cement, brick and plaster, which we do not furnish, this house can be built for about $1,615.00, including all material and labor.

For Our Offer of Free Plans See Page 3.

A POPULAR, inexpensive and graceful bungalow, well lighted and ventilated. The large overhanging roof serves for the porch roof also and is supported by beams, requiring no porch columns. The porch is 25 feet long and 8 feet 10 inches wide. Without extra cost we will furnish this bungalow with exterior as shown in Modern Home No. 208, illustrated below.

Main Floor.

Rooms on the main floor are ten feet from floor to ceiling. A large reception hall opens through a cased opening into an exceptionally large living room measuring 13 feet 6 inches by 27 feet and intended to be used as a combination living room and dining room. Note the beautiful Windsor front door glazed with leaded glass. All the windows are Queen Anne style. Interior doors are five-cross panel with soft pine stiles, rails and yellow pine panels. Floors and trim throughout are clear yellow pine. The bathroom is located between the two bedrooms.

Basement.

This house has an excavated cellar 12x24 feet. 7 feet high from floor to joists.

Built on a concrete foundation. Frame construction. Sided with narrow bevel edge cypress siding and has a cedar roof.

This house can be built on a lot 48 feet wide.

Complete Warm Air Heating Plant, for soft coal, extra	$ 69.13
Complete Warm Air Heating Plant, for hard coal, extra	71.23
Complete Steam Heating Plant, extra	159.05
Complete Hot Water Heating Plant, extra	199.83
Complete Plumbing Outfit, extra	115.59
Acetylene Lighting Plant, extra	47.10

MODERN HOME No. 208

MODERN HOME No. 191

$966⁰⁰

For $966.00 we will furnish all the material to build this Five-Room Bungalow, consisting of Lumber, Lath, Shingles, Mill Work, Flooring, Ceiling, Buffet, Finishing Lumber, Building Paper, Pipe, Gutter, Sash Weights, Hardware, Mantel and Painting Material. NO EXTRAS, as we guarantee enough material at the above price to build this house according to our plans.

By allowing a fair price for labor, cement, brick and plaster, which we do not furnish, this house can be built for about $1,800.00, including all material and labor.

For Our Offer of Free Plans See Page 3.

THIS Bungalow is of the California type and has many points to recommend it to the builder who desires a real home. It is sided with roof boards up to the height of 9 feet from the ground. Stonekote or stucco under the wide overhanging eaves. There are two entrances from the front porch, one being a French door which opens into the dining room and the other a Craftsman door which opens into the living room.

Main Floor.

A glance at the floor plans will show that this bungalow is admirably laid out. The living room with its beamed ceiling, rustic brick fireplace and built-in seat alongside the fireplace is a large airy apartment, having three large windows and two sash which admit an abundance of light and air. The dining room is also a good size room and has an attractive oak buffet facing the entrance. There are two bedrooms and a bathroom. Each of the two bedrooms have a good size clothes closet. The kitchen has a nice pantry in which is built a pantry case. Note the Craftsman oak front door, 1¾ inches thick. The French door leading to the dining room is also made of oak, 1¾ inches thick, and has small sash extending from top to bottom. All interior doors and trim are made of Craftsman oak. Oak flooring in the living room and dining room with maple floor in the bedrooms and kitchen. Mosaic tile floor is furnished for the bathroom. Floors are 9 feet from floor to ceiling.

Basement.

The basement under the entire house has a cement floor and is 7 feet from floor to joists. Lighted by basement sash.

Built on a concrete foundation. We furnish clear cedar shingles and the best No. 1 quality framing timbers and siding.

Stain and paint for outside, varnish and wood filler for the interior finish.

This house, while it is only 28 feet wide, requires a lot at least 40 feet wide to set it off properly.

Complete Warm Air Heating Plant, for soft coal, extra	$ 56.79
Complete Warm Air Heating Plant, for hard coal, extra	60.07
Complete Steam Heating Plant, extra	145.30
Complete Hot Water Heating Plant, extra	178.28
Complete Plumbing Outfit, extra	113.03
Acetylene Lighting Plant, extra	47.25

SEARS, ROEBUCK AND CO. **CHICAGO, ILLINOIS**

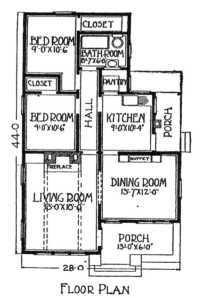

FLOOR PLAN

SUCCESSFUL BUILDING

A BOOK WRITTEN BY OUR CUSTOMERS

Send us your name and address and this book will go forward free by return mail. It contains facts you ought to know regarding the building business and explains how you can get $1.50 value for every dollar you spend with us.

Our customers are our best advertisers and they will be glad to tell you of the values we gave them and the splendid service we rendered.

Pictures of houses built according to our plans and with our materials, also letters from our customers, will be found in this book. Probably you will recognize some of the writers as your friends or neighbors. You ought to have this book. It is an endorsement of our business principles by the building public of the United States.

MODERN HOME No. 229

Built at Gary, Ind.

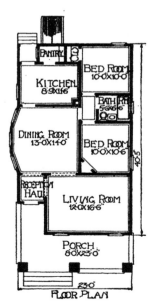

FLOOR PLAN

$670.00

For $670.00 we will furnish all the material to build this Five-Room Bungalow, consisting of Lumber, Lath, Shingles, Mill Work, Flooring, Ceiling, Finishing Lumber, Building Paper, Pipe, Gutter, Sash Weights, Hardware and Painting Material. NO EXTRAS, as we guarantee enough material at the above price to build this house according to our plans.

By allowing a fair price for labor, cement, brick and plaster, which we do not furnish, this house can be built for about $1,300.00, including all material and labor.

For Our Offer of Free Plans See Page 3.

MODERN HOME No. 229 is an attractive and inexpensive bungalow of five rooms with reception hall, bath and pantry. It has a front porch across the entire house, 23x8 feet, so arranged that it makes a combination porch and open terrace. We furnish a sufficient quantity of shingle stain, any color, for the sides, front and rear for the price quoted above, but not for the roof. Shingled houses are becoming quite popular and when stained with a suitable color have a very refined and comfortable appearance.

Main Floor.

A massive solid pine front door glazed with leaded crystal sheet glass leads from the handsome porch into the large reception hall. The two front windows are glazed to correspond with the front door. On entering the reception hall you find a cased opening leading to the living room and another leading into the dining room. There is also a cased opening leading into the dining room from the living room, making three cased openings in all. Note the triple bay window in the dining room. A swinging door leads from this room into the kitchen. The two bedrooms have good size closets. First quality yellow pine doors and trim throughout. All rooms are 9 feet from floor to ceiling.

Basement.

The excavated basement is 7 feet high from floor to joists. Lighted by basement sash.

Painted with two coats best paint on the outside. Shingles on sides stained green or brown. Varnish and wood filler for two coats of interior finish.

Built on a concrete block foundation with basement under the entire house. Cement floor. The entire house including the roof is covered with Star A Star cedar shingles.

This house can be built on a lot 27 feet wide.

Complete Warm Air Heating Plant, for soft coal, extra	$ 55.72
Complete Warm Air Heating Plant, for hard coal, extra	58.98
Complete Steam Heating Plant, extra	137.15
Complete Hot Water Heating Plant, extra	159.81
Complete Plumbing Outfit, extra	117.74
Acetylene Lighting Plant, extra	47.25

SEARS, ROEBUCK AND CO.   **CHICAGO, ILLINOIS.**

Skeptical Carpenters Won Over.

Forestburg, S. Dak.

Sears, Roebuck and Co., Chicago, Ill.

Dear Sirs:—I have received my bill of material and must say it is much better than I expected and better than I could get here from local dealers. Although my carpenters advised me not to send for it, they say it is a fine lot of mill work, especially the flooring and siding. The hardware all through is good—yes, fine, and I have saved at least one-half by buying it from you. Thanking you for kind and honest treatment, I am,

Very truly yours,   J. B. SHIRK.

$926⁰⁰

For $926.00 we will furnish all the material to build this Eight-Room Two-Story Bungalow, consisting of Mill Work, Ceiling, Siding, Flooring, Finishing Lumber, Building Paper, Pipe, Gutter, Sash Weights, Mantel, Hardware, Painting Material, Lumber, Lath and Shingles. NO EXTRAS, as we guarantee enough material at the above price to build this house according to our plans.

By allowing a fair price for labor, cement, brick and plaster, which we do not furnish, this bungalow can be built for about $2,035.00, including all material and labor.

For Our Offer of Free Plans See Page 3.

A MODERN style of eight-room bungalow of frame construction at a moderate price. The arrangement is ideal. Living room, dining room, library, kitchen and stair hall are located on the first floor; three bedrooms, trunk room and bathroom on second floor.

The large porch with panel columns, 30 feet long by 8 feet wide, has balusters extending down to the grade line, producing a very pleasing effect. Without extra charge we will furnish this house with exterior as shown in Modern Home No. 206 illustrated below.

First Floor.

The front vestibule leads directly into a wide hall which has cased opening with colonnades leading into a living room 11x14 feet and a dining room 11x12 feet, and also leading to stairway to second floor. Dining room has oak mantel, and plate rail around the entire room. The library, 8 feet 6 inches by 11 feet, is arranged directly in the rear of the living room, also with an entrance to back entry; can also be used as a bedroom. Kitchen, size 10 feet 4 inches by 11 feet. Directly off from the kitchen is the pantry with shelves and cupboards and door leading to rear entry. Inside stairway to basement from entry and also outside basement entrance.

Second Floor.

The stairs with landing leading to the second floor lead directly into a hall which connects with large bedroom 13x12 feet, with closet; also rear bedroom 11 feet by 14 feet 6 inches with large trunk room or closet, size 7 feet 6 inches by 8 feet, adjoining, and chamber 8 feet 10 inches by 11 feet, with closet. Directly at the head of the stairs is the door leading to bathroom, size 11x9 feet. All rooms on both floors are light and airy.

For the front door we specify four-cross panel sash door, 1¾ inches thick, glazed with etched glass. Rear door of similar design with double strength glass. All interior doors on both first and second floors are five-cross panel design, made of clear yellow pine with casing, base and all molding to match. Floors on first and second floors of clear yellow pine; for porches edge grain yellow pine. Porch ceiled overhead with yellow pine beaded ceiling.

Built on concrete block foundation. Sided with narrow bevel siding on first floor; roof, dormer and second story covered with cedar shingles. All framing material, including joists, studding, etc., made from No. 1 yellow pine.

Excavated basement under entire house and with concrete floor.

Height of Ceilings: Basement, 6 feet 6 inches from floor to joists; first floor, 9 feet from floor to ceiling; second floor, 8 feet from floor to ceiling. Paint furnished for two coats and stain for siding shingles. Your choice of colors. Also varnish and wood filler for two coats of inside hard oil finish.

MODERN HOME No. 206

MODERN HOME No. 144

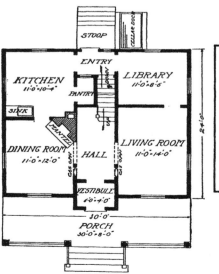

FIRST FLOOR PLAN

This house has been built at Aurora, Ill., Gary, Ind., Boston, Mass., Lynbrook, N. Y., West Pittsburgh, Penn., and Sioux Falls, S. Dak.

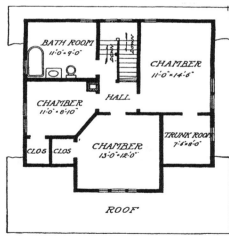

SECOND FLOOR PLAN

This house can be built on a lot 34 feet wide.

Complete Warm Air Heating Plant, for soft coal, extra....$ 86.62
Complete Warm Air Heating Plant, for hard coal, extra.. 88.78
Complete Steam Heating Plant, extra.................. 165.85
Complete Hot Water Heating Plant, extra............. 208.84
Complete Plumbing Outfit, extra........................ 127.68
Acetylene Lighting Plant, extra........................ 51.90

MODERN HOME No. 182

$902⁰⁰

For $902.00 we will furnish all the material to build this Five-Room Bungalow, consisting of Mill Work, Ceiling, Siding, Flooring, Finishing Lumber, Building Paper, Pipe, Gutter, Sash Weights, Buffet, Mantel, Medicine Cabinet, Pantry Case, Hardware, Painting Material, Lumber, Lath and Shingles. NO EXTRAS, as we guarantee enough material at the above price to build this house according to our plans.

By allowing a fair price for labor, cement, brick and plaster, which we do not furnish, this house can be built for about $1,850.00, including all material and labor.

For Our Offer of Free Plans See Page 3.

MODERN Home No. 182 is a very well arranged, solidly constructed house with a private front porch, 8x18 feet, the main entrance being on the right, as shown in the illustration. Stonekote and chimney brick are used in pleasing contrast with cypress siding for the outside finish.

First Floor.

French doors lead from the private porch into the spacious living room, in which there is a brick mantel. A cased opening leads into the dining room. The main attraction of this room is the massive buffet with bevel plate mirror. There is a pantry case provided for the pantry, and medicine cabinet for the bathroom. All interior doors and trim are of first quality yellow pine. Good size closets in the two bedrooms. Colonial windows are specified for this house to match the French doors and windows in the living room.

Built on concrete foundation and basement excavated under the entire house has a cement floor.

Framing timbers of No. 1 yellow pine. All outside walls covered with 1-inch dressed and matched sheathing boards lined with heavy building paper and sided with clear cypress bevel siding. *A* cedar shingles on the roof.

Basement, 7 feet from floor to joists. First floor, 9 feet from floor to ceiling.

Painted with two coats best paint on the outside. Varnish and wood filler for two coats for interior finish.

This house can be built on a lot 27 feet wide.

Complete Warm Air Heating Plant, for soft coal, extra	$ 56.43
Complete Warm Air Heating Plant, for hard coal, extra	59.69
Complete Steam Heating Plant, extra	149.10
Complete Hot Water Heating Plant, extra	184.37
Complete Plumbing Outfit, extra	114.39
Acetylene Lighting Plant, extra	47.25

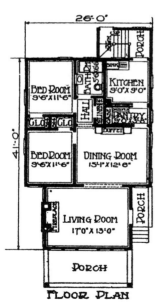

FLOOR PLAN

SEARS, ROEBUCK AND CO.   **CHICAGO, ILLINOIS**

MODERN HOME No. 201

$1,567⁰⁰

For $1,567.00 we will furnish all the material to build this Eight-Room Bungalow, consisting of Mill Work, Ceiling, Siding, Flooring, Finishing Lumber, Building Paper, Pipe, Gutter, Sash Weights, Buffet, Medicine Case, Pantry Case, Hardware, Painting Material, Lumber, Lath and Shingles. **NO EXTRAS**, as we guarantee enough material at the above price to build this house according to our plans.

By allowing a fair price for labor, cement, brick and plaster, which we do not furnish, this house can be built for about $3,300.00, including all material and labor.

For Our Offer of Free Plans See Page 3.

THIS modern bungalow is similar to our Modern Home No. 151, illustrated on page 18, but has two additional rooms on the second floor. The letter from Mr. August M. Schiller, West McHenry, Ill., telling of a saving of $1,500.00 on the materials which we furnished for this house, speaks for itself. There is no better type of a modern bungalow, conveniently arranged, perfectly lighted and ventilated with a great many large rooms.

First Floor.

A Craftsman oak veneered door leads from the large airy porch into the living room, which has Craftsman oak beamed ceiling. A beamed ceiling is also provided for the dining room, which is separated from the living room with an arched opening and four massive columns and balustrades. There is a rustic brick fireplace in the living room with seat on each side and leaded art sash over each seat. A Craftsman open stairway leads from the dining room to the second floor. The dining room has a massive oak buffet. Note the large front bedroom with bay windows. Closets are provided for all three bedrooms on this floor. Linen closet is provided for the bathroom. Doors and inside molding all of latest Craftsman design. Oak flooring for all rooms, excepting kitchen, back bedroom, bathroom and pantry, which have maple floors.

Second Floor.

The second floor is reached by the Craftsman oak open stairway in the dining room. The main room measures 22 feet by 24 feet 9 inches. There is also a convenient den which may be used as a library or sewing room. Clear yellow pine flooring and trim in these two rooms.

Painted two coats outside; your choice of color. Varnish and wood filler for interior finish.

Built on a concrete block foundation. Excavated basement under the entire house, 7 feet high to the joists with cement floor. Rooms on the main floor are 9 feet 4 inches from floor to ceiling. Sided with narrow bevel edge siding of clear cypress and shingled with **cedar shingles.**

This bungalow can be built on a lot 50 feet wide.

Complete Warm Air Heating Plant, for soft coal, extra	$ 77.72
Complete Warm Air Heating Plant, for hard coal, extra	80.47
Complete Steam Heating Plant, extra	204.80
Complete Hot Water Heating Plant, extra	245.12
Complete Plumbing Outfit, extra	104.70
Acetylene Lighting Plant, extra	48.70

SEARS, ROEBUCK AND CO.　　　　　**CHICAGO, ILLINOIS**

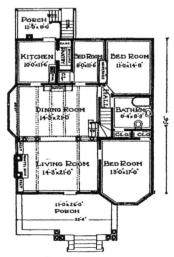

FIRST FLOOR PLAN

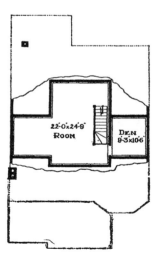

SECOND FLOOR PLAN

MODERN HOME No. 147

This house has been built at Kankakee, Ill., Great Bend, Kan., St. Louis, Mo., Mandan, N. Dak., and East Falls Church, Va.

FLOOR PLAN

$872⁰⁰

For $872.00 we will furnish all the material to build this Six-Room Bungalow, consisting of Mill Work, Siding, Flooring, Ceiling, Finishing Lumber, Building Paper, Pipe, Gutter, Sash Weights, Hardware, Painting Material, Lumber, Lath and Shingles. **NO EXTRAS,** as we guarantee enough material at the above price to build this house according to our plans.

By allowing a fair price for labor, cement, brick and plaster, which we do not furnish, this house can be built for about $1,530.00, including all material and labor.

For Our Offer of Free Plans See Page 3.

AN ATTRACTIVE cottage of frame construction and a popular design. The front elevation suggests the bungalow type of architecture. It has a large porch, 8 feet wide, extending across the front of the house which is sheltered by the projection of the upper story and supported with massive built-up square columns. Unique triple window in the attic and fancy leaded art glass windows add much to this pleasing design.

Main Floor.

From the front vestibule, which is 4x5 feet, you enter a large living room, 11 feet 6 inches by 14 feet. This room has a nook, 7x5 feet, with cased opening which can be used as a reading room or library. Living room leads directly into the dining room, back of which is a good size kitchen, 11 feet by 10 feet 10 inches, with combination cupboard which opens from both dining room and kitchen, a very convenient arrangement. This cupboard has four china closet doors glazed with leaded crystal glass facing the dining room. The kitchen side of the cupboard has six paneled cupboard doors and four small doors above. A double swinging door leads from the dining room to the kitchen. We furnish plate rail for the dining room. Note the arrangement of the two bedrooms, one in the front and one in the rear, the idea being to provide as much light and ventilation as possible. The front door is made of veneered birch, 1¾ inches thick, glazed with leaded art glass. All inside doors two-panel birch, with clear birch trim such as casing, baseboards, molding, etc., to match. All floors are made of clear yellow pine flooring laid on sub floor. Framing timbers are all No. 1 yellow pine. All rooms are 9 feet from floor to ceiling.

Basement.

The basement under the entire house has a cement floor and is 7 feet from floor to joists. Built on a concrete block foundation.

All outside walls covered with 1-inch dressed and matched sheathing boards lined with heavy building paper and sided with clear cypress bevel siding to the first story and *A* cedar shingles above first story line and on to the roof.

Paint for two coats best paint on the outside. Varnish and wood filler for two coats for interior finish.

This house can be built on a lot 27 feet wide.

Complete Warm Air Heating Plant, for soft coal, extra	$ 55.30
Complete Warm Air Heating Plant, for hard coal, extra	58.56
Complete Steam Heating Plant, extra	118.40
Complete Hot Water Heating Plant, extra	152.13
Complete Plumbing Outfit, extra	116.93
Acetylene Lighting Plant, extra	47.90

SEARS, ROEBUCK AND CO.　　　　　**CHICAGO, ILLINOIS**

MODERN HOME No. 165

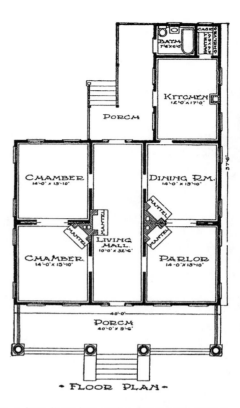

- FLOOR PLAN -

Built at New Braunfels, Texas; Lansdowne, Md.; and New Orleans, La.

$1,518.00

For $1,518.00 we will furnish all the material to build this Six-Room House, consisting of Mill Work, Ceiling, Siding, Flooring, Finishing Lumber, Building Paper, Pipe, Gutter, Sash Weights, Hardware, Mantels, Painting Material, Lumber, Lath and Shingles. **NO EXTRAS,** as we guarantee enough material at the above price to build this house according to our plans.

By allowing a fair price for labor, cement, brick and plaster, which we do not furnish, this house can be built for about $2,640.00, including all material and labor.

For Our Offer of Free Plans See Page 3.

A COLONIAL one-story house particularly planned for southern states. Plenty of room, light and ventilation are its chief characteristics. The large front porch with massive Colonial columns measures 40 feet by 9 feet 6 inches. A spacious rear porch is also provided.

Main Floor.

As will be seen by the floor plans, this house has a large living hall, parlor, dining room, kitchen, bathroom and two bedrooms. The large living hall extends the entire length of the house and when front and rear doors are open an abundance of air is admitted to all rooms, giving perfect ventilation. Four mantels are provided; one in the parlor, one in the dining room, one in the front bedroom and one in the living hall. There are double sliding doors between the two bedrooms and double sliding doors between the dining room and the parlor. Ceilings in all rooms are 12 feet high. Front and rear doors are all oak, glazed with leaded glass. Interior doors are six-cross panel veneered oak, with clear oak casing, base and molding. Clear yellow pine flooring. Outside blinds for all windows.

Basement.

There is an excavated basement under the entire house. Height from floor to joists, 7 feet.
Built on a concrete block foundation. Frame construction. Sided with narrow bevel edge cypress siding. Gables sided with cedar shingles and has cedar shingle roof.
Painted two coats outside; your choice of color. Varnish and wood filler for interior finish.

This house can be built on a lot 44 feet wide.

Complete Warm Air Heating Plant, for soft coal, extra	$122.34
Complete Warm Air Heating Plant, for hard coal, extra	125.12
Complete Steam Heating Plant, extra	286.65
Complete Hot Water Heating Plant, extra	328.62
Complete Plumbing Outfit, extra	99.39
Acetylene Lighting Plant, extra	47.90

SEARS, ROEBUCK AND CO.   **CHICAGO, ILLINOIS**

MODERN HOME No. 168

This house has been built at Lima, Colo., Westville, Conn., Chicago, Ill., La Grange, Ill., Watertown, Ill., Gary, Ind., Highland, Ind., Jeddo, Mich., Trenton, Mich., Rochester, Minn., Shelby, Neb., Medford, N. J., Irving, N. Y., Cincinnati, Ohio, East Petersburg, Penn., Elk Point, S. Dak., Madison, Wis., and other cities.

Saves 35 Per Cent and Gets a Better Grade Than the Local Market Could Furnish.

Silver Lane, Conn.

Sears, Roebuck and Co., Chicago, Ill.

Gentlemen:—In regard to the bill of lumber I bought of you people for my new house now built, will say I am very well satisfied with the quality of all the material that you sent me and compared with material that one can buy in this section it is much better grade of material, and I saved about 35 per cent by buying my material of you people. I am glad to say that the material was shipped promptly and came through to destination in only thirteen days.

Very truly yours,
JAMES P. PRATT.

FLOOR PLAN

$1,183.00

For $1,183.00 we will furnish all the material to build this Five-Room Bungalow, consisting of Mill Work, Ceiling, Flooring, Finishing Lumber, Building Paper, Pipe, Gutter, Sash Weights, Buffet, Medicine Case, Pantry Case, Hardware, Painting Material, Lumber, Lath and Shingles. NO EXTRAS, as we guarantee enough material at the above price to build this house according to our plans.

By allowing a fair price for labor, cement, brick and plaster, which we do not furnish, this house can be built for about $2,075.00 including all material and labor.

For Our Offer of Free Plans See Page 3.

A MODERN type of bungalow, sided with cedar shingles and having exterior brick chimney. Large porch, 16 feet 6 inches by 7 feet. Note the number of places where this house has been built. Every owner is well pleased with his investment.

First Floor.

A Craftsman front door glazed with leaded art glass opens from the porch into the living room, which has a convenient nook and window seat. Large bay window in this room, also in the dining room. The latter contains a Craftsman oak buffet and mantel. Colored leaded art glass sash on each side of the mantel. The front window in the living room has three colored leaded art sash. Pantry opens to the dining room and kitchen. There is an open closet off the hall with sash between this closet and pantry for light. The basement can be reached by inside stairs and also by outside cellar stairway under the porch. We furnish interior oak veneered doors of the latest Craftsman design for this house. Clear red oak floor for the living room and dining room. Clear maple for the kitchen and bathroom.

Built on a concrete foundation and is of frame construction, sided and roofed with cedar shingles; front gable is sided with stonekote, more commonly known as cement plaster.

The attic can be finished to very good advantage at a small cost, and the stairway could be placed directly over the cellar stairs, thereby doing away with the open closet which is now shown on the plan.

Painted two coats outside; your choice of color. Varnish and wood filler for interior finish.

Excavated basement under the entire house, 7 feet from floor to joists, with cement floor. Rooms on main floor are 9 feet from floor to ceiling.

This house can be built on a lot 34 feet wide.

Complete Warm Air Heating Plant, for soft coal, extra	$ 57.74
Complete Warm Air Heating Plant, for hard coal, extra	61.00
Complete Steam Heating Plant, extra	147.35
Complete Hot Water Heating Plant, extra	184.88
Complete Plumbing Outfit, extra	113.80
Acetylene Lighting Plant, extra	49.50

SEARS, ROEBUCK
AND CO.

CHICAGO,
ILLINOIS

—32—

MODERN HOME No. 140

Built at Gary, Ind.

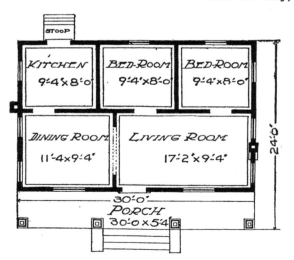

FLOOR PLAN

ADMIRED BY ALL.

Baltimore, Md.

Sears, Roebuck and Co.,

Chicago, Ill.

Gentlemen:—Enclosed you will find photo of my home built from your plans, slightly modified. I am well pleased with the way the materials show up. **The house is admired by all who see it.** I have talked a friend of mine into the idea of building and he wants one of your catalogs.

Very truly,

S. R. WANTZ, M. D.

$449.00

For $449.00 we will furnish all the material to build this Five-Rroom Bungalow, consisting of Lumber, Lath, Shingles, Mill Work, Flooring, Ceiling, Siding, Finishing Lumber, Building Paper, Pipe, Gutter, Sash Weights, Hardware and Painting Material. **NO EXTRAS,** as we guarantee enough material at the above price to build this house according to our plans.

By allowing a fair price for labor, cement, stone and plaster, which we do not furnish, this house can be built for about $900.00, including all material and labor.

For Our Offer of Free Plans See Page 3.

IN MODERN Home No. 140 we have an attractive cottage or bungalow sided with roughed 10-inch boards laid 8 inches to the weather and stained with dark creosote stain. A cobblestone foundation, porch pillars and chimney give this bungalow a rustic beauty seldom seen in buildings at such a low price.

First Floor.

A porch extends the entire length of the house, 5 feet 4 inches by 30 feet. The front door opens into the living room, which is separated from the dining room by a cased opening. Doors lead from the living room into the two bedrooms. A door leads from the dining room into the kitchen. The front door is made of clear pine 1¾ inches thick, glazed with bevel plate glass. Inside doors are five-cross panel style, clear yellow pine. Rear door is soft pine, 1¾ inches thick, and glazed with "A" quality double strength glass. The two windows in the front are glazed with leaded crystal sheet glass in the top sash and "A" quality double strength glass in the bottom sash. All flooring and trim used in this house are made of the best grade yellow pine.

Built on a cobblestone foundation. Not excavated. We furnish framing timbers and siding of No. 1 yellow pine. Shingles are of cedar.

Height from floor to ceiling, 9 feet. Stain and paint are furnished for the exterior. Varnish and wood filler for the interior finish.

The lot on which this house is built should be at least 40 feet wide.

Complete Warm Air Heating Plant, for soft coal, extra	$51.36
Complete Warm Air Heating Plant, for hard coal, extra	54.62
Acetylene Lighting Plant, extra	46.00

SEARS, ROEBUCK AND CO. **CHICAGO, ILLINOIS**

MODERN HOME No. 156

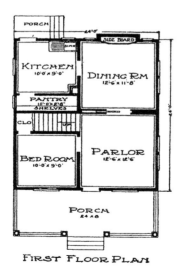

FIRST FLOOR PLAN

This house has been built at Elgin, Ill., Indianapolis, Ind., South Bend, Ind., Union, N. J., Schenectady, N. Y., Webster, N. Y., Dayton, Ohio, Marble Cliff, Ohio, and other cities.

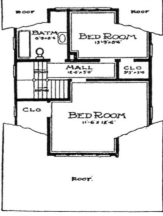

SECOND FLOOR PLAN

—34—

$779.00

For $779.00 we will furnish all the material to build this Six-Room Bungalow, consisting of Lumber, Lath, Shingles, Mill Work, Flooring, Ceiling, Siding, Finishing Lumber, Building Paper, Pipe, Gutter, Sash Weights, Hardware, Buffet and Painting Material. NO EXTRAS, as we guarantee enough material at the above price to build this house according to our plans.

By allowing a fair price for labor, cement, brick and plaster, which we do not furnish, this house can be built for about $1,500.00, including all material and labor.

For Our Offer of Free Plans See Page 3.

A MODERN six-room bungalow of frame construction, built along plain lines of good materials, yet at a price that is within reach of every purse. Every inch of space is used to the best advantage, the rooms being large in proportion to the exterior measurements of the house. The numerous windows, some of which are double, make every room light and airy. To bring out the bungalow effect our architect has designed a long sloping roof extending over the porch, and ornamented same by an attractive shingled dormer with four windows. The porch extends across the front of the house, measuring 24 feet long by 8 feet wide. Colonial porch columns and balusters are used with pleasing effect.

First Floor.

The front entrance leads directly into a large parlor, 12 feet 6 inches by 12 feet 6 inches, and separated from the dining room, which is arranged directly in the rear, with sliding door. The dining room, measuring 12 feet 6 inches by 11 feet 8 inches, has plate rail and buffet or china cabinet with small windows placed above plate rail at both sides of the cabinet and directly opposite the large sliding door, being plainly visible from the parlor. Directly off the dining room is located the kitchen with large pantry, also sink, which is placed directly in front of rear window. Glazed sash door leads from kitchen to back stoop. Directly off from parlor is a door leading to bedroom, 9 feet by 10 feet, with closet. This room can be used as a library or music room. The stairway leads from parlor to the second floor.

Second Floor.

Directly at the head of the stairs on the second floor is a hall which leads to front bedroom, size, 11 feet 6 inches by 12 feet 6 inches, with closet, and rear bedroom, 8 feet 6 inches by 13 feet 9 inches, with large closet. At the head of the stairs is a door leading to bathroom, 8 feet 9 inches by 8 feet 6 inches.

For the front door we furnish a heavy 1¾-inch door with etched design glass. Parlor and front bedroom, or library, have large cottage windows and double windows on the side. The interior doors are made of yellow pine and five-cross panels. All trim, including basewood, casings, interior molding and stair material, is made of yellow pine. Clear yellow pine flooring is used in all rooms and on porch. No. 1 yellow pine ceiling for porch.

Built on concrete block foundation. Sided with narrow bevel edge cypress siding and cedar shingles on the sides of dormer and on roof. All framing material, including joists, studding, etc., made from No. 1 yellow pine.

Height of Ceilings.

First floor, 9 feet from floor to ceiling.
Second floor, 8 feet from floor to ceiling.

We furnish two coats of paint for outside, your choice of color. Varnish and wood filler for interior finish.

This house can be built on a lot 27 feet 6 inches wide.

Complete Warm Air Heating Plant, for soft coal, extra	$ 81.55
Complete Warm Air Heating Plant, for hard coal, extra	83.99
Complete Steam Heating Plant, extra	155.55
Complete Hot Water Heating Plant, extra	187.42
Complete Plumbing Outfit, extra	105.02
Acetylene Lighting Plant, extra	47.90

SEARS, ROEBUCK AND CO.   **CHICAGO, ILLINOIS**

MODERN HOME No. 176

$2,141⁰⁰

For $2,141.00 we will furnish all the material to build this Eight-Room House, consisting of Lumber, Lath and Shingles, Mill Work, Flooring, Siding, Ceiling, Finishing Lumber, Building Paper, Pipe, Gutter, Sash Weights, Hardware, Brick Mantel, Buffet, Medicine Case, Painting Material, Bathroom Tile Floor. NO EXTRAS, as we guarantee enough material at the above price to build this house according to our plans.

By allowing a fair price for labor, cement, brick and plaster, which we do not furnish, this house can be built for about $3,800.00, including all material and labor.

For Our Offer of Free Plans See Page 3.

A LARGE modern type of square house with an open air dining porch in the rear and an open air sleeping porch on the second floor. The dining porch and sleeping porch may be enclosed with screen during the summer months and with sash during the winter. Note the Priscilla sash frames in each dormer, which gives this house a rich appearance and also affords a great deal of light in the attic, which is large enough for two small rooms.

First Floor.

In the large reception hall is an open oak stairway and large Colonial columns or colonnades reaching from the floor to the head casing. In the living room is a Colonial fireplace. The dining room is separated from the living room by double sliding doors. A Craftsman design oak buffet is provided for the dining room, which is further beautified by an oak beamed ceiling. A door leads from this dining room to the outside dining porch. The kitchen is exceptionally large, has a good size pantry with case on one side and shelving on the other and opens into the kitchen by way of cased opening opposite the rear window, making it light and well ventilated. A closet between the pantry and stairway is enclosed for a refrigerator and a storage for vegetables. The top sash of the two-light windows and also single windows are divided by wood bars, giving them a distinctly novel appearance. The flooring in the reception hall, living room and dining room is clear oak. The kitchen and pantry have clear maple flooring.

Second Floor.

The stairs from the kitchen join the landing of the main stairs, permitting one to go to the second floor from either the kitchen or reception hall. The bedrooms on the second floor have large closets. The two bedrooms on the left side of the house have mirror doors. Clear yellow pine flooring, with the exception of the bathroom, which is of beautiful white tile. Birch doors and clear birch trim throughout.

This house is built on a concrete block foundation and is of frame construction sided with clear cypress siding and has *A* cedar shingle roof. Excavated basement under the entire house, 7 feet from the floor to joists. Rooms on the first floor have 9-foot ceilings. Rooms on the second floor have 9-foot ceilings.

This house can be built on a lot 38 feet wide.

Complete Warm Air Heating Plant, for soft coal, extra................	$113.71
Complete Warm Air Heating Plant, for hard coal, extra................	116.09
Complete Steam Heating Plant, extra................	290.80
Complete Hot Water Heating Plant, extra................	336.58
Complete Plumbing Outfit, extra................	121.69
Acetylene Lighting Plant, extra................	50.30

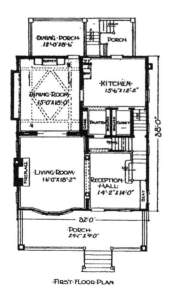

-FIRST-FLOOR-PLAN-

HAS BUILT THREE OF OUR MODERN HOMES AND IS NOW BUILDING THE FOURTH.

Hillsdale, Mich.

Sears, Roebuck and Co., Chicago, Ill.

Gentlemen:—I have built one house No. 111 Modern Home; made a few changes, but I will say that the plans are complete. I have built two houses after Modern Home No. 170 and am now starting the third. I am a contractor and builder. I have bought lots of mill work of you people and have always been satisfied. I now have an order and expect to send another this week. By buying your material, Modern Home No. 111 can be built in Hillsdale, Mich.; for $1,950.00; Modern Home No. 170 can be built for $1,600.00. Your blue prints are the finest I have ever seen. I have built two houses from plans bought from another well known firm for $30.00 and the prints are not worth one-fourth as much as yours.

S. E. FULLER.

-SECOND-FLOOR-PLAN-

—35—

SEARS, ROEBUCK AND CO.

CHICAGO, ILLINOIS

$1,779.00

MODERN HOME No. 146

For $1,779.00 we will furnish all the material to build this Seven-Room Residence, consisting of Lumber, Lath, Shingles, Mill Work, Ceiling, Siding, Flooring, Finishing Lumber, Buffet, Medicine Case, Building Paper, Pipe, Gutter, Sash Weights, Hardware and Painting Material. NO EXTRAS, as we guarantee enough material at the above price to build this house according to our plans.

By allowing a fair price for labor, cement, brick and plaster, which we do not furnish, this house can be built for about $3,960.00, including all material and labor.

For Our Offer of Free Plans See Page 3.

A GLANCE at the illustration will show that this is a strictly up to date residence. A spacious protected porch extends across the entire front and half way along the left elevation.

First Floor.

A beautiful front door opens from the porch into the reception hall, in which there is an open oak stairway of modern pattern leading to the second floor. The reception hall has a bay window and a window seat. The unique arrangement of the stairs permits one to reach the second floor from the kitchen or from the reception hall. The cellar stairs are placed directly under the main stairs. Large cased openings lead to the living room and dining room. The dining room has veneered oak beamed ceiling and a modern buffet with seats at each side. Colored leaded art glass over the buffet. This room also has a bay window with seat the entire length. The pantry between the dining room and kitchen effectively separates the kitchen from the rest of the house. A cased opening connects the pantry with the kitchen. The doors, staircase, window seats and interior trim of the first floor are furnished in the best quality of clear oak, Craftsman design, with clear oak flooring in the reception hall, living room and dining room. The kitchen and pantry floors are made of the best grade of maple.

Second Floor.

Four bedrooms, hall and bathroom are located on this floor. Like the rest of the plan, every foot of space is utilized to the very best advantage. Three large airy bedrooms each with windows on two sides, afford plenty of light and ventilation. Rooms have suitable closets and there is a plate glass mirror door in the front bedroom. The small bedroom or servant's room is lighted and ventilated from two sides also. The trim is of selected birch with six-cross panel birch doors to match. All flooring is made of clear maple.

Clear cypress siding from water table to second story window sills; balance of second story and roof shingled with cedar shingles. Edge grain fir flooring 1⅛ inches thick for porch.

Built on a concrete block foundation.

Excavated basement under the entire house, 7 feet high from floor to joists. First floor, 9 feet high from floor to ceiling; second floor, 8 feet high from floor to ceiling; attic room, 14x14 feet, 7 feet high from floor to collar beams. Gables and columns are sided with stonekote, the most modern style of construction.

This house can be built on a lot 46 feet wide.

Complete Warm Air Heating Plant, for soft coal, extra	$ 88.65
Complete Warm Air Heating Plant, for hard coal, extra	90.81
Complete Steam Heating Plant, extra	195.75
Complete Hot Water Heating Plant, extra	258.51
Complete Plumbing Outfit, extra	118.70
Acetylene Lighting Plant, extra	51.10

SEARS, ROEBUCK AND CO. **CHICAGO, ILLINOIS**

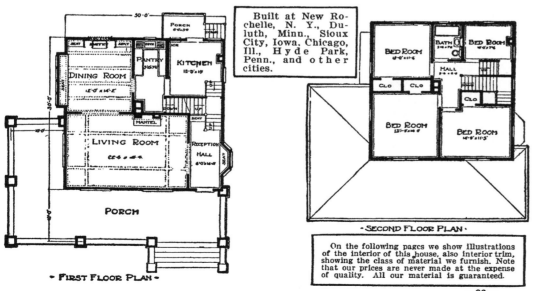

Built at New Rochelle, N. Y., Duluth, Minn., Sioux City, Iowa, Chicago, Ill., Hyde Park, Penn., and other cities.

- FIRST FLOOR PLAN -

- SECOND FLOOR PLAN -

On the following pages we show illustrations of the interior of this house, also interior trim, showing the class of material we furnish. Note that our prices are never made at the expense of quality. All our material is guaranteed.

—36—

THE INTERIOR OF OUR MODERN HOME No. 146

Our architects have devoted much careful study and spent considerable time in preparing the plans for all houses illustrated in this catalog. The specifications, working plans and itemized bill of material for every house shown herein have been proven by actual experience in erecting, eliminating all guesswork.

On the following pages we show some of the items of building materials which we furnish for this modern home. A comparison of prices will show that we can save you at least one-fourth in the cost of building materials with the use of our plans, as compared with what it would cost you if you purchased your building materials elsewhere and used the usual kind of incomplete plans.

MATERIAL SPECIFIED FOR MODERN HOME Nº 146

Birch Interior Door, 2 feet 8 inches by 7 feet, 1⅜ inches thick. Price...**$3.41**

Craftsman Oak Interior Door, 2 feet 8 inches by 7 feet, 1⅜ inches thick. Price ..**$6.00**

Closet Door for front chamber, birch, 2 ft. 4 in. x 7 ft., with beautiful full length bevel glass mirror. Price..**$14.50**

Rear Outside Door, 3x7 feet, 1¾ inches thick glazed. Price..**$4.95**

Two-Light Check Rail Window, 3 feet by 4 feet 6 inches, with glass. Price......**86c**

Craftsman Oak Buffet, bevel plate glass mirror, doors glazed with leaded glass. Price ..**$46.00**

The doors, buffet and other materials shown on this page represent a few of the items we furnish for Modern Home No. 146 shown on page 36.

Note our low prices. All our material is guaranteed. We furnish the very latest designs at half regular prices. For complete line see our Building Material Catalog.

⅞ × 5½
Stop

Inside Door Jambs.
Yellow pine...**$0.50**
Oak..........**.90**
Birch........**1.02**

QUALITY GUARANTEED

Colored Art Nouveau Leaded Glass over buffet.
Price, per foot.................................$1.65

Craftsman Oak Band Picture Mold. Price, per 100 feet..............$3.68

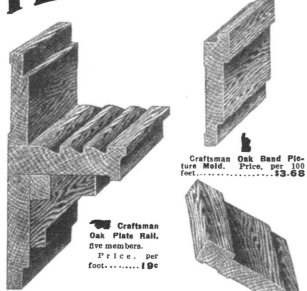

Craftsman Oak Plate Rail, five members. Price, per foot.........19c

Craftsman Oak Two-Member Casing. Price, per 100 feet..$3.85

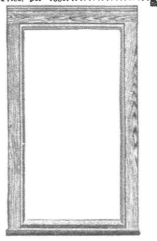

Outside Window Frame, 2 feet by 4 feet 6 inches, with pulleys. Price...................$1.62

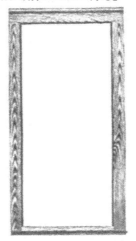

Outside Door Frame, 1⅛-inch outside casing, 1¾-inch thick oak sill. Price......$1.90

Craftsman Oak Window Stool. Price, per 100 feet.....$5.78

Craftsman Oak Three-Member Base. Price, per 100 feet.......$7.25

Craftsman Oak Window Apron. Price, per 100 feet...$2.85

Craftsman Oak Picture Molding. Price, per 100 feet.........$1.89

Clear Oak Flooring, 13-16x 2¼-inch face. Price, per 100 feet......$6.75

We specify the highest class of materials; strictly up to date designs. Our low prices explain why you can build a $5,000.00 house for $3,960.00 when you trade with us.

QUALITY GUARANTEED

Cupboard Door, 1 foot 6 inches by 2 feet 6 inches, 1⅛ inches thick. Price.....57c

The interior of a home finished with materials such as shown on this page is sure to please. There are none better made at any price. We guarantee to please our customers.

Clear Yellow Pine Flooring, 13-16x3¼-inch face. Price, per 100 feet.........$2.99

Craftsman Oak Stair Rail, 2½ x 3½ inches. Price, per lineal foot...........**14c**

WALL STRING
MOULDING
COVE
TREAD
RISER

OAK STAIRS.
Treads. Price, each..............**51c**
Risers. Price, each..............**24c**
Two-Member String Board. Price, per foot......................**13c**

Oak Thresholds. Price, each........**5c**

Front Door Lock Set, solid bronze trimming. Price......**$5.00**

Rear Door Lock Set, solid bronze trimming. Price....**$1.00**

Oak Stair Newel. Price......**$2.96**

Oak Angle Stair Newel. Price, **$1.81**

Sash Cord. Price, per 100 feet.....**60c**

Yellow Pine Kitchen Base, 7¼ inches high. Price, per 100 feet.........**$3.20**

Three-Member Cap Trim, yellow pine. Price, per 100 feet.........**$4.63**

Three-Member Birch Baseboard, 9½ in. high. Price, per 100 feet..**$9.20**

Yellow Pine Window Stool. Price, per 100 feet....**$2.64**

Yellow Pine Window Stop. ⅜ x 1⅜ inches. Price, per 100 feet.......**39c**

Yellow Pine Window Apron. Price, per 100 feet..**$1.68**

Yellow Pine Casing, 4¼ inches wide. Price, per 100 feet...............**$1.90**

Cove Molding. Price, per 100 feet........**35c**

Outside House Paint, guaranteed. In 5-gallon lots. Price, per gallon....**$1.09**

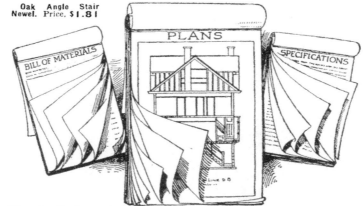

Plans, Specifications and Bill of Materials which we furnish free as offered on page 3.

Inside Door Lock Sets, plated bronze trimming. Price, each..........**50c**

Hinges and Screws to match trimming. Price, per pair........**23c**

SEARS, ROEBUCK AND CO.

CHICAGO, ILLINOIS

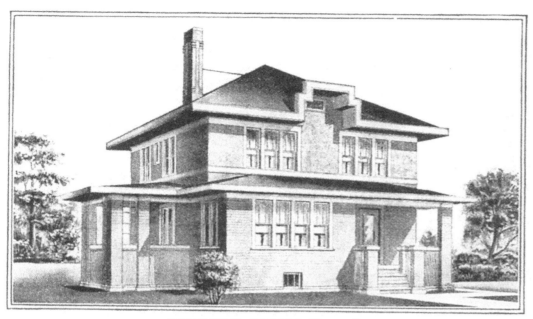

MODERN HOME No. 157

$1,866.00

For $1,866.00 we will furnish all the material to build this Eight-Room Residence, consisting of Mill Work, Ceiling, Siding, Flooring, Finishing Lumber, Building Paper, Pipe, Gutter, Sash Weights, Hardware, Mantel, Painting Material, Lumber, Lath and Shingles. **NO EXTRAS**, as we guarantee enough material at the above price to build this house according to our plans.

By allowing a fair price for labor, cement, brick and plaster, which we do not furnish, this house can be built for about $3,480.00, including all material and labor.

For Our Offer of Free Plans See Page 3.

THIS BIG roomy modern home is combination frame and stucco construction, which makes it specially attractive and the size makes it specially suited for a large family.

Main Floor.

This modern residence has an exceptionally large living room, 15 feet 6 inches by 26 feet 6 inches, and connects with the stairhall by means of a large cased opening. Another cased opening leads from the living room to the dining room. In the reception hall is a Colonial combination wardrobe and closet with leaded glass doors. A long hall seat built in an L shape on two walls at the foot of the stairway gives the reception hall an inviting and comfortable appearance. The living room is provided with a handsome mantel and beamed ceiling. From the living room you enter the veranda shown on the left. The main rooms on the first floor are trimmed with clear oak casing, baseboard and molding and have six-cross panel oak doors. Clear oak flooring for reception hall, living room and dining room. Maple flooring for kitchen and pantry. Rooms on this floor are 9 feet high.

Second Floor.

There are four bedrooms and a bathroom on the second floor, all of them having cypress casing, baseboard and molding, with five-cross panel clear cypress doors. Clear yellow pine floors. The large front bedroom has a mantel and two closets. All other rooms have one good size closet each. Ceilings are 8 feet 6 inches high. Attic is floored but not finished.

Basement.

Excavated basement under the entire house, 7 feet high from floor to joists. Lighted by basement sash.

Built on a concrete foundation; frame construction and is sided from the water table to window sills of the second story with narrow edge cypress siding. The remainder of the house is finished with stonekote, more commonly known as cement plaster, and has cedar shingle roof on main house and porches.

Painted two coats outside; your choice of color. Varnish and wood filler for two coats of interior finish.

This house can be built on a lot 45 feet wide.

Complete Warm Air Heating Plant, for soft coal, extra	$116.24
Complete Warm Air Heating Plant, for hard coal, extra	118.62
Complete Steam Heating Plant, extra	325.95
Complete Hot Water Heating Plant, extra	381.12
Complete Plumbing Outfit, extra	147.31
Acetylene Lighting Plant, extra	50.30

SEARS, ROEBUCK AND CO.   **CHICAGO, ILLINOIS**

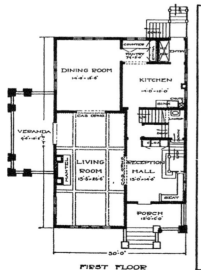

FIRST FLOOR

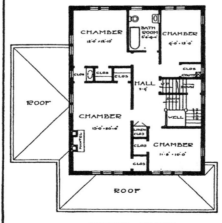

SECOND FLOOR

MODERN HOME No. 158

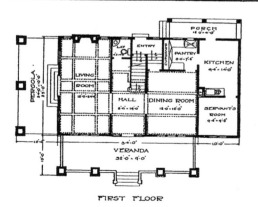

FIRST FLOOR

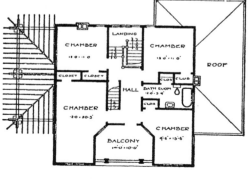

SECOND FLOOR

$1,845.00

For $1,845.00 we will furnish all the material to build this modern Nine-Room Residence, consisting of Lumber, Lath, Shingles, Mill Work, Ceiling, Siding, Flooring, Finishing Lumber, Building Paper, Pipe, Gutter, Sash Weights, Mantel, Hardware and Painting Material. NO EXTRAS, as we guarantee enough material at the above price to build this house according to our plans.

By allowing a fair price for labor, cement, brick and plaster, which we do not furnish, this house can be built for about $3,895.00, including all material and labor.

For Our Offer of Free Plans See Page 3.

MODERN HOME No. 158 is a high class residence in every sense of the word. Being a practically square design it can be built at a very reasonable price. The pergola, which is 24x10 feet, is a very popular feature in modern homes and in the present instance has the advantage of making the house look well balanced.

First Floor.

The rooms in this house are conveniently arranged with a reception hall opening into the dining room on one side and into a very large living room on the other side. The kitchen and pantry are practically separated from the remainder of the house with entrance from the kitchen to the dining room through the pantry. An open staircase leads from the reception hall to the second floor. The beamed ceiling is worked into one design for the living room, hall and dining room, the latter having a polished oak mantel. The front and side doors are veneered oak of the proper design to match the windows. Interior doors for the main rooms on the first floor are six-cross panel veneered oak with casing, baseboard, trim and stairs of clear oak also. Front door cylinder locks and all interior locks are genuine bronze. Other hardware to match. Ceilings are 9 feet high.

Second Floor.

The second floor contains four large chambers and a large balcony which can be screened in and used as an open air sleeping porch. Second floor doors are of clear birch, six-cross panel, with birch casing, baseboard and trim. All rooms have good size closets. Ceilings are 9 feet high.

Basement.

Excavated basement under the entire building, 7 feet high from floor to joists. Divided into three rooms; one for laundry, one for storage and the other for heating plant and coal.

Built on a concrete foundation and is of frame construction. The first story is covered with narrow bevel edge cypress siding, the second story with cedar shingles and has a cedar shingle roof.

Painted two coats outside; your choice of color. Varnish and wood filler for two coats of interior finish.

This house can be built on a lot 56 feet wide.

Complete Warm Air Heating Plant, for soft coal, extra	$101.75
Complete Warm Air Heating Plant, for hard coal, extra	103.91
Complete Steam Heating Plant, extra	294.50
Complete Hot Water Heating Plant, extra	336.28
Complete Plumbing Outfit, extra	121.31
Acetylene Lighting Plant, extra	52.70

SEARS, ROEBUCK AND CO.
CHICAGO, ILLINOIS

MODERN HOME No. 227

$978.00

For $978.00 we will furnish all the material to build this Eight-Room House, consisting of Lumber, Lath, Shingles, Mill Work, Ceiling, Siding, Flooring, Finishing Lumber, Building Paper, Pipe, Gutter, Sash Weights, Hardware, Mantel and Painting Material. NO EXTRAS, as we guarantee enough material at the above price to build this house according to our plans.

By allowing a fair price for labor, cement, brick and plaster, which we do not furnish, this house can be built for about $1,900.00, including all material and labor.

For Our Offer of Free Plans See Page 3.

A WELL designed house and one that will make a pleasant home. It is square in plan, giving the greatest amount of available space possible for the least money. The exterior presents a dignified and substantial appearance. Bevel siding is used for the first story, stonekote or cement for the second story. The large porch extending across the front is 23 feet wide by 8 feet deep. This house can be built with siding on the second story at about the same cost. The front door opens into a vestibule which separates the den from the hall. This vestibule could be dispensed with and the den would then be converted into a very nice reception hall. A large cased opening between the living room and dining room practically makes one large room of these two rooms. The pantry, which has plenty of shelving and a pantry case built in, is situated between the dining room and kitchen. This makes a very handy arrangement.

First Floor.

The front door is made of clear white pine, 1¾ inches thick, glazed with a long light of bevel plate glass. The vestibule door is also of clear white pine, glazed with "A" quality double strength glass. The inside doors are the five-cross panel design, made of the best quality yellow pine. Rear door, 1⅜ inches thick, made of soft pine and glazed with "A" quality double strength glass. Trim and flooring for the entire first floor are made of the best grade yellow pine.

Second Floor.

Stairway to second floor made of yellow pine, opens into a hall on the second floor, from which any of the four bedrooms, bathroom or linen closet may be entered. Three of the bedrooms have a good size clothes closet. All doors on the second floor are made of the best quality yellow pine in the five-cross panel style. Yellow pine trim and flooring.

Built on a concrete block foundation, excavated under the entire house. We furnish cypress siding and cedar shingles. Framing timbers of best quality yellow pine.

Height of Ceilings.

The basement has cement floor and is 7 feet from floor to joists. First floor is 9 feet from floor to ceiling; second floor, 8 feet 6 inches from floor to ceiling. Painted two coats outside, varnish and wood filler for interior finish.

Should be built on a lot about 35 feet wide.

Complete Warm Air Heating Plant, for soft coal, extra	$ 92.49
Complete Warm Air Heating Plant, for hard coal, extra	94.50
Complete Steam Heating Plant, extra	192.25
Complete Hot Water Heating Plant, extra	236.79
Complete Plumbing Outfit, extra	119.84
Acetylene Lighting Plant, extra	51.90

SEARS, ROEBUCK AND CO.   **CHICAGO, ILLINOIS**

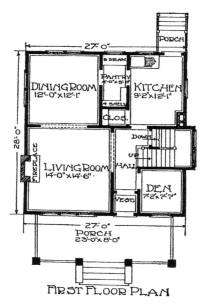

FIRST FLOOR PLAN

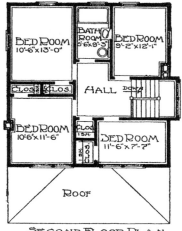

SECOND FLOOR PLAN

$992.00

For $992.00 we will furnish all the material to build this Eight Room House, consisting of Mill Work, Flooring, Ceiling, Siding, Finishing Lumber, Building Paper, Eaves Trough, Hardware, Painting Material, Lumber, Lath and Shingles. NO EXTRAS, as we guarantee enough material at the above price to build this house according to our plans.

By allowing a fair price for labor, cement, brick and plaster, which we do not furnish, this house can be built for about $1,980.00, including all material and labor.

For Our Offer of Free Plans See Page 3.

THIS GOOD substantial house of nice appearance is suitable for suburban residence or country home. Every bit of space has been used to the best advantage, leaving absolutely no waste space.

First Floor.

As one enters the hall the first thing to be seen is a nice open oak stairway with landing half way up to the second floor. Three nice rooms and a large hall on the first floor, all of which, excepting the kitchen, are finished in oak. Kitchen is finished in yellow pine, with maple flooring. Interior doors on this floor are two-panel oak, veneered. A combination china closet and cupboard is placed between the dining room and kitchen, opening into both rooms. This arrangement makes all parts of the cupboard accessible from either the kitchen or dining room, saving many steps. Ceilings are 9 feet high.

Second Floor.

There are four windows in each front bedroom on the second floor which admit plenty of light and air. The four bedrooms on this floor have clear yellow pine flooring and yellow pine five-cross panel doors. Ceilings are 8 feet high.

Basement.

Excavated basement under the entire house, 7 feet from floor to joists, with cement floor. Basement lighted by basement sash.

Built on a concrete block foundation. Frame construction. It is sided up to the second-story window sills with narrow bevel edge cypress siding and cedar shingles up the rest of the way to the cornice. Cedar shingles for roof.

This house can be built on a lot 28 feet wide.

Complete Warm Air Heating Plant, for soft coal, extra	$ 91.99
Complete Warm Air Heating Plant, for hard coal, extra	94.23
Complete Steam Heating Plant, extra	186.70
Complete Hot Water Heating Plant, extra	235.35
Complete Plumbing Outfit, extra	124.36
Acetylene Lighting Plant, extra	49.50

SEARS, ROEBUCK AND CO. **CHICAGO, ILLINOIS**

MODERN HOME No. 148

Built at Bellefonte, Penn., Des Plaines, Ill., Grand Rapids, Mich., Parker, S. Dak., Cleveland, Ohio, Logan, Iowa, Sioux Falls, S. Dak., and other cities.

SAVED ABOUT $700.00 ON MODERN HOME No. 148.
Cleveland, Ohio.
Sears, Roebuck and Co.,
Chicago, Ill.
Gentlemen:—I am now living in my house, E. 127 St., Kinsman Rd., and am pleased with it. Everybody who sees my home thinks it is very nice. **I saved between six and seven hundred dollars** by getting my lumber from you, and I recommend your lumber and material to all my friends.
Yours truly,
R. C. PITTMAN.

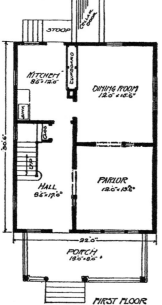

FIRST FLOOR

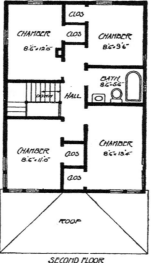

SECOND FLOOR

MODERN HOME No. 163

$1,282.00

For $1,282.00 we will furnish all the material to build this Eight-Room House, consisting of Mill Work, Flooring, Ceiling, Finishing Lumber, Building Paper, Pipe, Gutter, Sash Weights, Hardware, Mantel, Medicine Case, Lumber, Lath and Shingles. NO EXTRAS, as we guarantee enough material at the above price to build this house according to our plans.

By allowing a fair price for labor, cement, brick and plaster, which we do not furnish, this house can be built for about $2,675.00, including all material and labor.

For $64.00 extra we will furnish clear cypress bevel siding for the outside of this house.

For Our Offer of Free Plans See Page 3.

THIS HOUSE has two full stories and an attic. It is sided with stonekote, more commonly known as cement plaster. It can be sided with clear cypress bevel siding if desired for the amount specified above. A large front porch supported by massive stonekote columns extends across the entire front, 26 feet long by 8 feet wide. The balcony over the porch is protected by the main roof and is 12 feet 9 inches long by 5 feet 6 inches wide. This balcony makes a very desirable place for an open air sleeping porch when screened in.

First Floor.

In the vestibule an open oak stairway leads to the second floor and under this stairway is an inside cellar stairway. A cased opening leads from the hall into the parlor which is separated from the dining room by double sliding doors. Both parlor and dining room are lighted from two sides. A single door leads from the hall to the dining room so that it can be entered without passing through the parlor. The pantry is reached both from the kitchen and dining room by single doors. All interior doors are two-panel birch, with clear birch casing, baseboard and trim. The front door is a birch veneered door glazed with large bevel plate glass. Clear oak flooring for the main rooms with maple flooring for the kitchen and pantry. Clear yellow pine edge grain flooring for the porch. Rooms are 9 feet from floor to ceiling.

Second Floor.

When on the second floor landing you are within a very few feet of the entrance to all the four bedrooms and bathroom, also to the attic stairs. Colored leaded Art Nouveau sash at each stair landing and one about half way up the stairs, producing a beautiful mellow effect. Birch veneered front doors leaded with bevel plate glass open from the two front bedrooms onto the balcony. All rooms have good size closets. Flooring is clear maple for all rooms, with clear birch casing, baseboard and trim. Rooms are 8 feet 6 inches from floor to ceiling.

Basement.

Excavated basement under the entire house, 7 feet from floor to joists, with cement floor. Lighted with basement sash.
Built on a concrete block foundation with concrete blocks above the grade line. Frame construction and has cedar shingle roof.
Varnish and wood filler for two coats of interior finish.

This house can be built on a lot 32 feet wide.

Complete Warm Air Heating Plant, for soft coal, extra	$94.28
Complete Warm Air Heating Plant, for hard coal, extra	96.44
Complete Steam Heating Plant, extra	189.30
Complete Hot Water Heating Plant, extra	232.98
Complete Plumbing Outfit, extra	119.71
Acetylene Lighting Plant, extra	50.30

SEARS, ROEBUCK AND CO.　　　　　**CHICAGO, ILLINOIS**

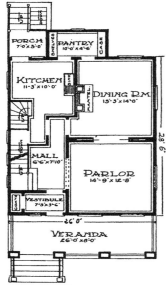

- FIRST FLOOR PLAN -

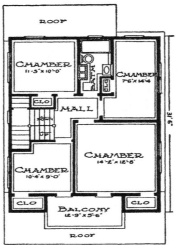

- SECOND FLOOR PLAN -

HE SAVED ALMOST ENOUGH TO PAY FOR THE LABOR.

Glen Park, N. Y.
Sears, Roebuck and Co.,
Chicago, Ill.

Gentlemen:—I am very much pleased with the building material you sent me for my house and can assure anyone who wishes to build that they can save enough on the cost of material bought from you to build their home. Have shown my house to a number of people and everyone was surprised at the fine grade of finish at such low prices.
I know from experience in dealing with you no one could ask for better service or be dealt with more fairly.

Respectfully,
ALBERT PEPIN.

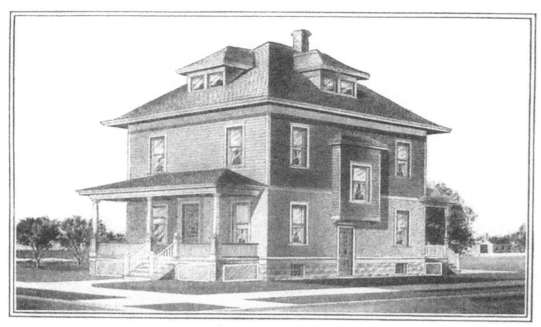

$1,209.00

For $1,209.00 we will furnish all the material to build this Eight-Room House, consisting of Mill Work, Ceiling, Siding, Flooring, Finishing Lumber, Building Paper, Pipe, Gutter, Sash Weights, Hardware, Painting Material, Lumber, Lath and Shingles. NO EXTRAS, as we guarantee enough material at the above price to build this house according to our plans.

By allowing a fair price for labor, cement, brick and plaster, which we do not furnish, this house can be built for about $2,345.00, including all material and labor.

For Our Offer of Free Plans See Page 3.

THIS is a conveniently arranged house of eight rooms at a very low cost compared with the accommodations it offers. A large front porch, 24 feet long and 6 feet wide, extends almost clear across the front of the house.

First Floor.

All interior doors on this floor are six-cross panel veneered oak, with clear plain sawed oak trim. Front door opens into a large hall in which there is an open oak stairway to the second floor. Under the main stairway cellar stairs lead to the side entrance and continue down into the basement. All rooms are well lighted by windows on two sides and are 9 feet 2 inches high from floor to ceiling.

Second Floor.

A stairway from the first floor leads to a central hall from which all bedrooms and bathroom can be instantly entered. The doors on this floor are five-cross panel solid yellow pine, with clear yellow pine trim. All rooms are well lighted, have good size closets and are 9 feet high from floor to ceiling.

Basement.

An excavated basement under the entire house, 7 feet 2 inches from floor to joists. Lighted with basement sash.

Paint for two coats of exterior work, your choice of color, varnish and wood filler for two coats of interior finish.

Built on a concrete block foundation and is of frame construction. The first story is sided with stonekote or cement plaster. The second story is sided with narrow bevel edge cypress siding. Cedar shingle roof.

This house is 28 feet wide by 38 feet 6 inches long and can be built on a lot 32 feet wide.

Complete Warm Air Heating Plant, for soft coal, extra	$ 97.43
Complete Warm Air Heating Plant, for hard coal, extra	99.59
Complete Steam Heating Plant, extra	207.80
Complete Hot Water Heating Plant, extra	247.62
Complete Plumbing Outfit, extra	118.21
Acetylene Lighting Plant, extra	50.30

SEARS, ROEBUCK AND CO.　　　　**CHICAGO, ILLINOIS**

MODERN HOME No. 111

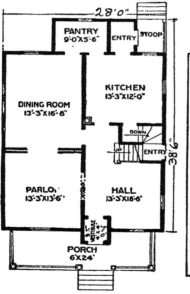

FIRST FLOOR PLAN

SAVED 25 PER CENT ON MODERN HOME No. 111.

1503 Holcomb Ave.,
Detroit, Mich.
Sears, Roebuck and Co.,
Chicago, Ill.

Gentlemen:—We are fully satisfied and find we saved 25 per cent on all building material we bought of you. If we build again we shall send for a full carload and especially mill work. Everything bought of you is up to your claim in every way. We will gladly answer any inquiries that may come to us. Yes, we are living in our house and the cypress doors are dandy finished. We shall finish our next house in cypress all through. We are sending a photograph of the house. Accept our thanks for your cordial treatment.

Respectfully yours,
W. A. TURK.

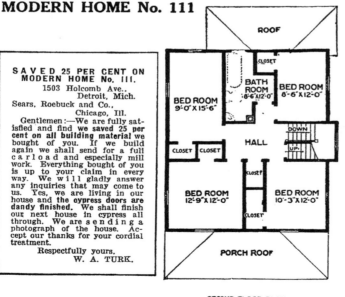

SECOND FLOOR PLAN

$1,057.00

For $1,057.00 we will furnish all the material to build this large Eight-Room House, consisting of Mill Work, Flooring, Ceiling, Siding, Finishing Lumber, Building Paper, Eaves Trough, Hardware, Painting Material, Lumber, Lath and Shingles. **NO EXTRAS**, as we guarantee enough material at the above price to build this house according to our plans.

By allowing a fair price for labor, cement, brick and plaster, which we do not furnish, this house can be built for about $2,170.00, including all material and labor.

For Our Offer of Free Plans See Page 3.

THIS HOUSE, which has been built in several states at a big saving to each builder, contains eight rooms, all conveniently arranged. It has a large front porch, 18 feet long by 6 feet wide, and a balcony of the same dimensions. Notice the wide panel cornice which is very becoming to this style of architecture. Without extra charge we will furnish this house with exterior as shown in Modern Home No. 207 illustrated below.

First Floor. Our Majestic oak veneered front door, glazed with bevel plate glass, leads from the porch into a spacious reception hall in which there is an open oak stairway to the second floor. The dining room can be entered from either the parlor or reception hall and connects with the reception hall by a 7-foot sliding door. Interior doors are made of clear solid yellow pine, five-cross panel, with clear yellow pine trim, such as baseboard, casing and molding. Clear yellow pine flooring for all rooms. Rooms are 9 feet, 2 inches high from floor to ceiling.

Second Floor. The large front bedroom, lighted by three windows, measures 19x11 feet and has two large closets, the front one being lighted by a Colonial window. Another Colonial window in the front bedroom. The two rear bedrooms have good size closets and there is also a closet off the hall. All doors, flooring and trim are clear yellow pine. Rooms are 8 feet high from floor to ceiling.

Basement. Excavated basement under the entire house, 7 feet from floor to joists. Lighted with basement sash.
Built upon a concrete block foundation. Frame construction. Sided with narrow bevel edge cypress siding and has cedar shingle roof.

This house is 27 feet 6 inches wide by 40 feet 6 inches long and can be built on a lot 30 feet wide.

Complete Warm Air Heating Plant, for soft coal, extra	$ 86.14
Complete Warm Air Heating Plant, for hard coal, extra	88.30
Complete Steam Heating Plant, extra	181.70
Complete Hot Water Heating Plant, extra	229.43
Complete Plumbing Outfit, extra	113.98
Acetylene Lighting Plant, extra	50.30

MODERN HOME No. 112

This house has been built at Birmingham, Ala., Deer Creek, Ill., Corunna, Ind., Rushville, Neb., New York, N. Y., Cohoes, N. Y., Granville, Ohio, Valley Springs, S. D., Enon, Ohio, Hartford City, Ind., Ponca, Neb., and other cities.

Two coats of paint for outside work. Varnish and wood filler for two coats of interior finish.

SAVED $1,000.00 ON MODERN HOME No. 112.

113 Bridge St., Cohoes, N. Y.
Sears, Roebuck and Co., Chicago, Ill.
Gentlemen:—I am sending you a photograph of the house built from material shipped from you and according to your plans. I am pleased to say that I was well satisfied with the quality of materials and your prompt shipment. Your plans are a great help to anyone that wants to build. After a close estimate I can say that I have saved on this property $1,000.00.

Very truly yours,
FRANK CHAMBERLAIN.

SEARS, ROEBUCK AND CO., CHICAGO, ILL.

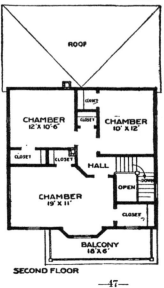

$1,243⁰⁰

For $1,243.00 we will furnish all the material to build this Ten-Room House, consisting of Mill Work, Flooring, Ceiling, Siding, Finishing Lumber, Building Paper, Pipe, Gutter, Sash Weights, China Closet, Hardware, Painting Material, Lumber, Lath and Shingles. **NO EXTRAS**, as we guarantee enough material at the above price to build this house according to our plans.

By allowing a fair price for labor, stone, brick and plaster, which we do not furnish, this house can be built for about $2,300.00, including all material and labor.

For Our Offer of Free Plans See Page 3.

A SQUARE house is always desirable. It is easy to build as the design is simple and requires less mechanical labor than other styles of architecture. It affords a great deal of room and has a good appearance for the amount of money invested. This house has ten good size conveniently arranged rooms. Front hall has sliding doors leading to the living room; also sliding doors to the parlor. Grille between the parlor and dining room. Kitchen connected with the dining room and large butler's pantry. Open stairway leading to the second floor. Four large bedrooms with two windows in each room. Large size bathroom and four closets on the second floor.

Queen Anne window in the hall on the second floor; leaded glass windows for the living room and parlor. Metropole front door, glazed with leaded glass. All interior doors are five-cross panel with soft pine stiles and rails, yellow pine panels. Clear pine trim throughout. Clear yellow pine flooring for the entire house and 1⅛-inch clear fir flooring for porches.

Painted two coats on the outside. Varnish and wood filler for two coats of interior finish.

Built on a stone foundation, frame construction, sided with narrow bevel edge clear cypress siding and has *A* cedar shingle roof. Large front porch, 26 feet 6 inches wide by 6 feet 3 inches deep; rear porch, 15 feet 6 inches long by 4 feet wide.

Excavated basement under the entire house, 7 feet 2 inches from floor to joists. Rooms on the first floor, 9 feet 3 inches from floor to ceiling; second floor, 8 feet 4 inches from floor to ceiling.

This house can be furnished with clear oak stairs and trim and oak flooring on the first floor. If you want it finished this way, order plans for Modern Home No. 150.

This house is 32 feet wide by 36 feet long and can be built on a lot 36 feet wide.

Complete Warm Air Heating Plant, for soft coal, extra	$ 80.32
Complete Warm Air Heating Plant, for hard coal, extra	82.35
Complete Steam Heating Plant, extra	222.75
Complete Hot Water Heating Plant, extra	276.70
Complete Plumbing Outfit, extra	117.55
Acetylene Lighting Plant, extra	51.10

SEARS, ROEBUCK AND CO.   **CHICAGO, ILLINOIS**

MODERN HOME No. 102 Trimmed Clear Nona White Pine. Price..$1,243.00
MODERN HOME No. 150 Oak Finish First Floor. Price............ 1,335.00

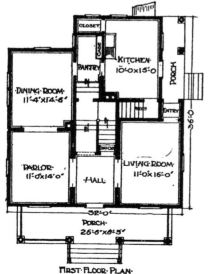

FIRST·FLOOR·PLAN·

Built at Norfolk, Conn., Belleville, N. J., Grand Rapids, Mich., Rockford, Ill., Shelby, Ohio, Plainview, Texas, and several other cities.

SAVED 30 PER CENT ON MODERN HOME No. 102.
No. 98 N. Gamble St., Shelby, Ohio.
Sears, Roebuck and Co., Chicago, Ill.
Gentlemen:—I am sending you a photograph of the house I built according to your House Plans No. 102. The quality of all the material was A 1, and I made a saving of 25 to 30 per cent, after paying freight. I have the best house that has been built around here for some time, for the price. You have been prompt and square with me in all my dealings with you.
Yours truly,
J. M. THORNHILL.

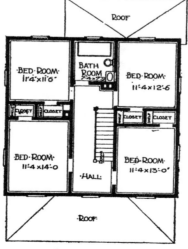

SECOND·FLOOR·PLAN·

$1,608.00

MODERN HOME No. 127

This house has been built at Colorado City, Colo., Lansing, Iowa, Owingsville, Ky., Demarest, N. J., Dunellen, N. J., Kingston, N. Y., Connellsville, Penn., and Sioux Falls, S. Dak.

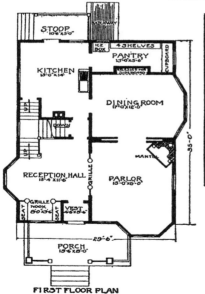

FIRST FLOOR PLAN

SECOND FLOOR PLAN

—49—

For $1,608.00 we will furnish all the material to build this Eight-Room House, consisting of Mill Work, Ceiling, Siding, Flooring, Finishing Lumber, Building Paper, Pipe, Gutter, Sash Weights, Mantel, Hardware, Painting Material, Lumber, Lath and Shingles. NO EXTRAS, as we guarantee enough material at the above price to build this house according to our plans.

By allowing a fair price for labor, cement, brick and plaster, which we do not furnish, this house can be built for about $3,050.00 including all material and labor.

For Our Offer of Free Plans See Page 3.

A STRICTLY modern residence, conveniently arranged. Has a large reception hall, 15 feet 4 inches by 11 feet 6 inches, separated from the parlor by a pair of colonnades and also separated from the nook, which is often used as a reading room, by a pair of colonnades. This nook has a seat built in on each end. Double sliding doors between parlor and dining room. Dining room has a sideboard built into the wall. A mantel in the parlor. Open oak staircase in the reception hall. Every part of this house is well lighted and ventilated by means of two or more windows in each room.

Ottawa front door glazed with leaded art glass. Interior doors on first floor, six-cross panel oak veneered; five-cross panel solid yellow pine doors on second floor. Oak trim, such as casing, baseboard and molding, throughout the first floor; second floor trimmed clear yellow pine baseboard, casing and molding. Oak flooring for main rooms on first floor; maple flooring for kitchen and pantry; clear yellow pine flooring for the second floor and porches. Note the stairs leading from the kitchen, which connect with the main stairs enabling one to go to the second floor from either the reception hall or kitchen.

Painted two coats outside; your choice of color. Varnish and wood filler for interior finish.

Built on a concrete block foundation, frame construction. Sided with narrow bevel edge cypress siding and has cedar shingle roof. Outside blinds for all windows except attic.

Excavated basement under the entire house, 7 feet 4 inches from floor to joists. First floor, 9 feet 6 inches from floor to ceiling; second floor, 8 feet 6 inches from floor to ceiling.

This house can be built on a lot 36 feet wide.

Complete Warm Air Heating Plant, for soft coal, extra	$104.84
Complete Warm Air Heating Plant, for hard coal, extra	107.00
Complete Steam Heating Plant, extra	260.35
Complete Hot Water Heating Plant, extra	286.57
Complete Plumbing Outfit, extra	117.93
Acetylene Lighting Plant, extra	50.30

SEARS, ROEBUCK AND CO.   **CHICAGO, ILLINOIS**

MODERN HOME No. 173

$1,009.00

For $1,009.00 we will furnish all the material to build this Six-Room House, consisting of Mill Work, Flooring, Ceiling, Finishing Lumber, Building Paper, Pipe, Gutter, Sash Weights, Hardware, Painting Material, Lumber, Lath and Shingles. NO EXTRAS, as we guarantee enough material at the above price to build this house according to our plans.

By allowing a fair price for cement, brick, plaster and labor, which we do not furnish, this house can be built for about $2,250.00, including all material and labor.

For Our Offer of Free Plans See Page 3.

A HIGH class six-room house with a large living room, 21 feet by 13 feet, opening into a large dining room with Roman colonnades between. A nice open staircase of oak in the front left hand corner of the living room, with a 5-foot stair landing which has four windows and a window seat on two sides.

The second floor contains three fair size bedrooms, four closets and bathroom.

The entire first floor trim, including front and inside doors, casings, base and open stairway, are of clear oak of modern Craftsman design. The entire second floor is trimmed with clear cypress casing, base, molding and cypress doors. Oak flooring in living room and dining room; yellow pine flooring for the kitchen, pantry, porches and entire second floor.

There is an entrance on the grade line, with a door under the main stairway which leads to the kitchen or to the basement.

This house is built on a concrete foundation and is of frame construction with stonekote finish, more commonly known as cement plaster, on the outside. Cedar shingle roof.

This house can be built on a lot 35 feet wide.

Complete Warm Air Heating Plant, for soft coal, extra.	$ 91.01
Complete Warm Air Heating Plant, for hard coal, extra.	93.17
Complete Steam Heating Plant, extra...................	147.95
Complete Hot Water Heating Plant, extra.............	184.53
Complete Plumbing Outfit, extra.....................	118.97
Acetylene Lighting Plant, extra......................	49.50

SEARS, ROEBUCK AND CO.   **CHICAGO, ILLINOIS**

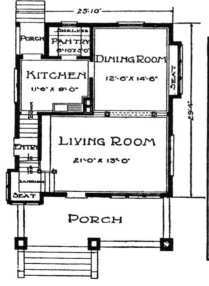

FIRST FLOOR PLAN

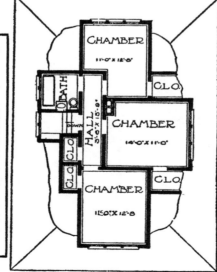

SECOND FLOOR PLAN

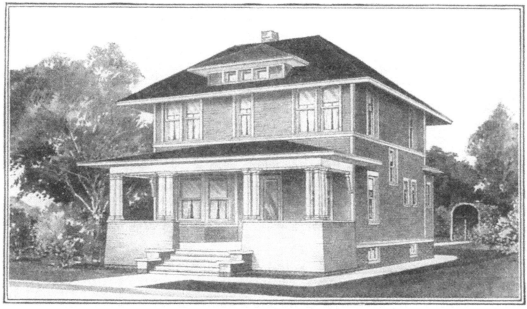

MODERN HOME No. 179

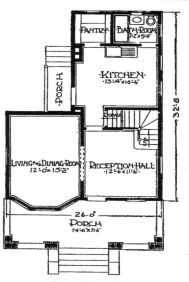

-FIRST-FLOOR-PLAN-

FAR BEYOND OUR EXPECTATIONS.

St. Marys, W. Va.

Sears, Roebuck and Co.,
Chicago, Ill.

Gentlemen:—We wish to say that the material for our Modern Home which we purchased from you was far beyond our expectations. The quality of the material is far ahead of anything we could have purchased here for the same money. We can truly say we have saved one-third or more by purchasing from you and are perfectly satisfied. I had plenty material to complete the house. We have always received prompt shipments from you.

Very truly yours,
JOANNA SCHUPBACH.

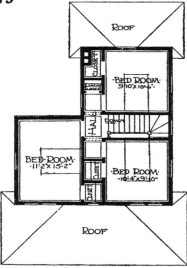

-SECOND-FLOOR-PLAN-
—51—

$1,003⁰⁰

For $1,003.00 we will furnish all the material to build this Six-Room House, consisting of Lumber, Lath, Shingles, Mill Work, Flooring, Ceiling, Siding, Finishing Lumber, Building Paper, Pipe, Gutter, Sash Weights, Hardware and Painting Material. NO EXTRAS, as we guarantee enough material at the above price to build this house according to our plans.

By allowing a fair price for labor, cement, brick and plaster, which we do not furnish, this house can be built for about $1,850.00, including all material and labor.

For Our Offer of Free Plans See Page 3.

WHILE this house can be built for a very reasonable amount, it has the appearance of a $3,000.00 house, arranged to give an abundance of light and ventilation in every room. Front porch is 24 feet wide by 7 feet 6 inches deep, and on account of its being sided up to the porch rail it could be screened in at very little expense. The front door opens into the reception hall, which has an attractive staircase leading to the second floor. The cased opening between the living room and reception hall practically makes one large room of these two rooms. The living room, which is also used as a dining room, is 12 feet wide by 15 feet 2 inches long. The kitchen is 13 feet 4 inches by 10 feet 6 inches and has a good size pantry. The bathroom is on the first floor.

First Floor.

Front door is made of soft pine, 1¾ inches thick, glazed with bevel plate glass. Inside doors are of the five-cross panel style and made of the best quality yellow pine, the same grade of yellow pine being used for inside trim and floors.

Second Floor.

The stairway from the first floor leads to a hall on the second floor from which any one of the three bedrooms and linen closet can be reached. These three bedrooms have splendid ventilation, there being windows on two sides of each room. Doors are five-cross panel and made of the best quality yellow pine, with trim and flooring to match.

Built on a brick foundation and excavated basement under entire house. We furnish clear cypress siding and cedar shingles, framing timbers of the best quality yellow pine. All windows "A" quality glass. Basement has cement floor.

Height of Ceilings.

Basement, 7 feet from floor to joists.
First floor, 9 feet from floor to ceiling.
Second floor, 8 feet from floor to ceiling.
Painted two coats of best paint outside, varnish and wood filler for interior finish.

This house can be built on a lot 35 feet wide.

Complete Warm Air Heating Plant, for soft coal, extra	$ 71.12
Complete Warm Air Heating Plant, for hard coal, extra	75.36
Complete Steam Heating Plant, extra	176.40
Complete Hot Water Heating Plant, extra	201.31
Complete Plumbing Outfit, extra	113.11
Acetylene Lighting Plant, extra	47.90

SEARS, ROEBUCK AND CO.   **CHICAGO, ILLINOIS**

MODERN HOME No. 209

$981⁰⁰

For $981.00 we will furnish all the material to build this Nine-Room House, consisting of Mill Work, Flooring, Ceiling, Finishing Lumber, Pipe, Gutter, Sash Weights, Hardware, Painting Material, Lumber, Lath and Shingles. NO EXTRAS, as we guarantee enough material at the above price to build this house according to our plans.

By allowing a fair price for labor, cement, brick and plaster, which we do not furnish, this house can be built for about $2,200.00, including all material and labor.

For Our Offer of Free Plans See Page 3.

A SQUARE concrete block residence with nine conveniently arranged rooms. Open stairway in the hall with closet underneath. Doors between stair hall and living room and between stair hall and bedroom. Double sliding doors between dining room and living room. Grade entrance opening to a landing with steps to the kitchen and also stairs to the cellar. Pantry in kitchen; closet in bedroom. On second floor are four bedrooms, four closets and bathroom.

Majestic front door, 1¾ inches thick, glazed with bevel plate glass. First floor inside doors, soft pine stiles and rails and five-cross yellow pine panels. Second floor doors, five-cross panels, clear soft pine. Clear yellow pine baseboard, casing and molding throughout the entire house. Yellow pine stairs of choice grain. Clear yellow pine flooring for first and second floors and porches.

Concrete block foundation made with 8x8x16-inch concrete blocks; cedar shingles for roof. Front porch, 27 feet 4 inches long by 9 feet wide; Colonial columns. Queen Anne attic and stair hall sash. Leaded Crystal front living room window.

Concrete block houses can be constructed at about one-third less than stone construction, and if properly built and well furred on the inside to make a dead air space between the blocks and the plaster, will be perfectly dry and healthful. A number of people apply the plaster directly to the block wall. We do not recommend this kind of construction unless you are sure that your concrete blocks are thoroughly waterproofed with a good waterproofing compound.

Excavated basement under the entire house, 7 feet 6 inches from floor to joists. Rooms on the first floor are 9 feet 4 inches from floor to ceiling; second floor, 8 feet 6 inches from floor to ceiling.

This house can be built on a lot 32 feet wide.

Complete Warm Air Heating Plant, for soft coal, extra	$100.36
Complete Warm Air Heating Plant, for hard coal, extra	102.52
Complete Steam Heating Plant, extra	186.40
Complete Hot Water Heating Plant, extra	241.95
Complete Plumbing Outfit, extra	125.30
Acetylene Lighting Plant, extra	51.10

SEARS, ROEBUCK AND CO. **CHICAGO, ILLINOIS**

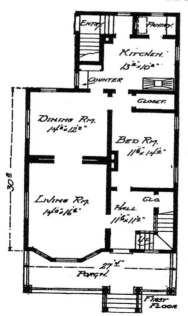

FIRST FLOOR.

> **ONE-HALF WHAT LOCAL DEALERS CHARGE.**
>
> Deans, N. J.
> Sears, Roebuck and Co.,
> Chicago, Ill.
>
> Dear Sirs:—I am very much pleased with your mill work. It has cost but one-half what local dealers charge for the same grade of material. It gives good satisfaction and is of good quality, also other materials, such as hardware, trimming, plumbing and finishing.
>
> Yours very truly,
> JAMES MORRELL,
> General Contractor and Builder.

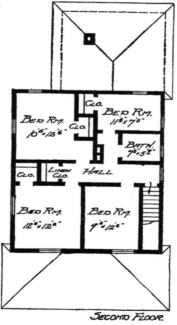

SECOND FLOOR.

$855.00

For $855.00 we will furnish all the material to build this Nine-Room House, consisting of Mill Work, Ceiling, Flooring, Finishing Lumber, Pipe, Gutter, Sash Weights, Hardware, Painting Material, Lumber, Lath and Shingles. NO EXTRAS, as we guarantee enough material at the above price to build this house according to our plans.

By allowing a fair price for labor, cement, brick and plaster, which we do not furnish, this house can be built for about $2,295.00 including all material and labor.

For Our Offer of Free Plans See Page 3.

A WELL proportioned and substantial city, suburban or country home with concrete porch 20 feet 6 inches by 7 feet. Concrete sides, steps and columns.

Oak open stairway in the reception hall. Cased opening between hall and parlor, and cased opening between dining room and parlor; door leading from the hall to the dining room. One bedroom and bathroom on the first floor. Closet in bedroom and one closet under the main stairs. Large china cupboard clear across one end of the kitchen, answering the purpose of a pantry. On the second floor are five bedrooms and five closets.

Beauty front door, 1¾ inches thick, veneered oak, glazed with bevel plate glass. Six-cross panel veneered oak inside doors for the first floor; clear oak trim with the exception of the cupboard. Oak floor for the first floor. Clear yellow pine doors, trim and flooring for the second floor.

Concrete block construction with rock face blocks up to the water table course and panel face blocks from the water table course to the second story window sill course. Plain face blocks the rest of the way up to cornice, and cedar shingle roof, with eaves curved at an 8-foot 9-inch radius, giving the roof a bell shape effect with 3-foot projection.

Our architects figured out the location and size of all doors and windows to come out just right by using full size and half size blocks, so that there will be no necessity of using any other size piece blocks. This makes the construction very easy and simple.

Excavated basement under the entire house, 7 feet 6 inches from floor to joists, with cement floor. Rooms on the first floor are 9 feet 5 inches from floor to ceiling; second floor, 8 feet 11 inches from floor to ceiling.

This house can be built on a lot 32 feet wide.

Complete Warm Air Heating Plant, for soft coal, extra	$ 97.63
Complete Warm Air Heating Plant, for hard coal, extra	99.79
Complete Steam Heating Plant, extra	189.95
Complete Hot Water Heating Plant, extra	239.72
Complete Plumbing Outfit, extra	119.89
Acetylene Lighting Plant, extra	51.90

SEARS, ROEBUCK AND CO. **CHICAGO, ILLINOIS**

MODERN HOME No. 143

REWARD FOR DEFECTS.

189 Spring Street.
Ossining, New York.

Sears, Roebuck and Co.,
Chicago, Ill.

Dear Sirs:—I put up a house for Mr. James M. Ferguson, he buying the lumber from you. We have offered a reward of one dollar for every knot as large as a 10-cent piece found on this house, but up to the present time no one has asked for a dollar, for the reason that a knot large enough to cover a 10-cent piece cannot be found on the whole house. It is the best lumber I have used in a long while.

Yours truly,
HENRY V. TILLOTSON.

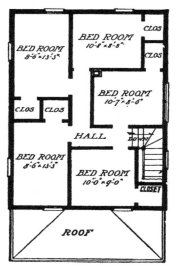

FIRST FLOOR PLAN

SECOND FLOOR PLAN

—53—

$1,251.00

MODERN HOME No. 137

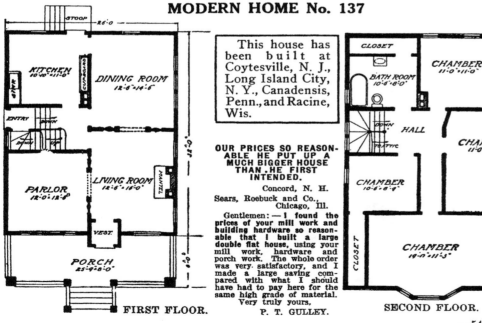

FIRST FLOOR.

SECOND FLOOR.

—54—

This house has been built at Coytesville, N. J., Long Island City, N. Y., Canadensis, Penn., and Racine, Wis.

OUR PRICES SO REASONABLE HE PUT UP A MUCH BIGGER HOUSE THAN HE FIRST INTENDED.

Concord, N. H.

Sears, Roebuck and Co., Chicago, Ill.

Gentlemen:—I found the prices of your mill work and building hardware so reasonable that I built a large double flat house, using your mill work, hardware and porch work. The whole order was very satisfactory, and I made a large saving compared with what I should have had to pay here for the same high grade of material.

Very truly yours,

P. T. GULLEY.

For $1,251.00 we will furnish all the material to build this Nine-Room House, consisting of Mill Work, Siding, Flooring, Ceiling, Finishing Lumber, Building Paper, Pipe, Gutter, Sash Weights, Hardware, Mantel, Painting Material, Lumber, Lath and Shingles. NO EXTRAS, as we guarantee enough material at the above price to build this house according to our plans.

By allowing a fair price for labor, cement, brick and plaster, which we do not furnish, this house can be built for about $2,750.00, including all material and labor.

For Our Offer of Free Plans See Page 3.

A COMBINATION siding and stonekote house with paneled gables; bay window in the front and side gables. Second story extends over the porch, forming the porch roof and making a great deal of room on the second floor. Queen Anne windows on the second floor with colored leaded art glass windows on the first floor, and front door also glazed with colored leaded art glass to match the windows.

Large living room with colonnade opening between the living room and parlor, and also colonnade between living room and dining room; mantel in living room. Open stairway and small hall connected with the living room, kitchen and dining room.

Ottawa front door. Two-panel veneered oak doors for the first floor; clear oak colonnades and stair trim. Five-panel yellow pine doors and yellow pine trim on the second floor. Oak flooring for the first floor; clear yellow pine flooring for the second floor and porches.

Built on a concrete block foundation, frame construction. First story sided with narrow bevel edge cypress siding; second story sided with stonekote and paneled with wood strips; cedar shingle roof.

Painted two coats outside; your choice of color. Varnish and wood filler for interior finish.

Excavated basement under the entire house, 7 feet 2 inches from floor to joists, with cement floor. Rooms on the first floor are 9 feet from floor to ceiling; second floor, 8 feet from floor to ceiling.

This house can be built on a lot 28 feet wide.

Complete Warm Air Heating Plant, for soft coal, extra	$ 94.83
Complete Warm Air Heating Plant, for hard coal, extra	96.99
Complete Steam Heating Plant, extra	182.10
Complete Hot Water Heating Plant, extra	239.10
Complete Plumbing Outfit, extra	119.72
Acetylene Lighting Plant, extra	49.50

SEARS, ROEBUCK AND CO.   **CHICAGO, ILLINOIS**

MODERN HOME No. 160

This house has been built at Long Island City, N. Y., Saratoga Springs, N. Y., South Bethlehem, Penn., and West Superior, Wis.

- FIRST FLOOR PLAN -

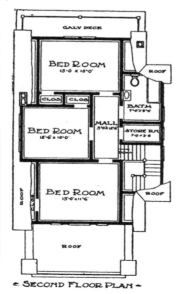

- SECOND FLOOR PLAN -

—55—

$1,265.00

For $1,265.00 we will furnish all the material to build this Seven-Room House, consisting of Mill Work, Ceiling, Flooring, Finishing Lumber, Building Paper, Pipe, Gutter, Sash Weights, Medicine Case, Buffet, Hardware, Mantel, Console, Painting Material, Lumber, Lath and Shingles. NO EXTRAS, as we guarantee enough material at the above price to build this house according to our plans.

By allowing a fair price for labor, cement, brick and plaster, which we do not furnish, this house can be built for about $2,695.00, including all material and labor.

For $48.00 extra we will furnish clear cypress bevel siding for the entire outside.

For Our Offer of Free Plans See Page 3.

A STRICTLY modern stonekote house with front porch 17x7 feet 6 inches, built-up columns and sided with stonekote to match the body of the house. Dublin front door glazed with bevel plate glass. Colored leaded Art Nouveau sash on each side of the center window on the second floor. Colored leaded art glass sash in stair hall, also over buffet in dining room.

Cased opening between the reception hall and parlor, also between parlor and living room. Double sliding doors between dining room and living room. Colonial buffet in the dining room. Mantel and fireplace in the living room. Console and large mirror in the parlor. Medicine case in bathroom. Oak open stairway in the hall with inside cellar stairs under the main stairs and outside cellar way in the rear. Inclosed rear porch.

Two-panel veneered oak interior doors and oak trim for first floor; five-cross panel yellow pine doors with soft pine stiles and rails and yellow pine trim for second floor. Oak flooring for main rooms first floor, with maple flooring for kitchen and pantry. Yellow pine flooring for the entire second floor and porches.

Varnish and wood filler for two coats of interior finish.

Built on a concrete foundation, frame construction, sided with stonekote, more commonly known as cement plaster, and has cedar shingle roof.

Excavated basement under the entire house, 7 feet from floor to joists, with cement floor. Rooms on the first floor are 9 feet from floor to ceiling; second floor, 8 feet 6 inches from floor to ceiling.

This house can be built on a lot 28 feet wide.

Complete Warm Air Heating Plant, for soft coal, extra	$ 90.64
Complete Warm Air Heating Plant, for hard coal, extra	92.80
Complete Steam Heating Plant, extra	211.90
Complete Hot Water Heating Plant, extra	252.06
Complete Plumbing Outfit, extra	124.34
Acetylene Lighting Plant, extra	51.10

SEARS, ROEBUCK AND CO.　　　**CHICAGO, ILLINOIS**

MODERN HOME No. 123

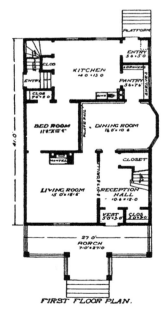

FIRST FLOOR PLAN.

SAVED $500.00 ON MODERN HOME No. 123. MATERIAL FIRST CLASS.

Box 6, Ossining, N. Y.
Sears, Roebuck and Co., Chicago, Ill.

Gentlemen:—Some time ago I had a picture taken of our house for which you furnished the plans and materials. I consider that I saved about $500.00 by purchasing my materials from you. I found them first class in every respect and they will stand comparison with any lumber I have ever seen.

I take pleasure in recommending Sears, Roebuck and Co. to anyone intending to build and thank you for the fair treatment I have received.

Very truly yours,
SAMUEL T. DAVIS.

Also built at Newark, N. J., Springfield, Ohio, Saratoga Springs, N. Y., Sharonville, Ohio, and other cities.

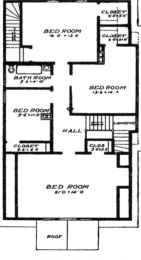

SECOND FLOOR PLAN

$1,404.00

For $1,404.00 we will furnish all the material to build this Nine-Room House, consisting of Lumber, Lath, Shingles, Mill Work, Flooring, Ceiling, Siding, Finishing Lumber, Building Paper, Pipe, Gutter, Sash Weights, Hardware and Painting Material. NO EXTRAS, as we guarantee enough material at the above price to build this house according to our plans.

By allowing a fair price for labor, cement, brick and plaster, which we do not furnish, this house can be built for about $2,835.00, including all material and labor.

For Our Offer of Free Plans See Page 3.

AN ATTRACTIVE two-story house of frame construction with gambrel roof, with return cornices. Arranged to give plenty of light and ventilation in every room in the house. Front porch, 27 feet long by 7 feet wide, is covered by the projection of the second story and supported by massive Colonial columns with square paneled base. The projection on porch is 10x5 feet and is in harmony with the general lines of the house.

Entrance on grade line on the left hand side leading to the kitchen and to the basement.

Front vestibule leads into large reception hall which has an attractive oak staircase leading to the second floor. To the right of the vestibule is a closet, also closet directly under stairs. Oak grille divides reception hall from living room. Living room has attractive quarter sawed oak mantel and tile fireplace and large fancy window. Large dining room, which is conveniently located, has a bay window, and is trimmed with plate rail. Between living room and kitchen is a good size bedroom which can be used as a library. The large kitchen has entrance to side and also to the rear, with stairs going to the basement and to second floor. Adjoining kitchen is a pantry with drawers and shelves, and entry leading to back steps.

First Floor.

Front door made of oak 1¾ inches thick, with bevel plate glass. Inside doors, with exception of kitchen and pantry, are six-cross panel oak with oak trim to match oak plate rail in dining room. Kitchen and pantry doors are five-cross panel white pine with trim to match. All floors, with the exception of kitchen, bedroom and pantry, are clear oak. Kitchen, bedroom and pantry floors are of clear maple, all laid on yellow pine floor lining.

Second Floor.

Stairs from first floor lead to hall on second floor. This hall leads to extra large bedroom in the front and three medium size bedrooms and bathroom. All bedrooms have closets, with shelf in each. All rooms are light and airy. All doors and trim are made of clear white pine; all floors are of clear yellow pine.

Built on concrete block foundation and excavated under entire house.

We furnish clear cypress siding and cedar shingles. Framing timbers of best quality yellow pine. Leaded Crystal glass front window. All windows "A" quality double strength glass.

Basement, 7 feet 4 inches from floor to joists, with cement floor.
First floor, 8 feet 6 inches from floor to ceiling.
Second floor, 8 feet 6 inches from floor to ceiling.
Painted with two coats of best paint outside. Varnish and wood filler for interior finish.

This house can be built on a lot 31 feet 6 inches wide.

Complete Warm Air Heating Plant, for soft coal, extra	$103.75
Complete Warm Air Heating Plant, for hard coal, extra	106.13
Complete Steam Heating Plant, extra	178.50
Complete Hot Water Heating Plant, extra	208.83
Complete Plumbing Outfit, extra	116.96
Acetylene Lighting Plant, extra	51.10

SEARS, ROEBUCK AND CO.

CHICAGO, ILLINOIS

MODERN HOME No. 122

$1,043.00

For $1,043.00 we will furnish all the material to build this Seven-Room House consisting of Lumber, Lath, Shingles, Mill Work, Siding, Flooring, Ceiling, Finishing Lumber, Building Paper, Pipe, Gutter, Sash Weights, Hardware, Mantel and Painting Material. NO EXTRAS, as we guarantee enough material at the above price to build this house according to our plans.

By allowing a fair price for labor, cement, brick and plaster, which we do not furnish, this house can be built for about $2,372.00, including all material and labor.

For Our Offer of Free Plans See Page 3.

A DESIGN that is popular in most all parts of the country, having a gambrel roof it is practical to build, as it can be built at a smaller cost than a full two-story house and yet contains practically the same amount of floor space.

The open birch stairway in the reception hall is a little out of the ordinary. Instead of the usual newel and rail it is paneled up 3 feet 6 inches high and finished with a wide ledge on top. Cased opening between the reception hall and living room. Cased opening between the living room and dining room. Door between living room and reception hall and one door between the reception hall and kitchen. This enables you to go to any room on the first floor or to the second floor without passing through any of the other rooms. Mantel and fireplace in the living room and plate rail in the dining room. On the second floor are three large bedrooms and large bathroom, also four closets.

Queen Anne windows in the front of second floor with leaded Crystal cottage window in the living room. Hamilton birch front door glazed with leaded glass. First floor inside doors, two panel birch. Clear birch trim. Doors on the second floor are five-cross panel yellow pine with clear yellow pine moldings and trim. Oak flooring for the main rooms on the first floor; clear maple flooring for the kitchen and pantry; clear yellow pine flooring for second floor and porches.

Painted two coats outside; your choice of color. Varnish and wood filler for interior finish.

Concrete block foundation, frame construction, sided with narrow bevel edge clear cypress siding and has cedar shingle roof. Excavated basement under the entire house, 7 feet 4 inches from floor to joists. First floor, 8 feet 7 inches from floor to ceiling; second floor, 8 feet 6 inches from floor to ceiling.

This house can be built on a lot 28 feet wide.

Complete Warm Air Heating Plant, for soft coal, extra	$ 88.24
Complete Warm Air Heating Plant, for hard coal, extra	90.40
Complete Steam Heating Plant, extra	178.50
Complete Hot Water Heating Plant, extra	211.63
Complete Plumbing Outfit, extra	116.96
Acetylene Lighting Plant, extra	51.10

SEARS, ROEBUCK AND CO.   **CHICAGO, ILLINOIS**

FIRST FLOOR PLAN

COMPLETE HOUSE COST HIM $2,100.00. IT IS VALUED AT $3,500.00.

307 Gibson St.,
Eau Claire, Wis.
Sears, Roebuck and Co.,
Chicago, Ill.

Gentlemen:—I am sending you photograph of my house which I built according to your plans. By buying mill work from you I saved $250.00. Every inch is clear lumber in the finishing as well as in the building lumber. It cost me $2,100.00 to build this house, and everybody thinks it cost at least $3,500.00. This I can prove any time.

Yours truly,
A. KORGER.

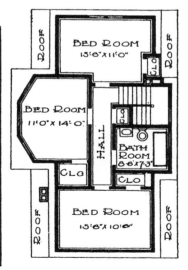

SECOND FLOOR PLAN

—57—

$1,270.00

MODERN HOME No. 113

Built at Dwight, Ill., Springfield, Mass., Elkland, Mo., Dunbar, Penn., and Harrisburg, Penn.

FIRST FLOOR.

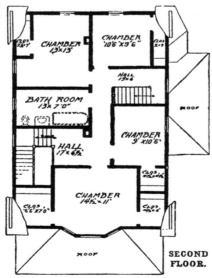

SECOND FLOOR.

Admired by All.

Elkland, Mo.

Sears, Roebuck and Co., Chicago, Ill.

Gentlemen: — My house built according to your plans for Modern Home No. 113, is a lovely residence and is admired by all the country round. It is located in an open prairie and can be seen for several miles. It cost me about $2,500.00. I am highly pleased with the plan. The material purchased from you was perfectly satisfactory and came in good condition. Should I build again, I will give you my order.

Yours very truly,
W. E. DAVISON.

For $1,270.00 we will furnish all the material to build this Eight-Room House, consisting of Lumber, Lath, Shingles, Mill Work, Siding, Flooring, Ceiling, Finishing Lumber, Building Paper, Pipe, Gutter, Sash Weights, Hardware and Painting Material. NO EXTRAS, as we guarantee enough material at the above price to build this house according to our plans.

By allowing a fair price for labor, brick, cement and plaster, which we do not furnish, this house can be built for about $2,475.00, including all material and labor.

For Our Offer of Free Plans See Page 3.

A MODERN house with gambrel roof, large front porch, 22 feet by 6 feet 6 inches, and side porch 15x6 feet. The side entrance makes it very convenient for city or suburban residence or country home. The side porch could be very easily arranged to open up to a driveway which might be made directly at side of the house.

The rooms are very conveniently arranged with a large parlor or living room, 22 feet long by 13 feet wide, with a large reception hall, dining room and kitchen, and a nook in front of the reception hall. Three fair size bedrooms on the second floor and one large bedroom across the front, with a bay window, also bathroom, size 7 feet by 13 feet. Five large closets on the second floor; one closet on the first floor. Inside cellar entrance leading from the side entry with rear stairs to the second floor from the dining room; also an outside cellar entrance.

We furnish our Windsor front door glazed with leaded glass. All interior doors for the first and second floors are of clear solid yellow pine, five-cross panel. Our Crystal leaded glass window for the large window in the parlor, hall, bay window in the dining room and bay window in the front bedroom of the second floor. All interior trim, such as baseboard, casing and molding, is clear yellow pine. Clear yellow pine flooring for entire house and for porches. Built on a concrete block foundation, frame construction. Sided with clear cypress siding and roofed with cedar shingles.

Main open stairs are of unique pattern of clear plain sawed oak.

Sufficient quantity of paint for two coats of exterior work. Varnish and wood filler for two coats of interior finish.

Excavated basement under the entire house, 7 feet 2 inches from floor to joists. Rooms on the first floor are 9 feet 2 inches from floor to ceiling; rooms on second floor, 8 feet from floor to ceiling.

This house is 27 feet 6 inches wide by 40 feet long and can be built on a lot 37 feet wide.

Complete Warm Air Heating Plant, for soft coal, extra	$ 89.35
Complete Warm Air Heating Plant, for hard coal, extra	91.51
Complete Steam Heating Plant, extra	223.30
Complete Hot Water Heating Plant, extra	280.09
Complete Plumbing Outfit, extra	119.32
Acetylene Lighting Plant, extra	51.10

SAVED $321.00 ON A $1,000.00 ORDER.

Uniontown, Penn.

Sears, Roebuck and Co., Chicago, Ill.

Gentlemen:—Last May I ordered the material to erect Modern Home No. 113. I have moved in and will say I am well pleased with the house in every detail. The material was much better than I could have gotten from our dealers here and I saved $321.00. The car of lumber came nice and new and bright, and the inside finish came ready to nail up and was a select grade, all sorted, and showed a uniform grain, all finished alike; was not short a single piece. In fact the whole house was much better than I expected. I must confess I gave you my check for $1,000.00 with some misgivings, but when I received the car of lumber eight days later I saw that I had made no mistake. I thank you for your promptness, fairness and willingness to please.

Yours truly,
S. B. WALTERS.

SEARS, ROEBUCK AND CO.　　　**CHICAGO, ILLINOIS**

MODERN HOME No. 103

Built at Waterbury, Conn., Indianapolis, Ind., Davenport, Iowa, Boston, Mass., Milwaukee, Wis., Rock Island, Ill., and other cities.

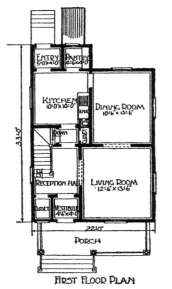

FIRST FLOOR PLAN

SAVES $250.00 ON MODERN HOME
No. 103.

Rockaway, N. J.
Sears, Roebuck and Co.,
Chicago, Ill.

Gentlemen:—I sent order for material for Modern Home No. 103, which I received in due time, all in good order. **The material was much better than I expected. There was about $250.00 difference between your price and the price of same grade of material around here, yours being the lowest.**
Yours truly,
THOMAS B. McGRATH.

SECOND FLOOR PLAN

—59—

$799⁰⁰

For $779.00 we will furnish all the material to build this Six-Room House, consisting of Lumber, Lath, Shingles, Mill Work, Ceiling, Siding, Flooring, Finishing Lumber, Building Paper, Pipe, Gutter, Sash Weights, Hardware and Painting Material. NO EXTRAS, as we guarantee enough material at the above price to build this house according to our plans.

By allowing a fair price for labor, cement, brick and plaster, which we do not furnish, this house can be built for about $1,400.00, including all material and labor.

For Our Offer of Free Plans See Page 3.

A POPULAR design two-story house with side dormer. Houses of this design are being built in very large numbers in several localities as they afford a great deal of room for the amount of money invested. Notice the arrangement of the rooms in this house. An open stairway in the reception hall with cased opening between the reception hall and living room and cased opening between living room and dining room. Closet at the foot of the main stairs. Two large bedrooms on the second floor, four large closets and bathroom.

Artistic front door glazed with sand blast design glass. Five-cross panel, yellow pine interior doors, clear yellow pine trim for both first and second floors. Clear yellow pine flooring for entire house and porches.

Painted two coats outside; your choice of color. Varnish and wood filler for interior finish.

Built on a brick foundation, frame construction, sided with narrow bevel clear cypress siding and has cedar shingle roof. Colonial porch columns.

Excavated basement under the entire house, 6 feet 6 inches from floor to joists. First floor, 9 feet from floor to ceiling; second floor, 8 feet 6 inches from floor to ceiling.

This house measures 22x33 feet and can be built on a lot 25 feet wide.

Complete Warm Air Heating Plant, for soft coal, extra	$ 61.81
Complete Warm Air Heating Plant, for hard coal, extra	72.07
Complete Steam Heating Plant, extra	146.90
Complete Hot Water Heating Plant, extra	180.90
Complete Plumbing Outfit, extra	118.76
Acetylene Lighting Plant, extra	48.70

SEARS, ROEBUCK AND CO.　　　　**CHICAGO, ILLINOIS**

MODERN HOME No. 226

$887⁰⁰

For $887.00 we will furnish all the material to build this Seven-Room House, consisting of Lumber, Lath, Shingles, Mill Work, Flooring, Ceiling, Siding, Finishing Lumber, Building Paper, Pipe, Gutter, Sash Weights, Brick Mantel, Hardware and Painting Material. NO EXTRAS, as we guarantee enough material at the above price to build this house according to our plans.

By allowing a fair price for labor, cement, brick and plaster, which we do not furnish, this house can be built for about $1,700.00, including all material and labor.

For Our Offer of Free Plans See Page 3.

A PLAIN gable roof house of good appearance, having seven rooms and bath, built along plain and simple lines, but with many attractive features. Another combination may be had by finishing the first story with siding instead of the stonekote. This will not change the cost of the completed building to any great extent. The large front porch can be screened in at a small cost and used as a sleeping porch. The side entrance is a practical feature.

The side entrance opens into the reception hall which is separated from the living room by a large cased opening. The living room is 21 feet long by 13 feet deep and has a large open brick fireplace. The entrance to front porch is through a pair of French doors, on both sides of which are French casement sash. The dining room is 13 feet 2 inches by 11 feet with cased opening to reception hall and door to kitchen. A good size pantry with a pantry case. Has inside stairway to cellar.

First Floor.

Main entrance door is made of white pine, 1¾ inches thick, glazed with a long light of bevel plate glass. The rear door is also of white pine, 1¾ inches thick; is glazed with "A" quality clear glass. Interior doors are clear yellow pine, with five-cross panels, and clear yellow pine trim to match. Floors are also of clear yellow pine.

Second Floor.

Stairs from the first floor to the second floor are clear yellow pine and lead into a small hall, from which any one of the four bedrooms or bathroom may be reached. All bedrooms have clothes closets. All rooms light and airy. Doors clear yellow pine, five-cross panel. Clear yellow pine trim and floors.

Built on a concrete foundation, excavated under entire house. We furnish cedar shingles and No. 1 yellow pine framing timbers.

Height of Ceilings.

Basement has cement floor and is 7 feet from floor to joists.
First floor is 9 feet from floor to ceiling. Second floor is 8 feet 6 inches from floor to ceiling.
Stain and paint furnished for the outside, varnish and wood filler for the interior finish.

This house can be built on a lot 32 feet wide.

Complete Warm Air Heating Plant, for soft coal, extra	$ 89.92
Complete Warm Air Heating Plant, for hard coal, extra	91.55
Complete Steam Heating Plant, extra	187.00
Complete Hot Water Heating Plant, extra	215.65
Complete Plumbing Outfit, extra	124.04
Acetylene Lighting Plant, extra	50.30

SEARS, ROEBUCK AND CO. **CHICAGO, ILLINOIS**

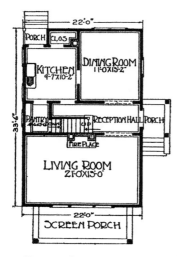

FIRST FLOOR PLAN

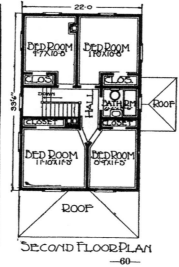

SECOND FLOOR PLAN

MODERN HOME No. 180

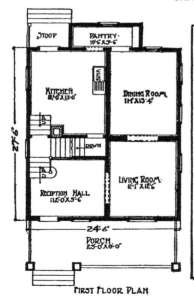

FIRST FLOOR PLAN

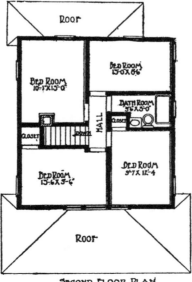

SECOND FLOOR PLAN

—61—

$907.00

For $907.00 we will furnish all the material to build this Eight-Room Two-Story House, consisting of Lumber, Lath, Shingles, Mill Work, Flooring, Ceiling, Siding, Finishing Lumber, Building Paper, Pipe, Gutter, Sash Weights, Hardware and Painting Material. NO EXTRAS, as we guarantee enough material at the above price to build this house according to our plans.

By allowing a fair price for labor, concrete, brick and plaster, which we do not furnish, this house can be built for about $1,700.00, including all material and labor.

For Our Offer of Free Plans See Page 3.

THIS attractive two-story frame house of eight rooms is of a very simple pattern. Every inch of space has been used to the best advantage. The large triple window frame on the second story and the peculiar treatment of the roof give this house its attractive appearance. All windows in the front and sides are of Colonial pattern.

First Floor.

As one enters the front door of this house he immediately has a favorable impression from the large reception hall and the open stairway which leads to the second floor. The living room is directly off the reception hall and separated from the reception hall by a cased opening. There is also a cased opening between the living room and dining room, and a large light pantry is conveniently situated between dining room and kitchen. The kitchen is 12 feet wide by 13 feet long and the entrance to the cellar is under the stairs leading to second floor. Hardwood flooring is furnished for the first floor.

Second Floor.

The second floor has four bedrooms of medium size, two closets and a nice bathroom. All interior doors for this house are of the five-cross panel design and made of clear yellow pine with yellow pine trim to match. Yellow pine flooring throughout for the second floor.

Built on a concrete foundation. Basement excavated and has cement floor. Cypress siding and cedar shingles.

Height of Ceilings.

Basement, 7 feet from floor to joists.
First and second floors, 8 feet from floor to ceiling.

Built at Duryea, Penn., Peoria, Ill., New York City, N. Y., Greensburg, Penn., Evansville, Ind., and Troy, N. Y.

This house can be built on a lot 30 feet wide.

Complete Warm Air Heating Plant, for soft coal, extra	$ 85.52
Complete Warm Air Heating Plant, for hard coal, extra	87.62
Complete Steam Heating Plant, extra	197.55
Complete Hot Water Heating Plant, extra	234.63
Complete Plumbing Outfit, extra	117.73
Acetylene Lighting Plant, extra	49.50

SEARS, ROEBUCK AND CO.　　　　　**CHICAGO, ILLINOIS**

$984.00

For $984.00 we will furnish all the material to build this Eight-Room House, consisting of Lumber, Lath, Shingles, Mill Work, Flooring, Ceiling, Siding, Finishing Lumber, Building Paper, Pipe, Gutter, Sash Weights, Hardware and Painting material. NO EXTRAS, as we guarantee enough material at the above price to build this house according to our plans.

By allowing a fair price for labor, cement, brick and plaster, which we do not furnish, this house can be built for about $1,850.00, including all material and labor.

For Our Offer of Free Plans See Page 3.

THIS house is very similar to our Modern Home No. 167, shown on page 5, excepting that it is 1½ feet wider and 2 feet longer. Our customers consider this house an ideal home as well as a good investment, having the appearance of a house costing $2,500.00 to build.

The front porch is 23 feet 6 inches by 8 feet, reception hall is 11 feet by 13 feet and has an open stairway leading to the second floor. The cased opening separates the reception hall from the parlor. The parlor or living room is 13 feet long by 11 feet 1 inch wide. The dining room is also a good size room, being 16 feet 1 inch by 11 feet 1 inch and has a large bay window extending almost the entire length of the room. Kitchen has a good size pantry. The stairway leading to the basement has its entrance in the pantry.

First Floor.

The front door is of white pine, 1¾ inches thick, glazed with bevel plate glass. Doors are of the four-panel design, made of the best quality yellow pine. All floors and inside trim are a clear grade of yellow pine.

Second Floor.

On the second floor there are two large bedrooms, each having large clothes closet, and one small bedroom. Also a good size bathroom, 8 feet wide by 11 feet long.

Stairs from the first floor lead to the hall on the second floor, from which the bathroom or any of the three bedrooms may be entered. All doors, trim and floors are of the best quality yellow pine.

Built on a brick foundation and excavated under entire house. We furnish clear cypress siding and cedar shingles; framing timbers of the best quality yellow pine. Leaded crystal glass front window. All windows "A" quality double strength glass.

Height of Ceilings.

Basement, 7 feet from floor to joists.
First floor, 9 feet from floor to ceiling.
Second floor, 8 feet from floor to ceiling.

Painted with two coats of the best paint outside, varnish and wood filler for interior finish.

This house can be built on a lot 30 feet wide.

Complete Warm Air Heating Plant, for soft coal, extra	$ 82.07
Complete Warm Air Heating Plant, for hard coal, extra	84.08
Complete Steam Heating Plant, extra	208.35
Complete Hot Water Heating Plant, extra	238.86
Complete Plumbing Outfit, extra	128.19
Acetylene Lighting Plant, extra	48.70

SEARS, ROEBUCK AND CO.　　　**CHICAGO, ILLINOIS**

MODERN HOME No. 188

Modern Home No. 188 is similar to our Modern Home No. 167, illustrated on page 5, excepting that it is wider and longer and the position of the rooms reversed. In addition to the places already named on page 5, Modern Home No. 167 has been built at Windsor, Conn., Dubuque, Ia., Auburn, Me., Steubenville, Ohio, Washington, Penn., and other cities.

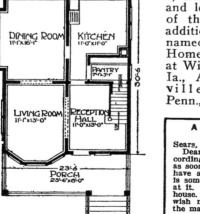

FIRST FLOOR PLAN

SECOND FLOOR PLAN

MODERN HOME No. 133

This house has been built at Gary, Ind., Des Moines, Iowa, Big Timber, Mont., Orange, N. J., Oneida, N. Y., Cincinnati, Ohio, Toledo, Ohio, Youngstown, Ohio, Philadelphia, Penn., Mt. Kisco, N. Y., Plainfield, N. J., and other cities.

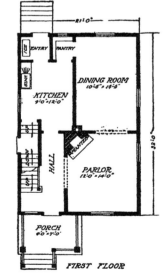

FIRST FLOOR

SAVED NEARLY ONE-FIFTH ON MODERN HOME No. 133.
Barrington, Ill.
Sears, Roebuck and Co.,
Chicago, Ill.

Gentlemen:—We built two houses from your plan No. 133. Material ordered from you was **better than first class, if that could be possible.** The entire shipment was received within fifteen days after being ordered. By using your plans, specifications, materials and blue prints we saved $150.00 on each house. Enclosed find photo of the two houses. Very truly yours,
ALVERSON & GROFF.

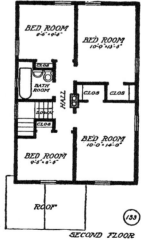

SECOND FLOOR

—63—

$831.00

For $831.00 we will furnish all the material to build this Eight-Room House, consisting of Mill Work, Flooring, Ceiling, Siding, Finishing Lumber, Building Paper, Pipe, Gutter, Sash Weights, Hardware, Mantel, Painting Material, Lumber, Lath and Shingles. NO EXTRAS, as we guarantee enough material at the above price to build this house according to our plans.

By allowing a fair price for labor, cement, brick and plaster, which we do not furnish, this house can be built for about $1,500.00, including all material and labor.

For Our Offer of Free Plans See Page 3.

A SIMPLE and well constructed house, which if built according to our plans and with our material will prove a very good paying investment, as it affords a great deal of room for the small amount of money. Fair size porch, 7x9 feet, with Colonial columns. Queen Anne windows in the front and leaded Crystal window in the parlor. Stair hall with door leading to the kitchen. Cased opening between the parlor and dining room. Grade entrance on the left side of the house leading to the kitchen, also down to the basement. Mantel and fireplace in the parlor. Four good size rooms on the second floor with bathroom and four closets.

Our Polk design front door. Five-cross panel yellow pine inside doors with clear yellow pine molding and trim throughout the house, and clear yellow pine stairs. Clear yellow pine flooring for the entire house and porches.

Painted two coats outside; your choice of color. Varnish and wood filler for interior finish.

Built on a concrete foundation, frame construction, sided with narrow bevel edge cypress siding to the belt course and sided with cedar shingles above the belt course, and has cedar shingle roof.

Excavated basement under the entire house, 6 feet 6 inches from floor to joists. First floor, 9 feet from floor to ceiling; second floor, 8 feet 6 inches from floor to ceiling.

This house can be built on a lot 25 feet wide.

Complete Warm Air Heating Plant, for soft coal, extra	$ 86.20
Complete Warm Air Heating Plant, for hard coal, extra	88.49
Complete Steam Heating Plant, extra	180.85
Complete Hot Water Heating Plant, extra	215.65
Complete Plumbing Outfit, extra	124.66
Acetylene Lighting Plant, extra	48.70

SEARS, ROEBUCK AND CO.   **CHICAGO, ILLINOIS**

MODERN HOME No. 135

$853.00

For **$853.00** we will furnish all the material to build this Seven-Room House, consisting of Mill Work, Siding, Flooring, Ceiling, Finishing Lumber, Building Paper, Pipe, Gutter, Sash Weights, Hardware, Painting Material, Lumber, Lath and Shingles. **NO EXTRAS**, as we guarantee enough material at the above price to build this house according to our plans.

By allowing a fair price for labor, cement, brick and plaster, which we do not furnish, this house can be built for about $1,620.00, including all material and labor.

For Our Offer of Free Plans See Page 3.

A VERY compact house with no space that cannot be used to the very best advantage. An extra large colonnade opening between the reception hall and living room, also between the living room and dining room, which practically throws these three rooms into one large room. In the reception hall there is an open stairway, the first tread having a circle end. Under the main stairs is an entrance on the grade line which leads to the kitchen or to the basement. When you land on the second floor at the head of the stairs you are within a very few feet from the entrance of all the bedrooms and bathroom. Each room has a large closet.

Queen Anne front window for the front bedroom. Leaded Crystal window for the living room on the first floor. Windsor front door glazed with leaded glass to match the leaded window. All interior doors are five-cross panel, soft pine stiles and rails, yellow pine panels. Clear yellow pine casing, baseboard and molding throughout the entire house. Clear yellow pine flooring for the entire house and porches.

Painted two coats outside; your choice of color. Varnish and wood filler for interior finish.

Built on a concrete foundation, frame construction, sided with narrow bevel clear cypress siding, and has cedar shingle roof.

Excavated basement under the entire house, 7 feet from floor to joists. First floor, 9 feet from floor to ceiling; second floor, 8 feet 4 inches from floor to ceiling.

This house can be built on a lot 26 feet wide.

Complete Warm Air Heating Plant, for soft coal, extra	$ 71.84
Complete Warm Air Heating Plant, for hard coal, extra	74.51
Complete Steam Heating Plant, extra	152.95
Complete Hot Water Heating Plant, extra	183.48
Complete Plumbing Outfit, extra	117.69
Acetylene Lighting Plant, extra	48.70

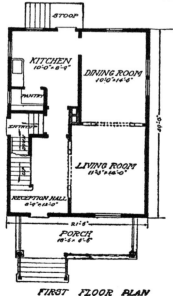

FIRST FLOOR PLAN

This house has been built at Chicago, Ill., Oak Park, Ill., Danbury, Conn., Davenport, Iowa, Acushnet, Mass., St. Louis, Mo., Oswego, N. Y., Carnegie, Penn., New Park, Penn., and Huntington, W. Va.

SAVED ABOUT $300.00 ON MODERN HOME No. 135 AND SECURED A SUPERIOR GRADE OF MATERIAL.

Huntington, W. Va.
Sears, Roebuck and Co., Chicago, Ill.

Gentlemen:—I have been told by contractors that the material furnished for this house was far superior to what I could get here. I can say that I have saved $250.00 to $300.00. My wife and I are very much pleased with our new house. Accept our thanks for your cordial treatment. I remain, Yours truly,
JAY INNIS.

SECOND FLOOR PLAN

— KITCHEN 10'0"x8'9"
— DINING ROOM 10'0"x14'6"
— PANTRY
— ENTRY
— LIVING ROOM 11'6"x14'0"
— RECEPTION HALL 6'4"x12'0"
— PORCH 18'6"x6'6"
— STOOP

— CHAMBER 10'0"x7'3"
— CLOS CLOS
— BATH ROOM
— CHAMBER 10'0"x12'6"
— CHAMBER 17'0"x12'0"
— CLOS
— ROOF

OUR MATERIAL SUPERIOR TO OTHERS AND SAVED 25 TO 30 PER CENT.

Peoria, Ill.
Sears, Roebuck and Co., Chicago, Ill.

Gentlemen:—I sent you an order for all lumber, mill work and hardware for House No. 115 and received shipment promptly. My house is now finished and I saved from 25 to 30 per cent on the material by buying from you. Your lumber is far superior to that of any other dealers. Yours truly,
ARTHUR LAHNE.

SEARS, ROEBUCK AND CO.   **CHICAGO, ILLINOIS**

MODERN HOME No. 199

$572.00

For $572.00 we will furnish all the material to build this Five-Room Cottage, consisting of Lumber, Lath, Shingles, Mill Work, Flooring, Ceiling, Siding, Finishing Lumber, Building Paper, Pipe, Gutter, Sash Weights, Hardware and Painting Material. NO EXTRAS, as we guarantee enough material at the above price to build this house according to our plans.

By allowing a fair price for labor, cement, brick and plaster, which we do not furnish, this house can be built for about $1,100.00, including all material and labor.

For Our Offer of Free Plans See Page 3.

A NICELY arranged home of five rooms and bath. This cottage can be built at a low cost and will go nicely on a 25-foot lot. Front d or opens into the living room which is 14 feet long by 11 feet wide. A large cased opening between the living room and dining room practically makes one large room of these two rooms. The kitchen is just a nice size, being 8 feet 7 inches wide by 9 feet 6 inches long. Has a good size pantry with pantry case built in. The cellar stairs have their entrance in the kitchen and are immediately under the stairs leading from the first floor to the second floor.

First Floor.

Front door is made of soft pine, 1⅜ inches thick, glazed with "A" quality double strength glass. All inside doors are made of yellow pine and are of the four-panel style, with best quality yellow pine trim and floors. Rear door is of soft pine 1⅜ inches thick and glazed with "A" quality double strength glass.

Second Floor.

The stairs open into the hall on the second floor, from which any of the bedrooms or the bathroom may be entered. Each of the bedrooms has a clothes closet. Bathroom is 6 feet 6 inches wide by 8 feet 2 inches long. All doors are of the four-panel style, made of the best quality of yellow pine. Yellow pine trim and floors.

Built on a concrete foundation. Excavated under the entire house. We furnish clear cypress siding and cedar shingles. Framing timbers are of the best quality yellow pine. Basement is 7 feet from floor to joists. First floor, 8 feet 6 inches from floor to ceiling; second floor, 8 feet from floor to ceiling.

Painted two coats of best paint outside, varnish and wood filler for interior finish.

This house can be built on a lot 25 feet wide.

Complete Warm Air Heating Plant, for soft coal, extra	$ 62.04
Complete Warm Air Heating Plant, for hard coal, extra	65.34
Complete Steam Heating Plant, extra	113.70
Complete Hot Water Heating Plant, extra	142.21
Complete Plumbing Outfit, extra	122.69
Acetylene Lighting Plant, extra	47.25

SEARS, ROEBUCK AND CO.   **CHICAGO, ILLINOIS**

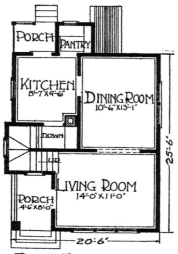

FIRST FLOOR PLAN

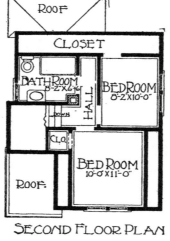

SECOND FLOOR PLAN

MODERN HOME No. 121

This house has been built at Chicago, Ill., Davenport, Iowa, Easthampton, Mass., Waterbury, Neb., Denville, N. J., Charlotte, N. Y., Westbury, N.Y., Gatesville, N. C., Almont, N. Dak., Coal Bluff, Penn., and other cities.

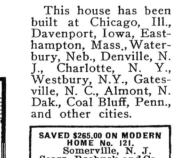

SAVED $265.00 ON MODERN HOME No. 121.
Somerville, N. J.
Sears, Roebuck and Co.,
Chicago, Ill.
Gentlemen:—It gives me pleasure to write that **you saved me $265.00** on the material for Modern Home No. 121. **The material was all you claimed it to be,** shipments were prompt and it was a pleasure to do business with you.
Yours very truly,
L. B. THATCHER.

FIRST FLOOR PLAN.

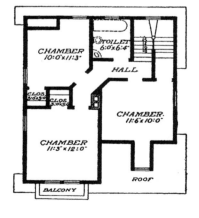

SECOND FLOOR PLAN.

—66—

$758.00

For $758.00 we will furnish all the material to build this Six-Room Cottage, consisting of Mill Work, Flooring, Siding, Ceiling, Finishing Lumber, Building Paper, Pipe, Gutter, Sash Weights, Mantel, Hardware, Painting Material, Lumber, Lath and Shingles. NO EXTRAS, as we guarantee enough material at the above price to build this house according to our plans.

By allowing a fair price for labor, cement, brick and plaster, which we do not furnish, this house can be built for about $1,602.00, including all material and labor.

For Our Offer of Free Plans See Page 3.

AN ATTRACTIVE six-room cottage for the family of moderate means. A good size front porch, 12 feet 3 inches by 7 feet, with a cluster of three Colonial columns on the outside corner and one column on each end next to the building. The front door enters directly into the dining room and there is a sliding door between the dining room and the parlor and a door from the dining room to the kitchen. Also a door connecting the parlor with the kitchen. Mantel and fireplace in the parlor. Closed stairway in the rear end of the dining room leading to the second floor. On the second floor are three good size chambers, bathroom and two closets.

Victoria front door glazed with leaded art glass. Five-cross panel inside doors; clear yellow pine trim throughout the house. Clear yellow pine flooring throughout the entire house and porches.

Painted two coats outside; your choice of color. Varnish and wood filler for interior finish.

Built on a concrete block foundation, frame construction, sided with narrow bevel edge cypress siding and has cedar shingle roof.

Excavated basement under the entire house, 7 feet from floor to joists. First floor, 8 feet 7 inches from floor to ceiling; second floor, 8 feet from floor to ceiling.

This house can be built on a lot 28 feet wide.

Complete Warm Air Heating Plant, for soft coal, extra	$ 78.67
Complete Warm Air Heating Plant, for hard coal, extra	81.10
Complete Steam Heating Plant, extra	151.75
Complete Hot Water Heating Plant, extra	193.48
Complete Plumbing Outfit, extra	115.74
Acetylene Lighting Plant, extra	46.75

SEARS, ROEBUCK AND CO.   **CHICAGO, ILLINOIS**

MODERN HOME No. 159

$699.00

For $699.00 we will furnish all the material to build this Six-Room Two-Story House, consisting of Lumber, Lath, Shingles, Mill Work, Ceiling, Siding, Flooring, Finishing Lumber, Building Paper, Pipe, Gutter, Sash Weights and Painting Material. NO EXTRAS, as we guarantee enough material to build this house according to our plans.

By allowing a fair price for labor, cement, brick and plaster, which we do not furnish, this house can be built for about $1,171.00, including all material and labor.

For Our Offer of Free Plans See Page 3.

THIS house is well arranged, having no waste space. Has six good size rooms, well lighted and ventilated with large windows. Is suitable for suburban or country home and has been frequently built in large numbers, proving to be a very good investment. It rents well, as it is practically two full stories high and of good appearance. It has a large front porch, 33 feet 6 inches long, with Colonial columns.

First Floor.

Parlor with staircase leading to second floor. Cased openings from parlor to dining room. Has a large front window facing the street. Dining room and kitchen are of good size.

Second Floor.

Has three good size bedrooms, three closets and bathroom.

At the above price we furnish a massive front door, 3x7 feet, 1¾ inches thick, glazed with bevel plate glass. Interior doors are five-cross panel with Nona pine stiles and rails and yellow pine panels. Clear yellow pine interior trim, such as baseboard, casing, molding and clear yellow pine staircase. Clear yellow pine flooring throughout house and porches.

This house is built on a concrete foundation, frame construction, sided with narrow bevel clear cypress siding and has cedar shingle roof.

Painted two coats outside; your choice of color. Varnish and wood filler for two coats of interior finish.

The rooms on the first floor are 9 feet from floor to ceiling; rooms on second floor, 8 feet from floor to ceiling.

This house can be built on a lot 27 feet wide.

Complete Warm Air Heating Plant, for soft coal, extra	$ 70.98
Complete Warm Air Heating Plant, for hard coal, extra	73.95
Complete Steam Heating Plant, extra	145.45
Complete Hot Water Heating Plant, extra	181.11
Complete Plumbing Outfit, extra	106.17
Acetylene Lighting Plant, extra	47.90

SEARS, ROEBUCK AND CO.　　　**CHICAGO, ILLINOIS**

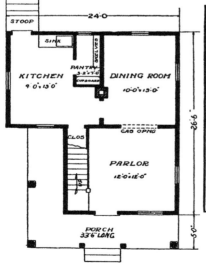

This house has been built at Aurora, Ill., Laporte, Ind., Boston, Mass., Ely, Minn., Fulton, Mo., Paterson, N. J., Bay Shore, L. I., N. Y., Canton, Ohio, Waynesboro, Penn., Mt. Pleasant, Tenn., and other cities.

FIRST FLOOR PLAN

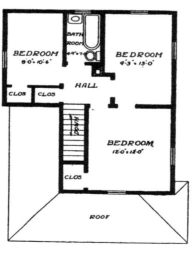

SECOND FLOOR PLAN

MODERN HOME No. 171

$597.00

For $597.00 we will furnish all the material to build this Six-Room Cottage, consisting of Mill Work, Flooring, Ceiling, Siding, Finishing Lumber, Building Paper, Pipe, Gutter, Sash Weights, Hardware, Painting Material, Lumber, Lath and Shingles. NO EXTRAS, as we guarantee enough material at the above price to build this house according to our plans.

By allowing a fair price for labor, cement, brick and plaster, which we do not furnish, this house can be built for about $950.00, including all material and labor.

For Our Offer of Free Plans See Page 3.

IN MODERN Home No. 171 we have a very neat appearing and up to date cottage at a very low cost. By reason of its simple outline and the entire absence of complicated details, the labor is but a small item of expense as compared with the average house of this size.

On the first floor there are three fair size rooms and pantry. Open stairway leading from the parlor to the second floor. The first and second floors are finished in yellow pine; doors have soft pine stiles and rails and yellow pine panels. In the parlor is a large cottage window; front door glazed with lace design glass. Three large size bedrooms on the second floor (another bedroom on first floor), each having a closet. The flooring for both the first and second floors and porches is of No. 1 yellow pine. This cottage is so arranged that the ventilation is perfect throughout the house, and yet so compact that it may be heated at a very low cost.

There is an excavated basement under the kitchen, 7 feet from floor to joists. This cottage is built on a concrete block foundation. Frame construction, sided with narrow bevel clear cypress siding and has cedar shingle roof.

This house can be built on a lot 28 feet wide.

Complete Warm Air Heating Plant, for soft coal, extra.............................$ 66.97
Complete Warm Air Heating Plant, for hard coal, extra.......................... 69.88
Complete Steam Heating Plant, extra.. 134.20
Complete Hot Water Heating Plant, extra... 150.67
Acetylene Lighting Plant, extra.. 47.25

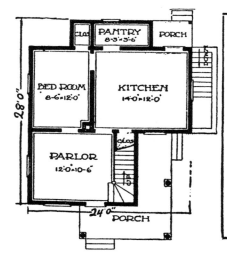

This house has been built at Windsor, Conn., Lansing, Ill., Freeport, Ill., Laporte, Ind., Sanborn, Iowa, S. Louisville, Ky., Virginia, Minn., Wrentham, Mass., Sterling, Neb., Franklin Furnace, N. J., Long Branch, N. J., Poughkeepsie, N. Y., Middlefield, Ohio, Painesville, Ohio, and other cities.

FIRST FLOOR

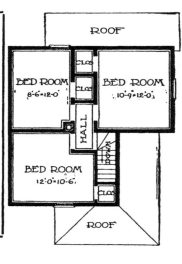

SECOND FLOOR

SEARS, ROEBUCK AND CO.   **CHICAGO, ILLINOIS**

$587⁰⁰

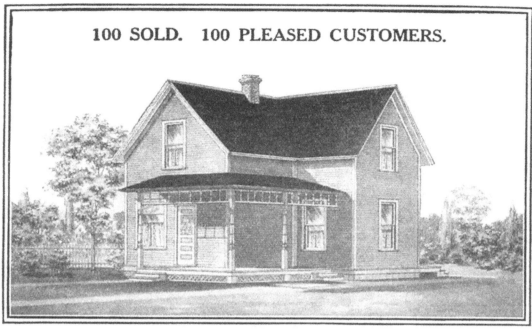

For \$587.00 we will furnish all the material to build this cozy Six-Room Story and a Half House with frame construction, consisting of Lumber, Lath, Shingles, Mill Work, Building Paper, Eaves Trough, Hardware and Painting Material. NO EXTRAS, as we guarantee enough material at the above price to build this house according to our plans.

By allowing a fair price for labor, cement, brick and plaster, which we do not furnish, this house can be built for about \$870.00, including all material and labor.

For Our Offer of Free Plans See Page 3.

A WELL and economically arranged six-room story and a half house, built of the same good material as specified in even our higher priced houses shown in this book. Over fifty houses of this design were built during the past year and every one of them has satisfied the owner in price, quality and the big saving we made them. Most of the houses were built at a lower price than we estimated.

A porch, 5 feet in width, extends across the front 11 feet, and 14 feet along the side, giving ample porch room.

100 SOLD. 100 PLEASED CUSTOMERS.

MODERN HOME No. 115

This house has been built at Washington, D. C., Normal, Ill., Ottawa, Ill., Gary, Ind., Dundee, Ill., Rockford, Ill., Star City, Ind., Bozeman, Mont., St. Louis, Mo., Canton, Ohio, Blue Ash, Ohio, Beechview, Penn., Rochester, Penn., Altoona, Penn., Racine, Wis., and other cities.

SAVED OVER 25 PER CENT ON MODERN HOME No. 115.

Star Route No. 7, Altoona, Penn.
Sears, Roebuck and Co., Chicago, Ill.
  Dear Sirs:—Under separate cover am mailing you a picture of our house built from your house plans No. 115. I was much pleased with all the materials and would also state that we saved fully 25 per cent on the present local prices in buying from your firm. Yours respectfully,
  E. N. HARRAR.

First Floor.

Front door leads to the parlor and to enclosed stairway leading to the second floor. Directly in the rear of the parlor is located a good size bedroom with closet, with doors leading from bedroom to parlor and from bedroom to kitchen. Kitchen measures 14 feet 1 inch by 12 feet, giving ample room for kitchen and dining room combined. Directly off kitchen is a large pantry with shelves, and a door leading to rear porch.

This house has an attractive white pine paneled front door with ornamental lace design glass. Rear outside door five-cross panel No. 1 yellow pine. Interior doors No. 1 quality four-panel yellow pine, all of which are 1⅜ inches thick. All casing, baseboards, molding and staircase are made of clear yellow pine. Yellow pine flooring throughout.

Second Floor.

On the second floor are located two medium size bedrooms with closets, all lathed and plastered, and one large room unfinished which can be used as a storage room or converted into a very large bedroom at little additional expense for lath and plaster. All doors, casing, baseboard, moldings and floors are of clear yellow pine and intended for oil finish.

Built on well constructed wood foundation and of frame construction. Covered with clear narrow bevel cypress siding and roof covered with *A* cedar shingles.
  Paint furnished for two coats for exterior work, your choice of colors. Sufficient wood filler and varnish furnished for two coats of interior finish.
  A saving of about \$25.00 can be made by using our 3½-ply Best-of-all Roofing instead of cedar shingles; same guaranteed to last equally as long as the best quality of cedar shingles.
  Excavated cellar, 7 feet 6 inches wide by 11 feet 6 inches long, 7 feet from floor to joists.
  First floor, 8 feet 6 inches from floor to ceiling.
  Second floor, 8 feet from floor to ceiling.

This house can be built on a lot 26 feet wide.

Complete Warm Air Heating Plant, for soft coal, extra	\$ 53.85
Complete Warm Air Heating Plant, for hard coal, extra	57.17
Complete Steam Heating Plant, extra	106.95
Complete Hot Water Heating Plant, extra	128.04
Acetylene Lighting Plant, extra	46.75

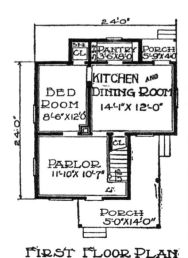

FIRST FLOOR PLAN

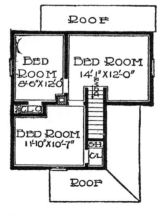

SECOND FLOOR PLAN

SEARS, ROEBUCK AND CO.   **CHICAGO, ILLINOIS**

MODERN HOME No. 105

$577⁰⁰

For $577.00 we will furnish all the material to build this Five-Room House, consisting of Mill Work, Siding, Flooring, Ceiling, Finishing Lumber, Building Paper, Pipe, Gutter, Sash Weights, Hardware, Painting Material, Lumber, Lath and Shingles. NO EXTRAS, as we guarantee enough material at the above price to build this house according to our plans.

By allowing a fair price for labor, stone, brick and plaster, which we do not furnish, this house can be built for about $1,190.00, including all material and labor.

For Our Offer of Free Plans See Page 3.

A TWO-STORY HOUSE having three rooms on the first floor with pantry and closet. Inside cellar stairway under the main stairs. Outside cellar entrance in the rear. Two rooms on the second floor and closet in each room, with two windows in each room, making them well lighted and perfectly ventilated. Front porch is 20x5 feet, with Colonial columns.

Our Cass front door. Yellow pine inside doors and trim. Clear yellow pine flooring throughout the entire house and porches.

Painted two coats outside; your choice of color. Varnish and wood filler for interior finish.

Built on a stone foundation, frame construction, sided with narrow bevel edge cypress siding and has a cedar shingle roof.

First story, 8 feet 6 inches from floor to ceiling.
Second story, 8 feet 6 inches from floor to ceiling.

This house is 22 feet wide by 27 feet 6 inches long and can be built on a lot 25 feet wide.

Complete Warm Air Heating Plant, for soft coal, extra	$ 54.98
Complete Warm Air Heating Plant, for hard coal, extra	58.22
Complete Steam Heating Plant, extra	109.49
Complete Hot Water Heating Plant, extra	140.28
Acetylene Lighting Plant, extra	46.75

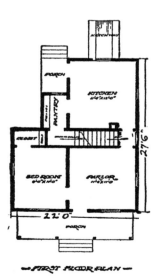

— FIRST FLOOR PLAN —

NO TROUBLE IN BUILDING WHEN OUR PLANS ARE USED.

Cowley, Wyo.

Sears, Roebuck and Co., Chicago, Ill.

Gentlemen:—I am mailing a picture of my new home built from your plans and materials. **By the use of your blue prints my carpenter was able to work without mistake or delay.** By the use of your bill of materials I was able to order just what I needed for my house and no more. By the use of your catalog and low prices I had my home complete, plaster, paint and all before cold weather came on. I saved as much as 60 per cent on some of the finishing lumber. If I build another home my mill work will come from Sears, Roebuck and Co. Yours truly,

BARTLETT D. DICKSON.

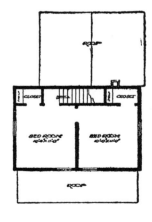

— SECOND FLOOR PLAN —

—70—

SAVED 35 PER CENT AND GOT A BETTER GRADE THAN THE LOCAL MARKET COULD FURNISH.

Silver Lane, Conn.

Sears, Roebuck and Co., Chicago, Ill.

Gentlemen:—In regard to the bill of lumber I bought of you people for my new house now built according to your plan No. 105, will say I am very well satisfied with the quality of all the material that you sent me and **compared with material that one can buy in this section it is much better grade of material, and I saved about 35 per cent** by buying my material of you people. I am glad to say that the material was shipped promptly and came through to destination in only thirteen days. Very truly yours,

JAMES P. PRATT.

SEARS, ROEBUCK AND CO.　　　　**CHICAGO, ILLINOIS**

$1,060⁰⁰

For $1,060.00 we will furnish all the material to build this large Eight-Room House, consisting of Mill Work, Flooring, Ceiling, Siding, Finishing Lumber, Building Paper, Eaves Trough, Mantel, Hardware, Painting Material, Lumber, Lath and Shingles. NO EXTRAS, as we guarantee enough material at the above price to build this house according to our plans.

By allowing a fair price for labor, cement, brick and plaster, which we do not furnish, this house can be built for about $1,930.00, including all material and labor.

For Our Offer of Free Plans See Page 3.

EIGHT large and well arranged rooms, with vestibule and pantry on the first floor. Bathroom and three closets on the second floor. A great deal of room for a small amount of money. The parlor contains a mantel and fireplace and the living room has an open stairway which also is connected with the stairway from the kitchen, enabling one to go to the second floor from either of these two rooms. Cellar stairs directly under the main stairs with a door leading to it from both the kitchen and living room. Double sliding doors between living room and dining room.

Taylor front door. Nona pine five-cross panel interior doors on first floor. Doors on second floor are four-panel solid yellow pine. Interior yellow pine trim and yellow pine stair material, also yellow pine flooring for entire house and porches. Queen Anne windows on the second floor for the sides and front.

Built on a concrete block foundation, frame construction, sided with narrow bevel clear cypress siding and has cedar shingle roof.

Painted two coats outside; color to suit. Varnish and wood filler for two coats of interior finish.

First story, 9 feet 6 inches from floor to ceiling.

Second story, 8 feet 6 inches from floor to ceiling.

Front porch, 10x14 feet; rear porch, 8 feet 4 inches by 7 feet 2 inches.

This house has been built at Brush, Colo., Plainville, Conn., Springerton, Ill., Peabody, Kan., Milford, Ky., Edmore, Mich., and Manitowoc, Wis.

This house can be built on a lot 34 feet wide.

Complete Warm Air Heating Plant, for soft coal, extra	$ 84.02
Complete Warm Air Heating Plant, for hard coal, extra	86.03
Complete Steam Heating Plant, extra	215.10
Complete Hot Water Heating Plant, extra	254.64
Complete Plumbing Outfit, extra	121.47
Acetylene Lighting Plant, extra	54.30

SEARS, ROEBUCK AND CO. **CHICAGO, ILLINOIS**

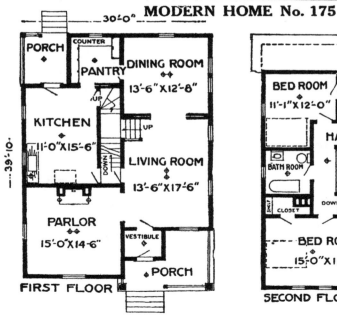

MODERN HOME No. 175

30'-0"

PORCH

COUNTER

PANTRY

DINING ROOM
13'-6"X12'-8"

UP

KITCHEN
11'-0"X15'-6"

UP

DOWN

LIVING ROOM
13'-6"X17'-6"

39'-10"

PARLOR
15'-0"X14'-6"

VESTIBULE

PORCH

FIRST FLOOR

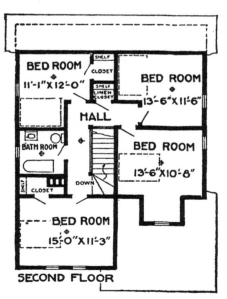

SHELF

BED ROOM
11'-1"X12'-0"

CLOSET

SHELF

LINEN CLOSET

BED ROOM
13'-6"X11'-6"

HALL

BATH ROOM

BED ROOM
13'-6"X10'-8"

DOWN

SHELF

CLOSET

BED ROOM
15'-0"X11'-3"

SECOND FLOOR

$1,026.00

For $1,026.00 we will furnish all the material to build this Eight-Room House, consisting of Mill Work, Siding, Flooring, Ceiling, Finishing Lumber, Building Paper, Pipe, Gutter, Sash Weights, Hardware, Painting Material, Lumber, Lath and Shingles. NO EXTRAS, as we guarantee enough material at the above price to build this house according to our plans.

By allowing a fair price for labor, cement, brick and plaster, which we do not furnish, this house can be built for about $1,900.00, including all material and labor.

For Our Offer of Free Plans See Page 3.

A GOOD, substantial house, suitable for town, suburban or country home. All rooms are of good size and well arranged for convenience. China closet built into the wall of the dining room. Large cased opening between the sitting room and dining room, which practically makes these two rooms into one large room. Has an open stairway in the sitting room which faces directly toward the entrance of the parlor. Inside cellar way leading to the basement from the hall. Bathroom on the first floor. Three large bedrooms on the second floor, all of which could be used with two beds if necessary.

Blaine front door, leaded Crystal front window. Interior doors on first floor have Nona pine stiles and rails with five-cross yellow pine panels. Second floor doors are our special high grade painted four-panel doors. Clear yellow pine trim for both first and second floors and yellow pine open stairs. Yellow pine flooring for entire house and porches.

Built on a concrete block foundation, frame construction, sided with narrow bevel edge cypress siding and has cedar shingle roof.

Painted two coats outside; color to suit. Varnish and wood filler for two coats of interior finish.

Excavated basement under the entire house, 6 feet 3 inches high. First floor, 9 feet from floor to ceiling; second floor, 8 feet from floor to ceiling. Outside measurement, 27 feet 6 inches by 47 feet.

This house is 27 feet 6 inches wide by 47 feet long and can be built on a lot 30 feet wide.

Complete Warm Air Heating Plant, for soft coal, extra	$ 91.13
Complete Warm Air Heating Plant, for hard coal, extra	93.10
Complete Steam Heating Plant, extra	188.45
Complete Hot Water Heating Plant, extra	244.02
Complete Plumbing Outfit, extra	118.23
Acetylene Lighting Plant, extra	51.10

SEARS, ROEBUCK AND CO.
CHICAGO, ILLINOIS

MODERN HOME No. 116

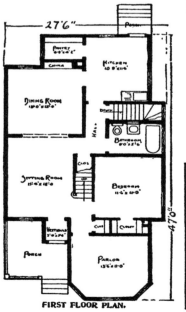

FIRST FLOOR PLAN.

This house has been built at Ponemah, Ill., Gary, Ind., Mishawaka, Ind., Hammond, Ind., Fenton, Iowa, Aurora, Neb., Ithaca, N. Y., Dresden, Ohio, and Fairmont, W. Va.

WE CUT HIS BILL DOWN TO ONE-HALF.

Sanborn, Iowa.
Sears, Roebuck and Co., Chicago, Ill.
Gentlemen:—A number of people sized up the building at the time I built and they were very much surprised that I bought the material for such a price. A dealer figured on the bill and made it about twice as much as your bill, and poor lumber at that. If anybody thinks about building in my vicinity refer him to me and I will do all I can for you.
Yours truly,
ERNEST BLOCK.

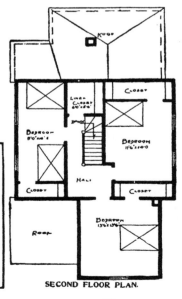

SECOND FLOOR PLAN.

$1,109⁰⁰

For $1,109.00 we will furnish all the material to build this Eight-Room House, consisting of Mill Work, Flooring, Ceiling, Finishing Lumber, Building Paper, Pipe, Gutter, Sash Weights, Hardware, Painting Material, Lumber, Lath and Shingles. **NO EXTRAS**, as we guarantee enough material at the above price to build this house according to our plans.

By allowing a fair price for labor, cement, brick and plaster, which we do not furnish, this house can be built for about $1,970.00, including all material and labor.

For Our Offer of Free Plans See Page 3.

A GOOD, well built, roomy house. Large parlor connects with the dining room by large cased opening. Good size kitchen and bedroom on the first floor. Reception hall connects with the parlor by sliding door and contains an open stairway of choice grain clear yellow pine.

Front door glazed with lace design glass. Interior doors for main rooms on first floor are five-cross panel with soft pine stiles and rails and yellow pine panels. Doors on the second floor are four-panel solid yellow pine. Clear yellow pine interior trim throughout the house. Our Crystal leaded glass sash for side bay window and front window in the parlor, with leaded glass sash in the stair hall to match. Three Queen Anne windows in the front bedroom of the second floor. Clear yellow pine flooring for the entire house and porches.

Built on a concrete block foundation, frame construction, sided with narrow bevel clear cypress siding and has cedar shingle roof. Colonial porch columns.

Painted two coats outside; color to suit. Varnish and wood filler for two coats of interior finish.

Excavated basement under the entire house, 7 feet from floor to joists. First floor, 9 feet from floor to ceiling; second floor, 8 feet 6 inches from floor to ceiling.

This house can be built on a lot 32 feet wide.

Complete Warm Air Heating Plant, for soft coal, extra	$ 84.89
Complete Warm Air Heating Plant, for hard coal, extra	86.92
Complete Steam Heating Plant, extra	191.60
Complete Hot Water Heating Plant, extra	214.25
Acetylene Lighting Plant, extra	50.30

SEARS, ROEBUCK AND CO.　　　　**CHICAGO, ILLINOIS**

MODERN HOME No. 170

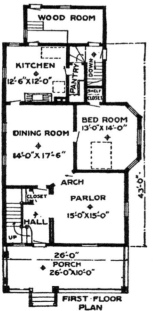

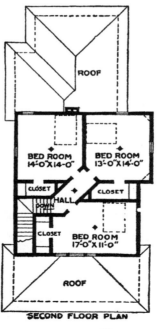

WRITE THIS MAN IF YOU ARE IN DOUBT.

15 Henery St.,
Fitchburg, Mass.
Sears, Roebuck and Co.,
Chicago, Ill.

Gentlemen:—I have moved into my new home No. 170 which I bought of you and find everything just as you represented, both in quality and saving. I am very well pleased with everything and am more than satisfied with the way you handled my order. When I ordered lumber I had you send studding two feet longer, so my house is two feet higher in second story, giving me square rooms with but very little cost. If any person interested in your building proposition is in doubt have him come to me or write and I will gladly give them all information. My contractor said the plans and specifications were the best he ever saw. Very truly yours,
PATRICK B. McNAMARA.

—73—

$910^{00}

For $910.00 we will furnish all the material to build this Eight-Room House, consisting of Lumber, Lath, Shingles, Mill Work, Ceiling, Siding, Flooring, Finishing Lumber, Building Paper, Pipe, Gutter, Sash Weights, Hardware and Painting Material. **NO EXTRAS**, as we guarantee enough material at the above price to build this house according to our plans.

By allowing a fair price for labor, stone, brick and plaster, which we do not furnish, this house can be built for about $1,875.00, including all material and labor.

For Our Offer of Free Plans See Page 3.

ROOMS are large and well proportioned. Front door enters directly into the living room. Sliding door between the living room and parlor, and sliding door between living room and library. Large kitchen, pantry, bathroom or storeroom on the first floor. Inside cellar stairs directly under the main stairs, and outside cellar entrance in the rear. On the second floor is one large front chamber with two medium size side bedrooms, three closets and large storeroom over kitchen which can be used as a bedroom.

Rich front door glazed with leaded art glass; clear yellow pine interior doors for both first and second floors. Yellow pine casing, baseboard and trim. Leaded Crystal front window for parlor. Yellow pine flooring for the entire house and porches.

Built on a stone foundation, frame construction, sided with narrow bevel cypress siding and cedar shingle roof.

Painted two coats outside; your choice of color. Varnish and wood filler for interior finish.

Excavated basement under the entire house, 6 feet 10 inches from floor to joists. First floor, 9 feet 2 inches from floor to ceiling; second floor, 8 feet 6 inches from floor to ceiling.

This house measures 26x44 feet and can be built on a lot 30 feet wide.

Complete Warm Air Heating Plant, for soft coal, extra.................$ 74.79
Complete Warm Air Heating Plant, for hard coal, extra................. 76.36
Complete Steam Heating Plant, extra.................................. 188.70
Complete Hot Water Heating Plant, extra............................. 232.98
Acetylene Lighting Plant, extra..................................... 49.50

SEERS, ROEBUCK AND CO.   **CHICAGO, ILLINOIS**

MODERN HOME No. 101

This house has been built at Ashland, Ill., Clifton, Ill., Crown Point, Ind., Wilton Junction, Iowa, Plummer, Minn., Rogers, Minn., Milford, Mich., and Cortland, N. Y.

This House Will Sell Four Others.

R. F. D. No. 1, Box, 78,
Kittanning, Penn.

Sears, Roebuck and Co., Chicago, Ill.
Gentlemen:—Everybody who has seen the material says it is the finest bought here at any price. I believe in buying from you one could save enough on the price of lumber to pay for the building of a house. There are **four people waiting to see this house** when it is completed and if the plans suit them there will be four more houses going up here in the spring just like it. I am a satisfied customer in every way. Yours truly,
JACOB S. STITT.

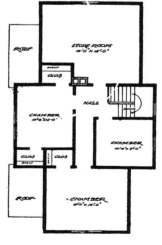

— FIRST FLOOR PLAN —

— SECOND FLOOR PLAN —

MODERN HOME No. 117

$921⁰⁰

For $921.00 we will furnish all the material to build this Seven-Room House, consisting of Mill Work, Lumber, Lath, Shingles, Flooring, Ceiling, Siding, Finishing Lumber, Eaves Trough, Hardware and Painting Material. NO EXTRAS, as we guarantee enough material at the above price to build this house according to our plans.

By allowing a fair price for labor, cement, brick and plaster, which we do not furnish, this house can be built for about $2,000.00, including all material and labor.

For Our Offer of Free Plans See Page 3.

THIS house is handily arranged, all rooms being of good size and so planned that there is hardly a foot of waste space. A large cased opening between the dining room and parlor makes these two rooms practically into one large room which is frequently used as a parlor and back parlor, and the kitchen being so large is often used as a kitchen and dining room, and the sitting room as a bedroom for the first floor. You will note the two large bedrooms on the second floor, each one extending clear across the house, one on the front and the other on the rear.

The front door is our Victoria design, glazed with colored leaded art glass. The inside doors are five-panel solid clear yellow pine for both first and second floors. All the interior trim, such as baseboard, casing, molding and stairs, is clear yellow pine. Front parlor window is our Crescent design, glazed colored leaded art glass. Clear yellow pine flooring for entire house and porches.

Painted two coats outside; your choice of color. Varnish and wood filler for interior finish.

This house is built on a concrete block foundation and is of frame construction, sided with narrow bevel clear cypress siding and has cedar shingle roof.

Excavated basement under the entire house, 7 feet from floor to joists. First floor, 9 feet 4 inches from floor to ceiling; second floor, 8 feet from floor to ceiling.

This house can be built on a lot 27 feet wide.

Complete Warm Air Heating Plant, for soft coal, extra	$ 88.79
Complete Warm Air Heating Plant, for hard coal, extra	90.80
Complete Steam Heating Plant, extra	177.55
Complete Hot Water Heating Plant, extra	226.13
Acetylene Lighting Plant, extra	48.70

SEARS, ROEBUCK AND CO. **CHICAGO, ILLINOIS**

This house has been built at Hartley, Iowa, Hillsdale, Mich., West Branch, Mich., Culbertson, Mont., and Orangeburg, N. Y.

SAVES ONE-HALF.

R. F. D. No. 1, Cypress, Ill.

Sears, Roebuck and Co.,
Chicago, Ill.

Gentlemen:—I am well pleased with every order which I sent you. I priced a bill of windows and doors here at four different houses. The very lowest price was $96.75, that was the best I could do, and I sent my order to you and the cost was $47.26, freight charges included. You can see what I saved by ordering from Sears, Roebuck and Co. I am a carpenter and contractor and I will send you another order in a short time. I can save one-half by ordering from you.

Very truly yours,
A. J. GREER.

FIRST FLOOR.

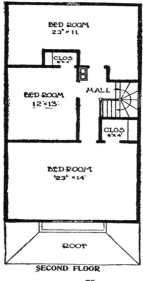

SECOND FLOOR

—75—

$826⁰⁰

For $826.00 we will furnish all the material to build this Seven-Room House, consisting of Lumber, Lath, Shingles, Mill Work, Flooring, Ceiling, Siding, Finishing Lumber, Building Paper, Pipe, Gutter, Sash Weights, Hardware and Painting Material. NO EXTRAS, as we guarantee enough material at the above price to build this house according to our plans.

By allowing a fair price for labor, stone, brick and plaster, which we do not furnish, this house can be built for about $1,615.00, including all material and labor.

For Our Offer of Free Plans See Page 3.

A COMFORTABLE home, suitable for a suburban or country residence. Has a large front porch, 25 feet long by 6 feet wide; Colonial porch columns. Rear porch, 11 feet by 4 feet 6 inches. Outside cellar entrance. Vestibule leads to the parlor and to the dining room. Cased opening between the dining room and parlor. Good size pantry and storeroom. Inside cellar stairs under the main stairs. Three bedrooms and two closets on the second floor, with an attic which is sometimes used as a storeroom or can be finished as a small bedroom, or it may be fitted up as a bathroom with little expense.

Windsor front door glazed with leaded glass. Inside doors are five-panel solid yellow pine; clear yellow pine molding and trim. Clear yellow pine flooring for the entire house and porches.

Painted two coats outside; your choice of color. Varnish and wood filler for interior finish.

Built on a stone foundation, frame construction, sided with narrow bevel edge cypress siding and has cedar shingle roof.

Excavated basement under the entire house, 6 feet 10 inches from floor to joists, with cement floor. First floor, 8 feet 6 inches from floor to ceiling; second floor, 8 feet from floor to ceiling.

This house is 24 feet 6 inches wide by 40 feet long and can be built on a lot 27 feet wide.

Complete Warm Air Heating Plant, for soft coal, extra	$ 67.68
Complete Warm Air Heating Plant, for hard coal, extra	70.59
Complete Steam Heating Plant, extra	138.40
Complete Hot Water Heating Plant, extra	172.42
Acetylene Lighting Plant, extra	51.10

SEARS, ROEBUCK AND CO.   **CHICAGO, ILLINOIS**

MODERN HOME No. 110

This house has been built at Rock Falls, Ill., Gary, Ind., Challis, I d a h o, Lawrence, Kan., Boston, Mass., Lansing, Mich., Nelson, Neb., Hamburg, N. J., Albany, N. Y., Shepard, Ohio, N. Milwaukee, Wis., and other cities.

24'6"

STORE RM.

KITCHEN
9'6"X13'0"

PANTRY

DINING ROOM
12'0"X13'0"

BED ROOM
11'0"X10'0"

40'0"

VESTIBULE
5'6"X5'6"

PORCH

PARLOR
13'0"X12'0"

PORCH

FIRST FLOOR PLAN

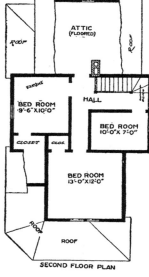

ATTIC
(FLOORED)

ROOF

ROOF

BED ROOM
9'6"X10'0"

HALL

BED ROOM
10'0"X 7'0"

CLOSET   CLOS.

BED ROOM
13'0"X12'0"

ROOF

ROOF

SECOND FLOOR PLAN

MODERN HOME No. 108

$835⁰⁰

For $835.00 we will furnish all the material to build this Seven-Room House, consisting of Mill Work, Siding, Flooring, Ceiling, Finishing Lumber, Building Paper, Pipe, Gutter, Sash Weights, Hardware, Painting Material, Lumber, Lath and Shingles. NO EXTRAS, as we guarantee enough material at the above price to build this house according to our plans.

By allowing a fair price for labor, stone, brick and plaster, which we do not furnish, this house can be built for about $1,750.00 including all material and labor.

For Our Offer of Free Plans See Page 3.

A SPACIOUS house with seven large and well proportioned rooms. Open stairway in the reception hall. Cased opening between the reception hall and living room; also cased opening between living room and dining room, and there is access from the reception hall to the kitchen and dining room without passing through any of the other rooms. A large pantry. Inside cellar stairs directly under the main stairs, also an outside cellar stairway. Large bay window in the dining room. On the second floor are three bedrooms, large bathroom and four closets.

Victoria front door glazed with colored leaded art glass. Interior doors are five-cross panel yellow pine. Clear yellow pine trim on first and second floors; yellow pine flooring throughout the entire house and porches.

Built on a stone foundation, frame construction, sided with narrow bevel edge cypress siding and has cedar shingle roof.

Painted two coats outside; your choice of color. Varnish and wood filler for interior finish.

Excavated basement under the entire house, 7 feet from floor to joists, with cement floor. First floor, 9 feet from floor to ceiling; second floor, 8 feet 5 inches from floor to ceiling.

This house is 26 feet 6 inches wide by 35 feet 6 inches long and can be built on a lot 31 feet wide.

Complete Warm Air Heating Plant, for soft coal, extra	$ 81.00
Complete Warm Air Heating Plant, for hard coal, extra	83.48
Complete Steam Heating Plant, extra	177.90
Complete Hot Water Heating Plant, extra	213.28
Complete Plumbing Outfit, extra	118.08
Acetylene Lighting Plant, extra	49.50

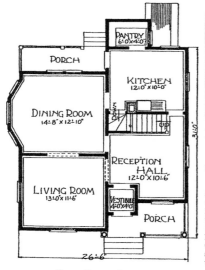

FIRST·FLOOR·PLAN

This house has been built at West Haverstraw, N. Y., Rossville, N. Y., and Shelby, Ohio.

Perfectly Fair and Square.

Grafton, Mass.
Sears, Roebuck and Co.,
Chicago, Ill.
Gentlemen: — The lumber and finishing material are much better than I could have gotten here. My contractor tells me I saved about $200.00. I will say right here that Sears, Roebuck and Co. are perfectly fair and square and have done everything that they agreed to do.
Yours respectfully,
D. S. CHASE.

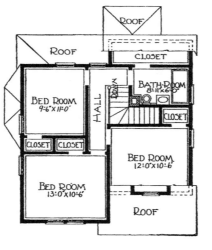

SECOND·FLOOR·PLAN
—77—

SEARS, ROEBUCK AND CO.　　　　**CHICAGO, ILLINOIS**

MODERN HOME No. 109

711\underline{\underline{00}}$

For $711.00 we will furnish all the material to build this Seven-Room House, consisting of Mill Work, Siding, Flooring, Ceiling, Finishing Lumber, Building Paper, Pipe, Gutter, Sash Weights, China Closet, Hardware, Painting Material, Lumber, Lath and Shingles. NO EXTRAS, as we guarantee enough material at the above price to build this house according to our plans.

By allowing a fair price for labor, stone, brick and plaster, which we do not furnish, this house can be built for about $1,465.00, including all material and labor.

For Our Offer of Free Plans See Page 3.

A GOOD, substantial, well built house with all rooms of a fair size and arranged to make the best possible use of all the available space.

We furnish our Windsor front door glazed with leaded glass for the front with solid yellow pine five-cross panel doors for the interior for both first and second floors. Our Crystal leaded glass front window for the living room, with clear yellow pine trim, such as baseboard, casing, molding, etc., throughout the entire house, with open stairway with choice grain. Clear yellow pine flooring for entire house and porches.

Painted two coats outside; color to suit. Varnish and wood filler for two coats of interior finish.

This house is built on a stone foundation, 24 feet wide by 33 feet long, is of frame construction, sided with narrow bevel edge cypress siding and has cedar shingle roof.

Excavated basement under the entire house, 6 feet 8 inches from floor to joists. First floor, 9 feet 4 inches from floor to ceiling; second floor, 8 feet 4 inches from floor to ceiling.

This house can be built on a lot 27 feet 6 inches wide.

Complete Warm Air Heating Plant, for soft coal, extra	$ 68.87
Complete Warm Air Heating Plant, for hard coal, extra	71.96
Complete Steam Heating Plant, extra	184.30
Complete Hot Water Heating Plant, extra	228.50
Acetylene Lighting Plant, extra	48.70

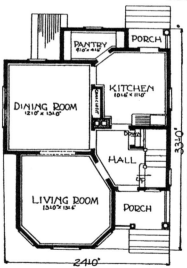

This house has been built at East Hampton, Conn., Belleville, Ill., Freeport, Ill., Oak Lawn, Ill., Muscatine, Iowa, Mt. Rainier, Md., Greenfield, Mass., Hadley, Mass., Hart, Mich., Novi, Mich., Dalbo, Minn., Ossining, N. Y., Wheatland, Penn., Westpoint, Va., and other cities.

FIRST FLOOR PLAN

SECOND FLOOR PLAN

—78—

SEARS, ROEBUCK AND CO.   CHICAGO, ILLINOIS

MODERN HOME No. 169

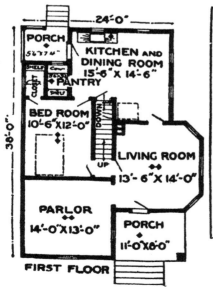

FIRST FLOOR

24'-0"

PORCH

KITCHEN AND DINING ROOM 15'-6" X 14'-6"

PANTRY

BED ROOM 10'-6" X 12'-0"

LIVING ROOM 13'-6" X 14'-0"

PARLOR 14'-0" X 13'-0"

PORCH 11'-0" X 6'-0"

38'-0"

This house has been built at Ellington, Conn., Modoc, Ill., Peru, Ind., Maple Grove, Ky., Fulda, Minn., Bay Port, Mich., Pleasanton, Neb., Morrisville, Penn., Boscobel, Wis., Aurora, S. Dak., Port Jefferson, N. Y., Janesville, Wis., and other cities.

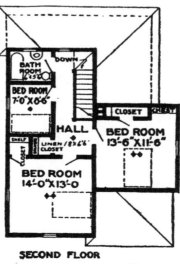

SECOND FLOOR

BATH ROOM

DOWN

BED ROOM 7'-0" X 6'-6"

HALL

CLOSET

BED ROOM 13'-6" X 11'-6"

LINEN CLOSET

BED ROOM 14'-0" X 13'-0"

—79—

$913.00

For $913.00 we will furnish all the material to build this Seven-Room House, consisting of Mill Work, Siding, Flooring, Ceiling, Finishing Lumber, Building Paper, Pipe, Gutter, Sash Weights, Hardware, Painting Material, Lumber, Lath and Shingles. **NO EXTRAS**, as we guarantee enough material at the above price to build this house according to our plans.

By allowing a fair price for labor, cement, brick and plaster, which we do not furnish, this house can be built for about $1,650.00, including all material and labor.

For Our Offer of Free Plans See Page 3.

THIS house makes a very comfortable country or suburban home, having large parlor, living room, kitchen and bedroom on the first floor, two large bedrooms, bathroom and one small bedroom on the second floor. While this house can be built for a very small cost it is well arranged to accommodate a large family. The building of this house at this low cost is made possible by our furnishing you a high grade of material at low prices.

This house has our Garfield front door and the interior doors on the first floor are five-cross yellow pine panel doors. Doors on the second floor are four-panel clear yellow pine. All interior trim, such as baseboard, casing, molding, etc., is clear yellow pine, and yellow pine stairs. Clear yellow pine flooring for entire house and porches.

Built on concrete block foundation, frame construction, sided with narrow bevel edge cypress siding and has cedar shingle roof.

Painted two coats outside; your choice of color. Varnish and wood filler for interior finish.

Excavated basement under the entire house. Rooms on the first floor, 9 feet from floor to ceiling; rooms on the second floor, 8 feet 8 inches from floor to ceiling.

This house can be built on a lot 32 feet wide.

Complete Warm Air Heating Plant, for soft coal, extra	$ 77.01
Complete Warm Air Heating Plant, for hard coal, extra	79.06
Complete Steam Heating Plant, extra	192.80
Complete Hot Water Heating Plant, extra	248.04
Complete Plumbing Outfit, extra	112.93
Acetylene Lighting Plant, extra	51.10

SEARS, ROEBUCK AND CO.

CHICAGO, ILLINOIS

MODERN HOME No. 161

Reproduced from photograph sent in by Mr. Homer J. Leeper,
Springfield, Mo. Read his letter below.

$969.00

For $969.00 we will furnish all the material to build this Seven-Room House, consisting of Mill Work, Ceiling, Siding, Flooring, Finishing Lumber, Building Paper, Pipe, Gutter, Sash Weights, Hardware, Painting Material, Lumber, Lath and Shingles. NO EXTRAS, as we guarantee enough material at the above price to build this house according to our plans.

By allowing a fair price for labor, cement, brick and plaster, which we do not furnish, this house can be built for about $1,870.00, including all material and labor.

For Our Offer of Free Plans See Page 3.

A COTTAGE that cannot help but please you if you are looking for an up to date, modern cottage. It has the appearance of a high priced house, both in exterior and interior. Large front porch, 17x7 feet, with square stonekote columns with panel tops.

Queen Anne windows. Birch Craftsman front door. Two-panel veneered birch interior doors and clear birch trim throughout the house.

First Floor.

The front door opens to a stair or reception hall that contains an open stairway made of clear birch of choice grain. Under the open stairway is a door and inside stairway leading to the basement. Door from the reception hall leads directly into dining room and a cased opening from the reception hall leads into the parlor. In the parlor are three large windows, affording plenty of light. A door leads from the parlor directly into the dining room. From the dining room there is a door leading to a bedroom, which can be used to advantage either for a library or den. There are two closets on the first floor, one opening into the bedroom and one into the dining room. A door leads from the dining room directly into the kitchen and at the end of the kitchen there is a large pantry which is also handy to the dining room. A door leads from the kitchen to the back porch, which is enclosed. The hall, parlor, dining room and bedroom have clear oak flooring. The kitchen and pantry have clear maple flooring.

Second Floor.

The head of the stairs ends in a hall which opens to each of the three large bedrooms or bath room. Each of these large bedrooms has one closet, and three windows in each room which afford plenty of light and ventilation. The bathroom is a large size room and has two windows and a small linen closet. Yellow pine flooring for the second floor.

Built on a concrete block foundation, frame construction, sided with narrow bevel edge cypress siding to the belt course and cedar shingles above the belt course. Gables sided with stonekote. Cedar shingle roof with the exception of the dormers, which are covered with galvanized steel roofing.

Painted two coats outside; your choice of color. Varnish and wood filler for interior finish.

Excavated basement under the entire house, 7 feet from floor to joists, with cement floor. Rooms on the first floor are 9 feet from floor to ceiling; second floor, 8 feet 6 inches from floor to ceiling.

This house can be built on a lot 30 feet wide.

Complete Warm Air Heating Plant, for soft coal, extra................	$ 77.24
Complete Warm Air Heating Plant, for hard coal, extra................	80.18
Complete Steam Heating Plant, extra..................................	161.75
Complete Hot Water Plant, extra......................................	201.10
Complete Plumbing Outfit, extra......................................	119.33
Acetylene Lighting Plant, extra......................................	50.30

SEARS, ROEBUCK AND CO.   **CHICAGO, ILLINOIS**

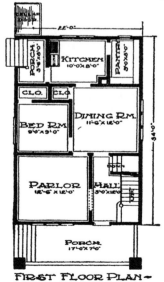

FIRST FLOOR PLAN

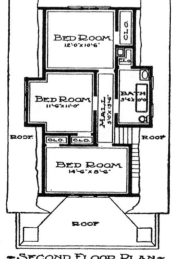

SECOND FLOOR PLAN

MODERN HOME No. 190

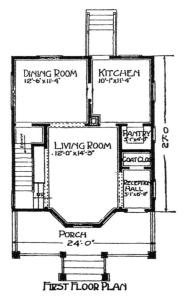

FIRST FLOOR PLAN

DINING ROOM 12'-6"x11'-4"
KITCHEN 10'-1"x11'-4"
PANTRY 5'-1"x4'-5"
LIVING ROOM 12'-0"x14'-3"
COAT CLOS.
RECEPTION HALL 5'-1"x6'-11"
PORCH 24'-0"

PEOPLE TRAVEL 120 MILES TO SEE THIS HOUSE.

Coldwater, Kan.
Sears, Roebuck and Co.,
Chicago, Ill.

Gentlemen:—My house has attracted a good deal of attention and favorable comment, and has been visited by people from quite a distance, farthest being 120 miles. Everybody is surprised at the quality of mill work, nothing like it being obtainable here for natural wood finish. **Saved $419.00 on lumber, net.**

Yours truly,
A. A. WARD.

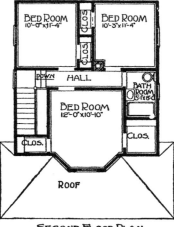

SECOND FLOOR PLAN

BED ROOM 10'-0"x11'-4"
BED ROOM 10'-3"x11'-4"
CLOS.
DOWN
HALL
BATH ROOM 5'-1"x8'-0"
BED ROOM 12'-0"x10'-10"
CLOS.
CLOS.
ROOF

$894.00

For $894.00 we will furnish all the material to build this Six-Room House, consisting of Lumber, Lath, Shingles, Mill Work, Flooring, Ceiling, Siding, Finishing Lumber, Building Paper, Pipe, Gutter, Sash Weights, Hardware and Painting Material. NO EXTRAS, as we guarantee enough material at the above price to build this house according to our plans.

By allowing a fair price for labor, cement, brick and plaster, which we do not furnish, this house can be built for about $1,700.00, including all material and labor.

For Our Offer of Free Plans See Page 3.

THIS comfortable little home is pleasing and homelike. It has a large bay window on both the first and second floors. The porch is 24 feet wide by 7 feet 6 inches deep. This house has a small reception hall 5 feet 1 inch wide by 6 feet 11 inches long. Directly off this reception hall is the large roomy coat closet. A cased opening separates the reception hall from the living room. The living room is 14 feet 3 inches long by 12 feet wide. By referring to the floor plan you will note that the left hand side of the living room has a large cased opening 10 feet wide by 7 feet high which opens on to the stairway leading to the second floor. The dining room and kitchen are both fair size rooms; the kitchen has a pantry 4 feet by 5 feet 1 inch in which a pantry case is built. All rooms on the first floor will be perfectly cool on the hottest days, the ventilation being perfect. The entrance to the basement is through the dining room; basement stairs being immediately under the stairs leading from the first floor to the second floor.

First Floor.

Front door made of clear white pine, 1¾ inches thick, glazed with bevel plate glass. Inside doors are of the five-cross panel design, made of the best quality yellow pine with yellow pine trim to match. Yellow pine flooring for first floor.

Second Floor.

Stairs from first floor lead to hall on second floor, the entrance to each of the three bedrooms being off this hall. Each of the two rear bedrooms has a clothes closet; the front bedroom has two large clothes closets. All doors, trim and flooring are made of yellow pine, the doors being five-cross panel design.

Built on a concrete block foundation with basement under the entire house. We furnish cypress siding and cedar shingles, framing timbers of best quality yellow pine. Basement has cement floor.

Height of Ceilings.

Basement, 7 feet from floor to joists.
First floor, 9 feet from floor to ceiling.
Second floor, 8 feet 6 inches from floor to ceiling.

Painted with two coats of best quality paint outside, varnish and wood filler for interior finish.

This house can be built on a lot 28 feet wide.

Complete Warm Air Heating Plant, for soft coal, extra	$ 70.88
Complete Warm Air Heating Plant, for hard coal, extra	74.18
Complete Steam Heating Plant, extra	170.01
Complete Hot Water Heating Plant, extra	210.22
Complete Plumbing Outfit, extra	127.36
Acetylene Lighting Plant, extra	50.30

SEARS, ROEBUCK AND CO. 　　　　**CHICAGO, ILLINOIS**

MODERN HOME No. 185

$683.00

For $683.00 we will furnish all the material to build this Seven-Room House, consisting of Lumber, Lath, Shingles, Mill Work, Flooring, Ceiling, Siding, Finishing Lumber, Building Paper, Pipe, Gutter, Sash Weights, Hardware and Painting Material. NO EXTRAS, as we guarantee enough material at the above price to build this house according to our plans.

By allowing a fair price for labor, cement, brick and plaster, which we do not furnish, this house can be built for about $1,250.00, including all material and labor.

For Our Offer of Free Plans See Page 3.

IN MODERN Home No. 185 we have a cottage of low cost, suitable for a 30-foot lot and is particularly adapted for a large family of moderate means. It will be seen from the floor plans that there is a large porch extending almost entirely across the front of the house. The front door opens into the living room. Either of the two bedrooms on the first floor or kitchen may be entered from the living room. A boxed stairway to the second floor has its entrance from the kitchen.

First Floor.

Front and rear doors are made of soft pine, 1⅜ inches thick, glazed with "A" quality double strength glass. Inside doors are of the five-cross panel style, and made of the best grade of yellow pine with yellow pine trim and flooring to match.

Second Floor.

The stairway opens into the small hall on the second floor, from which any of the three second floor bedrooms may be entered. Each bedroom on the second floor has a large closet. All doors on the second floor are made of the best grade of yellow pine, of the five-cross panel style. Floors and trim are also of yellow pine.

Built on a concrete block foundation. Not excavated. We furnish clear cypress siding and cedar shingles. Framing timbers are of the best quality yellow pine. "A" quality double strength glass used in all the windows. First floor height from floor to ceiling, 8 feet 6 inches. Second floor, 8 feet from floor to ceiling. Outside painted with two coats of the best paint. Varnish and wood filler for interior finish.

This house can be built on a lot 30 feet wide.

Complete Warm Air Heating Plant, for soft coal, extra	$ 65.58
Complete Warm Air Heating Plant, for hard coal, extra	67.88
Complete Steam Heating Plant, extra	146.50
Complete Hot Water Heating Plant, extra	175.74
Acetylene Lighting Plant, extra	47.90

SEARS, ROEBUCK AND CO.   **CHICAGO, ILLINOIS**

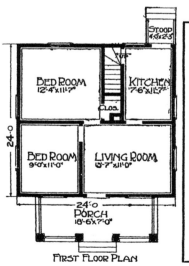

FIRST FLOOR PLAN

WE HAVE THE GOODS.

Belleville, Ill.
Sears, Roebuck and Co.,
Chicago, Ill.

I received the third shipment today from you and must say that the doors, thirty in all, are the best that I have seen. When I sent you the order for Nona pine doors I thought I would never use those doors in a $3,400.00 house. I took twenty-six doors from this order and the owner is more than pleased with them. I purchased the goods from you because I know that you do what is right to all concerned. I also send you another order for this year. In the near future I will send you more orders, because I am convinced now that you have the goods. Yours respectfully,

E. F. DREWES.

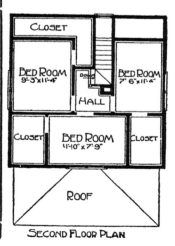

SECOND FLOOR PLAN

MODERN HOME No. 141

This house has been built at Wilmington, Del., Steger, Ill. Streator, Ill., Burlington, Iowa, Hastings, Neb., Salineville, Ohio, Cincinnati, Ohio, Central Falls, R. I., Warrenton, Va., N. Milwaukee, Wis., and other cities.

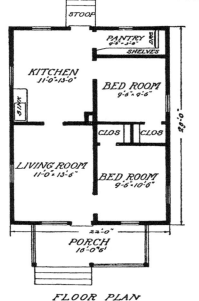

FLOOR PLAN

$531⁰⁰

For $531.00 we will furnish all the material to build this Four-Room Cottage, consisting of Mill Work, Flooring, Siding, Ceiling, Finishing Lumber, Building Paper, Pipe, Gutter, Sash Weights, Hardware, Painting Material, Lumber, Lath and Shingles. **NO EXTRAS**, as we guarantee enough material at the above price to build this house according to our plans.

By allowing a fair price for labor, brick and plaster, which we do not furnish, this house can be built for about $900.00, including all material and labor.

For Our Offer of Free Plans See Page 3.

A FOUR-ROOM COTTAGE with large pantry and two closets. Good size front porch 16x6 feet. This house has a large attic which can be finished into two good size rooms at an extra cost of $94.00 for stairs and other material needed. Note the letter from James E. Craig, Indianapolis, Ind., claiming that we saved him $150.00 on the bill of material for this house.

First Floor.

Our Metropole door glazed with sand blast design glass leads from the front porch into the living room. A door leads from the living room into the kitchen and another door from the living room into the front bedroom. The rear bedroom is reached by a door from the kitchen. We specify clear yellow pine inside molding and trim with clear yellow pine flooring for the house and porches. For size of rooms see floor plan.

Painted two coats outside; your choice of color. Varnish and wood filler for interior finish.

Built on a frame foundation. Frame construction, sided with narrow bevel clear cypress siding and has cedar shingle roof. Rooms are 9 feet from floor to ceiling.

This house can be built on a lot 25 feet wide.

Complete Warm Air Heating Plant, for soft coal, extra	$ 45.43
Complete Warm Air Heating Plant, for hard coal, extra	48.16
Complete Steam Heating Plant, extra	95.05
Complete Hot Water Heating Plant, extra	118.82
Acetylene Lighting Plant, extra	46.00

SEARS, ROEBUCK AND CO.   **CHICAGO, ILLINOIS**

MODERN HOME No. 200

Built at Oak Park, Ill.

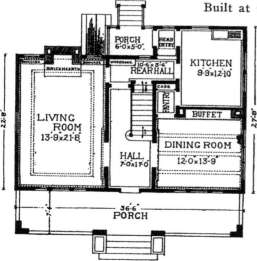

FIRST FLOOR PLAN

SECOND FLOOR PLAN

—84—

$1,528.00

For $1,528.00 we will furnish all the material to build this Seven-Room House, consisting of Lumber, Lath, Shingles, Ceiling, Siding, Flooring, Finishing Lumber, Building Paper, Pipe, Gutter, Sash Weights, Buffet, Cabinet Work, Hardware, Mosaic Tile Flooring, and Painting Material. NO EXTRAS, as we guarantee enough material at the above price to build this house according to our plans.

By allowing a fair price for labor, cement, brick and plaster, which we do not furnish, this house can be built for about $3,000.00, including all material and labor.

For Our Offer of Free Plans See Page 3.

THIS large residence is similar in design to our Modern Home No. 230, illustrated on page 90, but the private veranda and open sleeping porch are omitted. A front porch extending the full length of the house is added.

Built on a concrete block foundation, veneered with brick from the grade to the first floor joists. Framing timbers are of the best quality yellow pine. Cedar shingle roof. Clear cypress siding.

Excavated basement with cement floor under entire house, and is 7 feet from floor to joists. First floor is 9 feet 3 inches from floor to ceiling. Second floor, 8 feet 9 inches from floor to ceiling.

Stain and paint for exterior; varnish and wood filler for interior included in above price.

First Floor.

Front door is made of oak, 1¾ inches thick. Craftsman style, glazed with plate glass. French doors, glazed with heavy plate glass, between living room and hall and between hall and dining room. Compound oak doors between living room and rear hall, and between pantry and living room. Oak floors and trim in living room, dining room and hall. Dining room contains a modern built-in buffet, also plate rail and beamed ceiling. Kitchen, rear hall and pantry have yellow pine doors and trim, and maple floors. Built-in wardrobe in rear hall. Built-in cupboard in pantry. Open stairway of oak to second floor.

Second Floor.

Open stairway to hall on second floor from which the bathroom, linen closet or any of the bedrooms may be entered. French doors glazed with heavy plate glass open on to balcony in the rear. Two mirror doors glazed with heavy plate glass mirrors in front bedroom at the left. Tile floor in bathroom. Medicine cabinet built in the bathroom. Clothes chute to the basement is situated between the two bedrooms at the right. Yellow pine floors in the hall, closets and all four bedrooms. Two-panel birch doors with trim to match used for entire second floor. Open stairway to attic. Attic is floored.

This house requires either a corner lot 50 feet wide or inside lot 75 feet wide to set off building properly.

Complete Warm Air Heating Plant, for soft coal, extra............................$101.52
Complete Warm Air Heating Plant, for hard coal, extra............................103.53
Complete Steam Heating Plant, extra...225.95
Complete Hot Water Heating Plant, extra.......................................282.58
Complete Plumbing Outfit, extra..119.16
Acetylene Lighting Plant, extra..50.30

SEARS, ROEBUCK AND CO.　　　　**CHICAGO, ILLINOIS**

$1,731.00

For $1,731.00 we will furnish all the material to build this Ten-Room House, consisting of Mill Work, Siding, Flooring, Ceiling, Finishing Lumber, Building Paper, Pipe, Gutter, Sash Weights, Hardware, Painting Material, Lumber, Lath and Shingles. **NO EXTRAS**, as we guarantee enough material at the above price to build this house according to our plans.

By allowing a fair price for labor, cement, brick and plaster, which we do not furnish, this house can be built for about $3,345.00, including all material and labor.

For Our Offer of Free Plans See Page 3.

THIS is a good substantial design, constructed with a view to economy and affording a great deal of room. It has a large front porch, 7 feet wide by 24 feet long, with balcony over part of it 8 feet 6 inches by 12 feet.

First Floor.

The front door is made of clear red oak and glazed with leaded art glass. A large reception hall in which there is an open oak stairway leading to the second floor. A convenient closet is located right under this stairway. We furnish a grille for the opening leading from the reception hall into the parlor, in which there is a handsome mantel. There is a cased opening between the sitting room and parlor. Crescent cottage window glazed with colored leaded art glass for the front parlor. There is a bay window in the sitting room. The kitchen can be entered from both the sitting room and dining room. Large pantry and storeroom located convenient to the kitchen. We furnish six-cross panel clear oak interior doors for the first floor with oak trim and molding. Oak plate rail for the dining room. All flooring for the main rooms on the first floor is of clear oak; the pantry and kitchen have clear maple flooring.

Second Floor.

This floor has five bedrooms, three of which are quite large and two of medium size. All rooms have closets, and in one of the front bedrooms a door leads to the balcony above the porch. A bathroom is located in the rear of this floor. Doors on this floor are clear yellow pine with clear yellow pine trim to match. Clear yellow pine flooring.

Painted two coats outside. Varnish and wood filler for two coats of interior finish.

Built on a concrete block foundation, frame construction, sided with narrow bevel edge cypress siding and has cedar shingle roof.

Excavated basement under the entire house, 7 feet 4 inches from floor to joists. First floor, 9 feet 6 inches from floor to ceiling; second floor, 9 feet from floor to ceiling.

This house can be built on a lot 35 feet wide.

Complete Warm Air Heating Plant, for soft coal, extra	$121.81
Complete Warm Air Heating Plant, for hard coal, extra	125.17
Complete Steam Heating Plant, extra	289.65
Complete Hot Water Heating Plant, extra	331.12
Complete Plumbing Outfit, extra	120.16
Acetylene Lighting Plant, extra	55.10

SEARS, ROEBUCK AND CO. **CHICAGO, ILLINOIS**

MODERN HOME No. 119

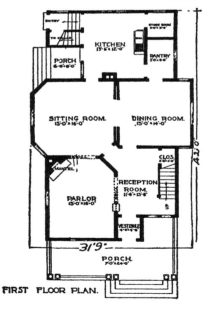

FIRST FLOOR PLAN.

SAVED 33⅓ PER CENT ON MODERN HOME NO. 119.

Hereford, Texas.
Sears, Roebuck and Co.,
Chicago, Ill.

Gentlemen:—We have now completed our new home, built from your Modern Home Plan No. 119. We could not have been better suited by employing a first class architect at many times the cost. We could not have gotten better material anywhere than we got from you, and we have saved on an average 33⅓ per cent after paying freight.

Very truly yours,

C. H. CARL.

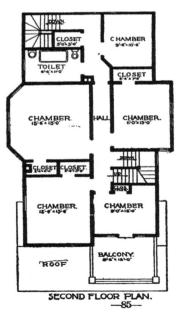

SECOND FLOOR PLAN.
—85—

$2,290⁰⁰

For $2,290.00 we will furnish all the material to build this Twelve-Room House, consisting of Lumber, Lath, Shingles, Mill Work, Flooring, Ceiling, Siding, Finishing Lumber, Building Paper, Pipe, Gutter, Sash Weights, Mantel, Medicine Case, China Closet, Console, Hardware and Painting Material. NO EXTRAS, as we guarantee enough material at the above price to build this house according to our plans.

By allowing a fair price for labor, cement, brick and plaster, which we do not furnish, this house can be built for about $4,480.00, including all material and labor.

For Our Offer of Free Plans See Page 3.

A LARGE, roomy house, well designed and suitable for a corner lot, having large front porch 42x9 feet, and large bay window in the dining room, with an outside door opening from the porch into the living room, front door opens into the reception hall. Large colonnade between the hall and parlor. Well designed oak open stairway. The hall leads to the living room, parlor or second floor. Cased opening between the living room and parlor. Sliding doors between the living room and library; sliding doors between the living room and dining room. China closet or sideboard set into the wall of the dining room. Colored leaded art glass sash on each side of sideboard above plate rail. Rear stairway leading to the second floor from the kitchen with cellar stairs directly underneath. Toilet on the first floor. On the second floor there are four large bedrooms, sewing room, storeroom or trunk room, and bathroom which has medicine case built into the wall.

Two front doors of veneered oak, glazed with bevel plate glass. Two-panel veneered oak inside doors and clear oak casing, baseboard and molding throughout the entire house. Quarter sawed oak flooring for the main rooms on the first floor and clear yellow pine flooring for the second floor and porches. Mantel in living room, and console with large mirror in parlor.

Painted two coats outside. Varnish and wood filler for two coats of interior finish.

Built on a concrete block foundation, frame construction, sided with narrow bevel edge siding of clear cypress and has cedar shingle roof.

Excavated basement under the entire house, 7 feet from floor to joists, with cement floor. First floor, 10 feet from floor to ceiling; second floor, 9 feet from floor to ceiling.

This house can be built on a lot 50 feet wide.

Complete Warm Air Heating Plant, for soft coal, extra	$112.86
Complete Warm Air Heating Plant, for hard coal, extra	115.40
Complete Steam Heating Plant, extra	345.70
Complete Hot Water Heating Plant, extra	407.63
Complete Plumbing Outfit, extra	159.26
Acetylene Lighting Plant, extra	55.10

SEARS, ROEBUCK AND CO. **CHICAGO, ILLINOIS**

MODERN HOME No. 132

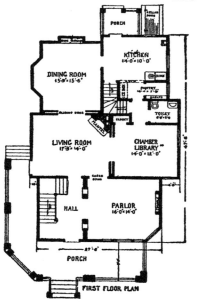

Built at Paxton, Ill., Douglas, Wyo., Rochester, Minn., Port Union, Ohio, Frankfort, So. Dak., Lincoln, Ill., and Ransom, Ill.

SAVED $800.00 ON MODERN HOME No. 132.

Colorado Springs, Colo.
Sears, Roebuck and Co.,
Chicago, Ill.

Gentlemen:—I will state that I am more than pleased with my home built by your plans and with your material. I have saved on my order given you about $800.00, and the quality of the material furnished by you far surpasses any that is being furnished for other houses being built right here. I received my entire order in a little more than two weeks from the time you shipped it from your factory and not a single article was damaged and was packed in fine shape.

Yours truly,
JOHN M. CLEAR.

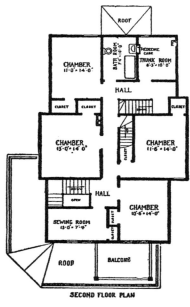

FIRST FLOOR PLAN

SECOND FLOOR PLAN

MODERN HOME No. 215

Built at Buffalo, N. Y., and Boston, Mass.

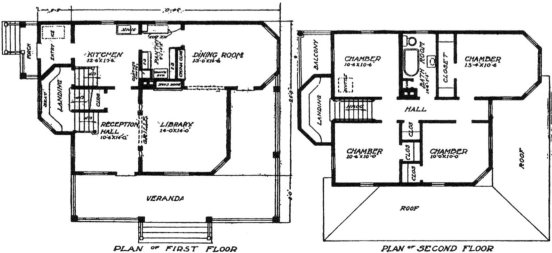

PLAN OF FIRST FLOOR   PLAN OF SECOND FLOOR

—87—

$1,561⁰⁰

For $1,561.00 we will furnish all the material to build this Eight-Room House, consisting of Mill Work, Ceiling, Siding, Flooring, Finishing Lumber, Bookcase, China Closet, Building Paper, Pipe, Gutter, Sash Weights, Hardware, Painting Material, Lumber, Lath and Shingles. NO EXTRAS, as we guarantee enough material at the above price to build this house according to our plans.

By allowing a fair price for labor, stone, cement, brick and plaster, which we do not furnish, this house can be built for about $2,970.00, including all material and labor.

For Our Offer of Free Plans See Page 3.

A LARGE modern residence with very large front porch, 46 feet long by 8 feet wide, with Colonial columns. Superba front door, 3x7 feet, 1¾ inches thick, veneered oak, glazed bevel plate glass. Julien dining room door, glazed with lace design glass. Leaded Crystal windows for front of reception hall, library, stair landing and dining room bay. For attic, Queen Anne sash.

Large reception hall opening directly into the library with colonnade opening between them. A well designed open stairway leading to the second floor.

The kitchen stairs leading to the landing of the main stairs enable one to go to the second floor from either the front hall or kitchen. This stair landing contains a long seat on the three sides of the bay, with a large mirror on the entry side of the landing bay which reflects directly into the reception hall.

Six-cross panel oak interior doors for the first floor with clear oak trim, molding, colonnade and open stair material; oak floor. Second floor finished with five-cross panel solid clear yellow pine doors and yellow pine trim, with clear yellow pine flooring for the second floor and porches. Dining room contains a china closet. The library has built in bookcase with leaded glass doors.

Painted two coats outside; your choice of color. Varnish and wood filler for interior finish.

Built on a stone foundation, frame construction, sided with narrow bevel edge cypress siding and has cedar shingle roof.

Excavated basement under the entire house, 7 feet 2 inches from floor to joists, with cement floor. First floor, 9 feet 2 inches from floor to ceiling; second floor, 8 feet from floor to ceiling.

This house can be built on a lot 48 feet wide.

Complete Warm Air Heating Plant, for soft coal, extra	$ 92.14
Complete Warm Air Heating Plant, for hard coal, extra	94.87
Complete Steam Heating Plant, extra	221.55
Complete Hot Water Heating Plant, extra	274.81
Complete Plumbing Outfit, extra	139.47
Acetylene Lighting Plant, extra	52.70

SEARS, ROEBUCK AND CO.   CHICAGO, ILLINOIS

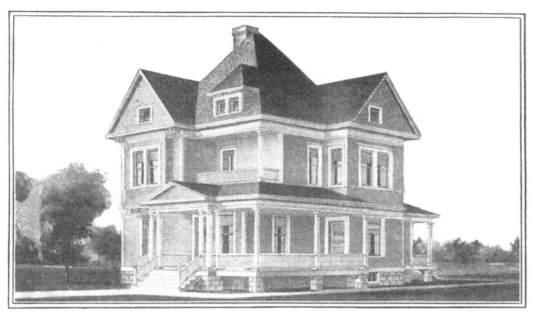

MODERN HOME No. 118

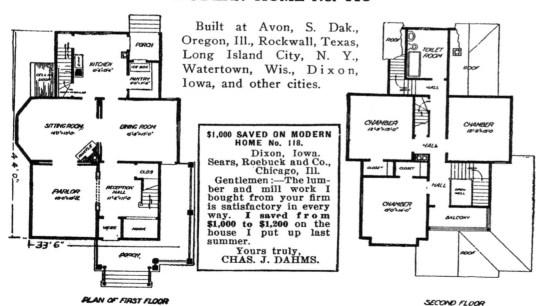

Built at Avon, S. Dak.,
Oregon, Ill., Rockwall, Texas,
Long Island City, N. Y.,
Watertown, Wis., Dixon,
Iowa, and other cities.

PLAN OF FIRST FLOOR

SECOND FLOOR
—88—

$1,575.00

For $1,575.00 we will furnish all the material to build this Nine-Room House, consisting of Lumber, Lath, Shingles, Mill Work, Siding, Flooring, Ceiling, Finishing Lumber, Building Paper, Pipe, Gutter, Sash Weights, Hardware, Mantel and Painting Material. **NO EXTRAS**, as we guarantee enough material at the above price to build this house according to our plans.

By allowing a fair price for labor, cement, brick and plaster, which we do not furnish, this house can be built for about $3,060.00, including all material and labor.

For Our Offer of Free Plans See Page 3.

MODERN Home No. 118 is a well proportioned house, suitable for any locality. One is immediately impressed on approaching this house by its quiet dignity and comfort. The large, roomy porch, 7 feet wide by 33 feet long, seems to invite one to its cool shade.

Upon entering the reception hall we find to the right a nice open stairway of oak leading to the second floor. At the foot of the stairs there is a little nook which will make a nice cozy corner.

On the first floor there are five large rooms, including the reception hall. The sitting room has a large bay window extending entirely across one side of the room. In the corner of the sitting room is an oak mantel and open fireplace. Leading from the reception hall to parlor is a cased opening with oak columns. Between parlor and living room is placed sliding doors. The kitchen is very handily arranged, having a large pantry. This pantry has a small opening in the back which admits of filling the ice chest from the back porch, doing away with having the ice carried across the kitchen floor.

The second floor has three large bedrooms and a good size bathroom; two of the bedrooms have large closets.

All the rooms on the first floor, excepting the kitchen, are finished in oak with oak flooring and six-cross panel veneered oak doors. Outside doors are of elegant design made of clear oak. Oak plate rail is furnished to go entirely around the dining room. Maple flooring is furnished for the kitchen and pantry. The second floor is finished in yellow pine, solid five-cross panel yellow pine doors. Clear yellow pine flooring for the second floor and porches.

Painted two coats outside. Varnish and wood filler for two coats interior finish.

This house is of frame construction, sided with narrow bevel edge siding and has cedar shingle roof. Built on a concrete block foundation.

Excavated basement under the entire house, 7 feet 4 inches from floor to joists. First floor, 9 feet from floor to ceiling; second floor, 8 feet 6 inches from floor to ceiling.

This house can be built on a lot 38 feet wide.

Complete Warm Air Heating Plant, for soft coal, extra	$103.06
Complete Warm Air Heating Plant, for hard coal, extra	105.11
Complete Steam Heating Plant, extra	293.70
Complete Hot Water Heating Plant, extra	337.21
Complete Plumbing Outfit, extra	120.47
Acetylene Lighting Plant, extra	53.50

SEARS, ROEBUCK AND CO.   **CHICAGO, ILLINOIS**

MODERN HOME No. 177

$1,461.00

For $1,461.00 we will furnish all the material to build this large Six-Room House, consisting of Lumber, Lath, Shingles, Mill Work, Flooring, Siding, Ceiling, Finishing Lumber, Building Paper, Pipe, Gutter, Sash Weights, Brick Mantel, Buffet, Medicine Case and Painting Material. NO EXTRAS, as we guarantee enough material at the above price to build this house according to our plans.

By allowing a fair price for labor, brick, cement and plaster, which we do not furnish, this house can be built for $3,100.00, including all material and labor.

For Our Offer of Free Plans See Page 3.

THIS combination of frame and cement plaster with wood panel strips, the latest style of construction, has proven a great success. A wide front porch extends across the entire front. No columns in the center of the porch to obstruct the view.

The windows are of a design that are in harmony with the rest of the architectural scheme. The top sash of all two-light windows has divided wood bars, adding much to its appearance. In this house we specify the best clear narrow bevel cypress siding, the very best siding made. Roofs are covered with *A* cedar shingles. Porch floors are made of edge grain yellow pine flooring, ⅞ inch thick. Every room is perfectly lighted and well ventilated.

A glance at the floor plans will show that all rooms are very large and well located. The living room is 25 feet long by 14 feet 6 inches wide. The dining room is 16 feet 6 inches long by 12 feet wide. Bedrooms on the second floor are large size. A beautiful rustic fireplace with two colored art glass windows, one on each side, adorns this large and beautiful living room. Directly in the rear of the dining room is placed an oak buffet of the latest Craftsman design, and on each side of this buffet is placed seats. The buffet with the built-in seats covers the entire end of the room. The bay window in the dining room has four windows, making it a very well lighted room. Directly below these windows are built-in window seats. In addition to all this, this room has the latest style beam ceiling.

Beautiful double French design doors are placed between the living room and dining room, adding much to the beauty of both rooms. Cased openings lead from the living room to the stair hall, and cased openings from the stair hall to the dining room. Inside entry to the basement is conveniently placed directly under the main stairs. The latest Craftsman design clear red oak doors, stairwork and trim are furnished for the first floor. The doors and trim on the second floor are made of clear birch throughout. Clear oak flooring furnished for the living room, dining room and stair hall. Clear maple flooring furnished in kitchen, pantry and on the entire second floor. Bathroom floor is made of pure white tile. This house is built on a concrete foundation which extends 7 inches above the grade line and brick from that point to the wall sill.

Basement excavated 7 feet from the floor to joists. First floor rooms, 9 feet to ceiling; second floor rooms, 8 feet 6 inches to ceiling.

We furnish paint for two coats for outside work and sufficient filler and varnish for interior work.

This house can be built on a lot 32 feet wide.

Complete Warm Air Heating Plant, for soft coal, extra	$ 96.13
Complete Warm Air Heating Plant, for hard coal, extra	98.82
Complete Steam Heating Plant, extra	213.77
Complete Hot Water Heating Plant, extra	258.09
Complete Plumbing Outfit, extra	118.15
Acetylene Lighting Plant, extra	48.70

SEARS, ROEBUCK AND CO. **CHICAGO, ILLINOIS**

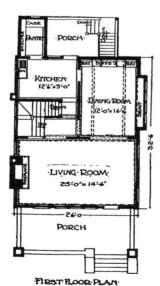

FIRST FLOOR PLAN

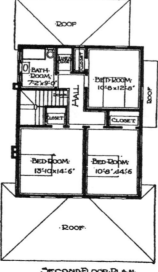

SECOND FLOOR PLAN

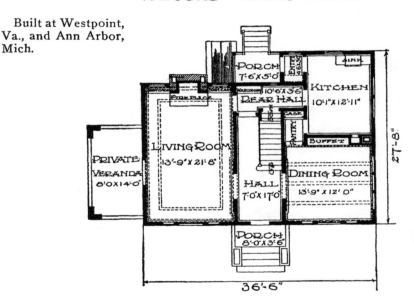

SECOND FLOOR PLAN

Built at Westpoint, Va., and Ann Arbor, Mich.

FIRST FLOOR PLAN

$1,718⁰⁰

MODERN HOME No. 230

For $1,718.00 we will furnish all the material to build this Seven-Room House, consisting of Lumber, Lath, Shingles, Ceiling, Siding, Flooring, Finishing Lumber, Building Paper, Pipe, Gutter, Sash Weights, Buffet, Cabinet Work, Hardware, Mosaic Tile Flooring, and Painting Material. NO EXTRAS outside of plumbing and heating, as we guarantee enough material at the above price to build this house according to our plans.

By allowing a fair price for labor, cement, brick and plaster, which we do not furnish, this house can be built for about $3,275.00, including all material and labor.

FOR OUR OFFER OF FREE PLANS SEE PAGE 3.

THIS modern home was designed by one of Chicago's leading architects. It is up to date, attractive and well arranged for good ventilation and convenience. It contains many features found only in the more expensive houses and, considering the low cost at which this house can be built, it makes a fine investment as well as a desirable home.

First Floor.

Front door is made of oak, 1¾ inches thick, Craftsman style, glazed with plate glass. French doors, glazed with heavy plate glass, between veranda and living room, between living room and hall and between hall and dining room. Compound oak doors between living room and rear hall, and between pantry and dining room. Oak floors and trim in living room, dining room and hall. Dining room contains a modern built-in buffet, also plate rail and beamed ceiling. Kitchen, rear hall and pantry have yellow pine doors and trim, and maple floors. Built-in wardrobe in rear hall. Built-in cupboard in pantry. Open stairway of oak to second floor.

Built on a concrete block foundation, veneered with brick from the grade to the first floor joists. Framing timbers are of the best quality yellow pine. Cedar shingle roof. Clear cypress siding.

Excavated basement with cement floor under entire house and under veranda, and is 7 feet from floor to joists. First floor is 9 feet 3 inches from floor to ceiling. Second floor, 8 feet 9 inches from floor to ceiling.

Stain and paint for exterior; varnish and wood filler for interior included in above price.

This house requires either a corner lot 50 feet wide or inside lot 75 feet wide to set off building properly.

Second Floor.

Open stairway to hall on second floor from which the bathroom, linen closet or any of the bedrooms may be entered. French doors glazed with heavy plate glass open onto sleeping porch, also on balcony in the rear. Two mirror doors glazed with heavy plate glass mirrors in front bedroom at the left. Tile floor in bathroom. Medicine cabinet built in the bathroom. Clothes chute to the basement is situated between the two bedrooms at the right. Yellow pine floors in the hall, closets and all four bedrooms. Two-panel birch doors with trim to match used for entire second floor. Open stairway to attic. Attic is floored.

Complete Warm Air Heating Plant, for soft coal, extra	$101.52
Complete Warm Air Heating Plant, for hard coal, extra	103.53
Complete Steam Heating Plant, extra...........$300.45	Complete Plumbing Outfit, extra..................123.09
Complete Hot Water Heating Plant, extra.........346.09	Acetylene Lighting Plant, extra..................53.50

—90—

SEARS, ROEBUCK AND CO.

CHICAGO, ILLINOIS

MODERN HOME No. 174

$940.00

For $940.00 we ewill furnish all the material to build this Five-Room House with attic, consisting of Mill Work, Flooring, Ceiling, Siding, Finishing Lumber, Buffet, Medicine Case, Pantry Case, Building Paper, Pipe, Gutter, Sash Weights, Hardware, Mantel, Painting Material, Lumber, Lath and Shingles. NO EXTRAS, as we guarantee enough material at the above price to build this house according to our plans.

By allowing a fair price for labor, concrete blocks, brick and plaster, which we do not furnish, this house can be built for about $1,800.00, including all material and labor.

For Our Offer of Free Plans See Page 3.

MODERN Home No. 174 was designed particularly for a narrow lot. It is possible to build this house on a lot 22 feet wide. A large porch 18 feet long by 7 feet deep extends across the entire front of the house. Nearly all the windows are of Colonial pattern. Front door is our Dublin pattern oak, glazed with bevel plate glass. As will be seen by the picture, the glass extends from the top of the door down to within 18 inches of the bottom. All the inside doors are of clear yellow pine. Open stairway leading from the hall to the second floor. The casing, base, window stool; in fact, all the inside trim and flooring is of clear yellow pine. The doors are of the five-cross panel style. Double sliding doors separate the dining room from the parlor. We particularly call your attention to the many nice features in the large dining room. Brick mantel and fireplace in the corner. A beautiful buffet is built in, with plate rail around the entire room. The window seat extends entirely across the bay. The kitchen is a small room 10 feet 6 inches by 10 feet, having a fair size pantry and closet.

On the second floor are two good size bedrooms, each having a clothes closet. The bathroom is at the end of the hall. The front bedroom on the second floor has an alcove 6 feet by 6 feet 3 inches in one corner with window seats.

Painted two coats outside; your choice of color. Varnish and wood filler for interior finish.

Built on a concrete block foundation, frame construction, sided with narrow bevel edge cypress siding. Cedar shingles for roof and porches.

Rooms on first floor, 9 feet from floor to ceiling; second floor, 8 feet from floor to ceiling.

Excavated basement under the entire house with cement floor, 7 feet from cement floor to rafters.

This house can be built on a lot 22 feet wide.

Complete Warm Air Heating Plant, for soft coal, extra.	$ 67.10
Complete Warm Air Heating Plant, for hard coal, extra	69.58
Complete Steam Heating Plant, extra	167.50
Complete Hot Water Heating Plant, extra	211.76
Complete Plumbing Outfit, extra......................	122.09
Acetylene Lighting Plant, extra......................	49.50

SEARS, ROEBUCK AND CO. **CHICAGO, ILLINOIS**

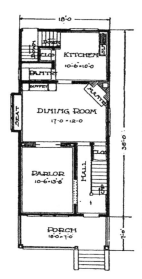

FIRST FLOOR

RECOMMENDS US TO HIS FRIENDS.
Syracuse, N. Y.

Sears, Roebuck and Co., Chicago, Ill.

Gentlemen:—I have just built a house for myself. I am not in the house building business, but if I were you may feel sure that I would get all my building material from your house. I was perfectly satisfied with everything that I got from you and I never tire in telling my neighbors and friends of the quality and perfection of anything that you handle. I have told some of my friends who are going to build in the spring that the best thing they could do is to get all their mill work from your house, and I take great pleasure in demonstrating to them that your goods are the best on any market.

Yours truly,
JOHN G. FAY.

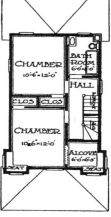

SECOND FLOOR

—91—

MODERN HOME No. 128

$429⁰⁰

For $429.00 we will furnish all the material to build this Three-Room Bungalow, consisting of Lumber, Lath, Shingles, Mill Work, Flooring, Ceiling, Siding, Finishing Lumber, Building Paper, Pipe, Gutter, Sash Weights, Hardware and Painting Material. NO EXTRAS, as we guarantee enough material at the above price to build this house according to our plans.

By allowing a fair price for labor, cement, brick and plaster, which we do not furnish, this house can be built for about $900.00, including all material and labor.

For Our Offer of Free Plans See Page 3.

A TWENTIETH century bungalow. The popularity of cobblestones and boulders for foundations, pillars, chimneys and even for open fireplaces is unquestioned, and the effect obtained here through using cobblestones for a foundation and as porch pillars, in combination with shingles stained a rich brown as a siding, lends to its beauty.

The porch is 10 feet 4 inches wide by 5 feet 6 inches deep. The front door is made of clear white pine, 1¾ inches thick, and glazed with bevel plate glass. The combination living and dining room is 10 feet 4 inches wide by 19 feet long. The kitchen and bedroom are both of fair size, being each 9 feet wide by 10 feet 3 inches long. The bathroom is 7 feet 4 inches by 6 feet.

The interior doors are of the five-cross panel design, clear yellow pine, with yellow pine trim to match. The rear door is of soft pine, 1¾ inches thick, and glazed with clear glass. Yellow pine floors for entire house.

We furnish No. 1 yellow pine framing timbers. Cedar shingles for the roof and siding. Built on a cobblestone foundation, not excavated; 9 feet from floor to ceiling.

In order to have this house look its best, it should be built on a lot about 35 feet wide.

Complete Warm Air Heating Plant, for soft coal, extra	$ 47.89
Complete Warm Air Heating Plant, for hard coal, extra	51.20
Complete Steam Heating Plant, extra	107.55
Complete Hot Water Heating Plant, extra	126.35
Complete Plumbing Outfit, extra	101.27
Acetylene Lighting Plant, extra	45.00

SEERS, ROEBUCK AND CO. **CHICAGO, ILLINOIS**

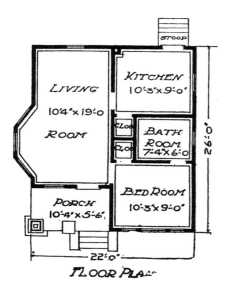

FLOOR PLAN

EVERYTHING ARRIVED O. K.

R. F. D. No. 9, Grand Rapids, Mich.
Sears, Roebuck and Co., Chicago, Ill.
Gentlemen:—Enclosed you will find picture of our home at North Park. We found the lumber perfectly satisfactory, it was put up in a very substantial manner for shipping, **not even a window glass was broken in the whole carload.** We know we saved considerable money. We saved just one-half on the bathroom outfit and are well pleased with it. The Acme Hummer furnace is all you claim. It heats our house to 70 degrees in the coldest weather and is very simple and easy to control. We saved $30.00 on furnace.
Yours truly,
C. J. MAURER.

MODERN HOME No. 129

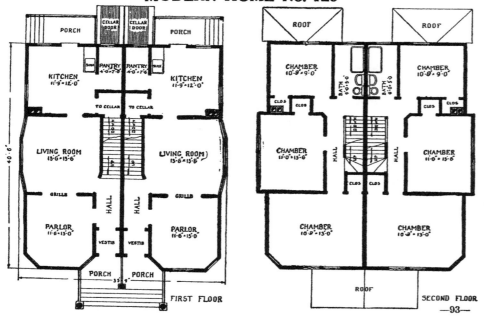

FIRST FLOOR

SECOND FLOOR

—93—

$1,744.00

For $1,744.00 we will furnish all the material to build this Twelve-Room Duplex House, consisting of Mill Work, Siding, Flooring, Ceiling, Finishing Lumber, Building Paper, Pipe, Gutter, Sash Weights, Hardware, Painting Material, Lumber, Lath and Shingles. NO EXTRAS, as we guarantee enough material at the above price to build this house according to our plans.

By allowing a fair price for labor, cement, brick and plaster, which we do not furnish, this house can be built for about $3,670 00, including all material and labor.

For Our Offer of Free Plans See Page 3.

A COZY double house for two families. Three rooms on the first floor and three rooms on the second floor for each family. Door leading from the stair hall to the parlor and another door leading from the stair hall to the living room, with grille between the parlor and living room. Large kitchen and pantry. Inside cellar stairway under the main stairs. Each room on the second floor opens directly into the stair hall. Large front bedroom; medium size rear bedroom and medium size middle bedroom. Each bedroom has a closet. Attic stairs directly over the main stairs.

Windsor front doors glazed with leaded glass. Blaine vestibule doors. Five-panel doors with yellow pine panels and soft pine stiles and rails. Clear yellow pine trim throughout the house. Yellow pine plate rail in the dining rooms. Yellow pine flooring for entire house and porches. Leaded Crystal windows for parlors and leaded Crystal attic sash.

Built on a concrete block foundation, frame construction, sided with narrow bevel edge cypress siding and has cedar shingle roof.

Painted two coats outside; your choice of color. Varnish and wood filler for interior finish.

Excavated basement under the entire house separated in two, making a private basement for each family. Basement, 7 feet 2 inches from floor to joists. First floor, 9 feet from floor to ceiling; second floor, 8 feet 6 inches from floor to ceiling. Large roomy attic separated in two, making a private attic for each family.

This house can be built on a lot 42 feet wide.

Complete Warm Air Heating Plant, for soft coal, extra	$170.32
Complete Warm Air Heating Plant, for hard coal, extra	175.00
Complete Steam Heating Plant, extra	314.40
Complete Hot Water Plant, extra	361.46
Complete Plumbing Outfit, extra	228.17
Acetylene Lighting Plant, extra	69.20

SEARS, ROEBUCK AND CO.

CHICAGO, ILLINOIS

MODERN HOME No. 154

$2,702.00

For $2,702.00 we will furnish all the material to build this Fourteen-Room Double House, consisting of Mill Work, Ceiling, Siding, Flooring, Finishing Lumber, Building Paper, Pipe, Gutter, Sash Weights, Medicine Cases, Buffets, Mantels, Hardware, Painting Material, Lumber, Lath and Shingles. NO EXTRAS, as we guarantee enough material at the above price to build this house according to our plans.

By allowing a fair price for labor, cement, brick and plaster, which we do not furnish, this house can be built for about $4,950.00, including all material and labor.

For Our Offer of Free Plans See Page 3.

A DOUBLE house built for two families. Has three rooms, stair hall and pantry on the first floor and three bedrooms, sewing room and bathroom on the second floor for each family. In this house we offer a very handy arrangement with a stair hall leading direct to the kitchen, dining room and parlor without having to pass through any of the other rooms. Inside cellar stairs directly under the main stairs. Large roomy closet off the center hall. On the second floor is a sewing room which is often used for a library; three good size bedrooms, a closet for each bedroom and a closet in each hall. Both bathrooms are close to each other so that the same pipes can be used for both, thereby making it possible to put in the plumbing at the very lowest possible cost. Each dining room contains a mantel, fireplace and buffet, with French bevel plate mirror.

Two Beauty front doors, veneered oak, glazed with bevel plate glass; leaded colored art glass transom overhead. The latest design of Queen Anne windows for front and sides. The six main rooms and halls are trimmed with oak Craftsman design of casing, baseboard and molding and two-panel veneered oak doors. Kitchen, pantry and entire second floor are trimmed with clear birch casing, baseboard and molding and two-panel veneered birch doors. Each front hall has an open oak staircase. Clear oak flooring for the front rooms and hall; maple flooring for kitchens and pantries; clear yellow pine flooring for the entire second floor and porches.

Hardware, lemon color brass finish.

This house presents the appearance of a large single residence and has practically no appearance of a double house from the exterior. Has a large front porch, 39 feet long by 9 feet wide, with Ionic columns put up in groups.

Built on a concrete block foundation, frame construction, sided with narrow bevel edge cypress siding from the water table to the second story window sills, and with stonekote, more commonly known as cement plaster, the rest of the way up. Gables sided with cedar shingles. Has a cedar shingle roof.

Painted two coats outside; your choice of color. Varnish and wood filler for two coats of interior finish.

Excavated basement under the entire building separated in two and making each basement private, 7 feet 6 inches from floor to joists, with cement floor. Rooms on the first floor are 9 feet 6 inches from floor to ceiling; second floor, 9 feet from floor to ceiling. A very large attic separated in two.

This house can be built on a lot 48 feet wide.

Complete Warm Air Heating Plant, for soft coal, extra	$181.78
Complete Warm Air Heating Plant, for hard coal, extra	184.04
Complete Steam Heating Plant, extra	347.70
Complete Hot Water Heating Plant, extra	434.40
Complete Plumbing Outfit, extra	223.26
Acetylene Lighting Plant, extra	74.00

SEARS, ROEBUCK AND CO.　　　　**CHICAGO, ILLINOIS**

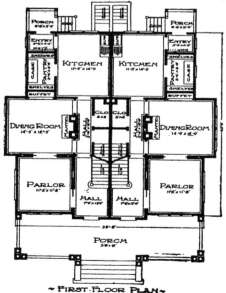

~FIRST·FLOOR·PLAN~

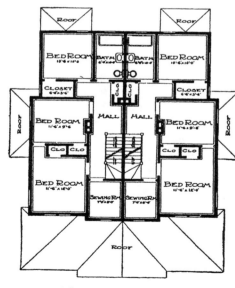

~SECOND·FLOOR·PLAN~

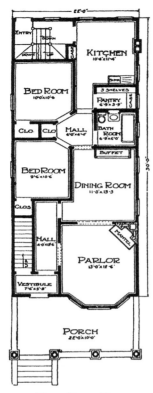

~ FIRST FLOOR PLAN ~

This house has recently been built, with some modifications, by Judge W. F. Barry, Luzerne, Penn., at a saving of $750.00. It has also been built at Freeport, Ill., Newton Highlands, Mass., and Providence, R. I.

MODERN HOME No. 149

$1,894.00

For $1,894.00 we will furnish all the material to build this Eleven-Room Two-Family Flat Building, consisting of Mill Work, Ceiling, Siding, Flooring, Finishing Lumber, Hardware, Building Paper, Sash Weights, Medicine Cases, Buffets, Mantels, Painting Material, Lumber, Lath and Shingles. NO EXTRAS, as we guarantee enough material at the above price to build this house according to our plans.

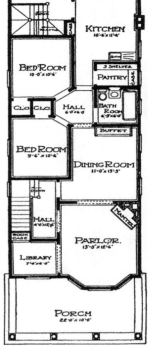

~ SECOND FLOOR PLAN ~

By allowing a fair price for labor, cement, brick and plaster, which we do not furnish, this house can be built for about $3,520.00, including all material and labor.

For Our Offer of Free Plans See Page 3.

A MODERN two-family flat building in the Colonial style of architecture. Every inch of space is utilized to the best advantage.

Every room is very handy to the other rooms. Note the small amount of hall space compared with what is usually put into a building of this kind. A large vestibule with entrance to flat on the first floor and entrance to stairs for the second floor.

Each flat contains a mantel in the parlor, buffet in the dining room and medicine case in the bathroom. The library on the second floor contains bookcase built in the wall over the stairway leading from the first floor. The rear stairs are built inside of the house, enabling all the occupants of the building to go to the basement or to the attic without going outside.

Everything is up to date. Craftsman design veneered oak doors are specified. The vestibule, parlor and dining room on the first floor and the parlor, dining room and library on the second floor are trimmed with clear oak casing, base and moldings, with clear oak flooring. The remainder of both the first and second floors is trimmed with clear yellow pine casing, baseboard and molding, with five-cross yellow pine panel doors, clear maple flooring. The front stairs are clear oak and the rear stairs are clear yellow pine.

Note the large front porch, 22 feet long by 10 feet wide, with a balcony for the second floor of the same size, with a pair of double French doors leading from the library to this balcony. This affords the same amount of convenience and comfort for all occupants of the building. The columns on the front porch and balcony are of a heavy Colonial pattern, 10 inches in diameter. Porch floors are of clear yellow pine edge grain flooring.

The top sash of all the windows on the front and sides is divided into three lights and the bottom in one large light. This is a very late pattern and matches well with the Colonial style of building.

The rear entrance of the building is on the grade line, doing away with rear outside steps.

This house is built on a concrete block foundation and is of frame construction. The main body is sided with bevel siding. The porch column bases and panels are covered with stonekote plaster. The balcony front and gables are sided with cedar shingles. Balance sided with narrow bevel edge cypress siding. Cedar shingles for the roof.

This house has an excavated basement under the entire house, 7 feet from floor to ceiling, with cement floor. Rooms on the first floor, 9 feet from floor to ceiling; rooms on second floor, 9 feet from floor to ceiling, with a very large attic, 8 feet from floor to collar beams, having ten sash, which makes a very convenient place for drying clothes and also a nice dry room for storage, etc.

Painted two coats outside; your choice of color. Varnish and wood filler for two coats of interior finish.

This house can be built on a lot 25 feet wide.

Complete Steam Heating Plant, extra	$265.55
Complete Hot Water Heating Plant, extra	286.06
Complete Plumbing Outfit, extra	216.03
Acetylene Lighting Plant, extra	69.20

SEARS, ROEBUCK AND CO.	**CHICAGO, ILLINOIS**

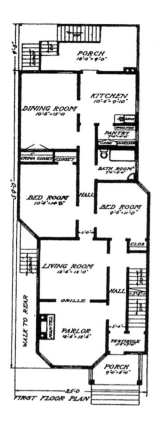

FIRST FLOOR PLAN

MODERN HOME No. 131

$1,870.00

This house has been built at Chicago, Ill., Boston, Mass., Woburn, Mass., and New York, N. Y.

SECOND FLOOR PLAN

For $1,870.00 we will furnish all the material to build this Thirteen-Room Two-Family Flat Building, consisting of Mill Work, Siding, Flooring, Ceiling, Finishing Lumber, Roofing, Building Paper, Pipe, Gutter, Sash Weights, Lumber, Lath, Hardware and Painting Material. NO EXTRAS, as we guarantee enough material at the above price to build this house according to our plans.

By allowing a fair price for labor, cement, brick and plaster, which we do not furnish, this house can be built for about $3,475.00, including all material and labor.

For Our Offer of Free Plans See Page 3.

THESE flats are conveniently arranged so that the parlor and living room with a large grille between practically make one large room with one bedroom on each side of the hall, having the windows on an angle, which assures that the light and ventilation will not be shut off in case other buildings are erected alongside. The dining room opens direct into the kitchen with two large windows on the rear, which makes a well lighted dining room. The bathrooms being directly over each other makes it possible for the same pipes to be used for the plumbing on the first and second floors, thereby making it possible to do the plumbing in the most economical manner. The parlor in each flat contains a mantel, each dining room contains a china closet and a large pantry opens into the kitchen.

Beauty front door, veneered oak, glazed with bevel plate glass, is furnished for the front door. Interior doors for both flats are our Wilcox two-panel veneered birch of a very choice grain. The entire house is finished with clear birch casing, baseboard and moldings, with oak flooring in all rooms except kitchens, which is of maple.

This design of flat building is being put up in large numbers in many localities.

Built on a concrete block foundation and is of frame construction, sided with narrow bevel clear cypress siding and covered with 3½-Ply Best-of-all Roofing. Front porch, 9x6 feet, with Ionic columns and balcony overhead the same size as porch, and a large rear porch for each flat. Clear yellow pine flooring for porches.

The two front windows have a leaded colored art glass top of our Crescent design. All fair size windows, glazed with clear "A" quality double strength glass.

Painted two coats outside; your choice of color. Varnish and wood filler for two coats of interior finish.

Excavated basement under the entire building, 7 feet high from floor to joists, with a concrete floor. The rooms on the first floor are 9 feet from floor to ceiling; rooms on the second floor are 9 feet from floor to ceiling.

This flat building can be built on a lot 25 feet wide.

Complete Steam Heating Plant, extra	$300.15
Complete Hot Water Heating Plant, extra	350.32
Complete Plumbing Outfit, extra	200.93
Acetylene Lighting Plant, extra	69.20

SEARS, ROEBUCK AND CO.

CHICAGO, ILLINOIS

MODERN HOME No. 214

$1,299.00

For $1,299.00 we will furnish all the material to build this Ten-Room Two-Family Flat Building, consisting of Mill Work, Ceiling, Siding, Flooring, Finishing Lumber, Building Paper, Pipe, Gutter, Sash Weights, Hardware, Painting Material, Lumber, Lath and Shingles. **NO EXTRAS,** as we guarantee enough material at the above price to build this house according to our plans.

By allowing a fair price for labor, cement, brick and plaster, which we do not furnish, this house can be built for about $2,530.00, including all material and labor.

For Our Offer of Free Plans See Page 3.

A FLAT building arranged for one family on the first floor and one family on the second floor. Five rooms, bathroom, pantry and vestibule on the first floor. Five rooms, bathroom, pantry and alcove on the second floor. All rooms arranged to make use of every bit of space in the building. Large living rooms and kitchens. The rear bedroom in each flat can be very conveniently used for a dining room. The rear stairs built on the inside of the building enable the families in both flats to go to the basement or up to the attic without going outside.

Madison front door, 3x7 feet, 1¾ inches thick, glazed with lace design glass. All interior doors are five-cross panel clear yellow pine, and clear yellow pine trim, such as baseboard, casing, molding and stairs. Clear yellow pine flooring for porch floor and interior floors.

Built on a concrete block foundation, frame construction, and sided with narrow bevel clear cypress siding. Front gable has fancy window with a single sash on each side and is sided with stonekote, more commonly known as cement plaster. Cedar shingle roof. Front porch, 16 feet by 5 feet 6 inches, with Colonial columns.

Painted two coats outside; your choice of color. Varnish and wood filler for two coats of interior finish.

This house is built on very simple and plain lines of architecture, can be constructed at a very low cost and will prove a very good paying investment.

This house can be built on a lot 32 feet wide.

Complete Warm Air Heating Plant, for soft coal, extra	$119.25
Complete Warm Air Heating Plant, for hard coal, extra	124.04
Complete Steam Heating Plant, extra	267.25
Complete Hot Water Heating Plant, extra	277.60
Complete Plumbing Outfit, extra	202.39
Acetylene Lighting Plant, extra	55.90

SEARS, ROEBUCK AND CO. **CHICAGO, ILLINOIS**

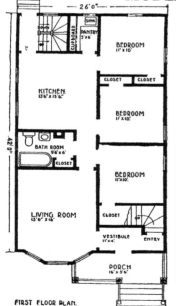

FIRST FLOOR PLAN.

No Better House in Town.

Halifax, Penn.

Sears, Roebuck and Co.,
Chicago, Ill.

Gentlemen:—I am sending you a picture of my new house built according to your plans. **There is no better house in town,** and it is admired by all. This you may think is putting it pretty strong but it is nevertheless a fact. Many have put the cost of my house as high as $3,500.00. I have a fine home and have been congratulated many times for the design, fine appearance, fine lumber and trimmings.

Yours respectfully,
N. E. NOBLET.

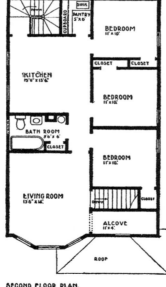

SECOND FLOOR PLAN.

MODERN HOME No. 130

This house has been built at Great Falls, Mont., Boston, Mass., Woonsocket, R. I., and New Richmond, Wis.

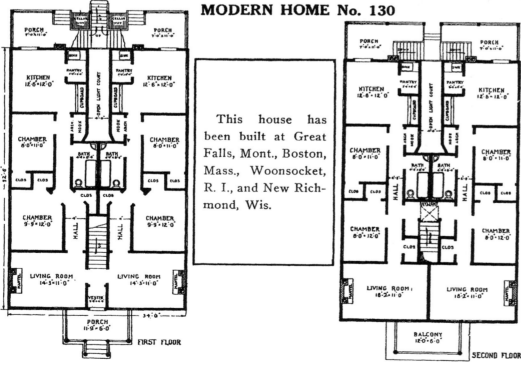

FIRST FLOOR

SECOND FLOOR

$2,152⁰⁰

For $2,152.00 we will furnish all the material to build this Sixteen-Room Apartment Building, consisting of Mill Work, Flooring, Ceiling, Siding, Finishing Lumber, Building Paper, Roofing, Pipe, Gutter, Sash Weights, Hardware, Mantels, Painting Materials, Lumber and Lath. NO EXTRAS, as we guarantee enough material at the above price to build this house according to our plans.

By allowing a fair price for labor, cement, brick and plaster, which we do not furnish, this house can be built for about $4,510.00, including all material and labor.

For Our Offer of Free Plans See Page 3.

A FOUR-FAMILY apartment house with four rooms for each family, that can be built at a very low cost and will make an exceptionally good paying investment. The building of this house at a low cost is made possible by the economical arrangement of the plans, such as one single stairway to be used for both families on the second floor, and with but one front door and one vestibule. Having the two bathrooms on the first floor adjoining the same wall and the bathrooms on the second floor directly over the bathrooms on the first floor, thereby making it possible to use one set of plumbing pipes for all four bathrooms. One rear stair opening to each side to accommodate all the families in the building.

Each flat contains a mantel and fireplace in the living room. Two bedrooms, each with closet. One closet in the hall. Bathroom, nook, which is often used as an open closet, with a cased opening. Cupboard in the kitchen. A light court from the rear extending 18 feet 6 inches from the front to the rear, giving light and ventilation for the pantry, alcove, hall and bathrooms.

Majestic front door, 1¾ inches thick, glazed with bevel plate glass. Inside doors have soft pine stiles and rails with five-cross yellow pine panels. Clear yellow pine trim throughout the building. Clear yellow pine flooring throughout the building and porches.

Built on a concrete block foundation, frame construction, sided with narrow bevel clear cypress siding. Best-of-all Roofing. Front porch, 11 feet 9 inches by 6 feet. Colonial columns and newels. Colored leaded art Crescent window for the center window of each living room with Queen Anne side windows for each side of the triple windows.

Painted two coats outside; your choice of color. Varnish and wood filler for interior finish.

Excavated basement under the entire house, 7 feet 4 inches from floor to joists, with concrete floor and separated in two parts, each half being for two of the families in the building. Rooms on first floor, 9 feet from floor to ceiling; second floor, 9 feet from floor to ceiling. Skylight over stair hall.

This house can be built on a lot 36 feet wide.

Complete Warm Air Heating Plant, for soft coal, extra	$214.00
Complete Warm Air Heating Plant, for hard coal, extra	225.95
Complete Steam Heating Plant, extra	353.25
Complete Hot Water Heating Plant, extra	414.43
Complete Plumbing Outfit, extra	377.22
Acetylene Lighting Plant, extra	78.80

SEARS, ROEBUCK AND CO. **CHICAGO, ILLINOIS**

GREATER ECONOMY=BIGGER PROFITS

By Building Two or More Houses at the Same Time. All Live Real Estate Operators and Contractors Are Now Building on a Larger Scale Wherever Possible.

DO LIKE THE LARGEST REAL ESTATE OPERATORS ARE NOW DOING. Improve your property by building on a little larger scale and reap the big benefits either in the way of increasing your profits or doubling percentage of earnings on your investment. Houses built one at a time under ordinary conditions which would earn you 10 per cent would easily earn you 15 or 50 per cent more profit if the same quality of house was built six at one time.

THERE ARE MANY REASONS WHY YOU CAN LOWER YOUR BUILDING COSTS by this procedure. Here are just a few illustrations. For instance, excavating. While laborers, horses, scoops and other implements are on the ground, six basements can be excavated at a slight advance over a lesser number. As much as 25 per cent can be saved on this procedure alone. The cost of foundation walls, especially when made of concrete, can be considerably reduced in price when the forms for concrete work can be used for a number of houses, as the cost of lumber for making the forms, and the labor, can be entirely saved for all additional houses, and by placing a larger order for concrete or masonry work, any up to date contractor is willing to make big concessions in price.

BUILDING ON A LARGER SCALE enables the various contractors and subcontractors to proceed from one building to the next without loss or delay. Carpenters can lay out their framing work for six houses at one time. While one house is in the course of framing, another house will be under its roof, and carpenters during inclement weather can always be worked to the very best possible advantage, which means low building cost for carpenter labor. Plasterers and painters proceed in a like manner, all of them doing the work to the very best advantage and at the very lowest cost. Furthermore, much closer supervision can be had when a number of houses are built close together at one time, as the contractor or foreman can carefully watch the work as it progresses, making every penny paid for labor count to the very best advantage.

WE ARE SELLING MANY OF THE HOUSES SHOWN IN THIS BOOK in lots of fifteen to twenty-five houses, all of which are built in numbers of five to ten at one time. Realty operators and contractors building in this manner claim an actual saving of from 10 to 25 per cent, and claim to give the owner far better satisfaction than would be possible if building one house at a time. On pages 100 and 101 we show these very same houses separately with a larger illustration and quote a total price for all the material to complete these houses. In designing these houses it has been our aim to have Modern Homes No. 193, No. 194 and No. 196 with foundations of exactly the same dimensions, thus enabling a contractor when laying out his work and making his form to use the same forms on the three different houses, all different in design from an exterior viewpoint yet similar in foundation and arrangement on the inside. We also have planned Modern Homes No. 192, No. 195 and No. 197 in a similar manner, which enables realty operators or individuals who are building on a larger scale for the purpose of renting, speculation or selling, to do the work in the most economical manner at the very lowest possible cost and still be in position to erect the six houses one next to the other without being confronted with the monotony that is found in many localities where the same scheme has been followed out by making slight changes in the front elevation, but not sufficient to make the house look as though each one was an entirely different pattern or design, as we aim to do, and as illustrated above. The above illustration shows six modern homes shown on pages 100 and 101 erected one next to the other on adjoining lots. One can see at a glance that there is no monotony or similarity in their appearance, yet they are constructed on similar foundations and three of each have identical interior arrangements.

IMPROVE YOUR VACANT PROPERTY. If you adopt this scheme of building two or more houses at a time your houses will be sold long before they are completed or, if rented, they will double the interest on your money. Investments of this kind are readily financed by banking institutions or money lenders, as they realize that the security is the best that can be had.

DON'T FORGET that when building in this manner you are cutting out all delays, you are saving in the cost of bringing the scaffolding and tools from one job to the other, you are practically building six houses with the same amount of trouble and attention that is necessary when building one.

TO THOSE WHO ONLY WANT TO BUILD ONE HOUSE FOR RESIDENCE OR OTHER PURPOSES, you can make no mistake in selecting any one of the designs on the following pages. Each one of them is considered very good, of a convenient arrangement, and the excellent material used puts these houses on a par with any other house we show in this book. We simply have pointed out the advantages of building more than one house at a time, which is now being practiced by all the largest and most up to date realty operators in this country.

SEARS, ROEBUCK AND CO.   —99—   **CHICAGO, ILLINOIS**

YOUR CHOICE! $656.00 for Material to Build Any One of These Three Houses

MODERN HOME No. 193

All Three Houses on This Page Have Exactly the Same Floor Plan and Interior Arrangement as Shown.

MODERN HOME No. 194

ONE-HALF WHAT LOCAL DEALERS CHARGE.

Deans, N. J.

Sears. Roebuck and Co., Chicago, Ill.
Dear Sirs:—I am very much pleased with your mill work. It has cost but **one-half what local dealers charge** for the same grade of material. It gives good satisfaction and is of good quality, also other materials, such as hardware, trimming, plumbing and finishing. Yours very truly,
JAMES MORRELL,
General Contractor and Builder.

SEARS, ROEBUCK AND CO.

CHICAGO, ILLINOIS

MODERN HOME No. 196

For $656.00 we will furnish all the Lumber, Lath, Shingles, Mill Work, Flooring, Ceiling, Siding, Finishing Lumber, Building Paper, Pipe, Gutter, Sash Weights, Hardware and Painting Material to build the house selected. **NO EXTRAS,** as we guarantee enough material at the price shown to build any one of these houses according to our plans.

By allowing a fair price for labor, cement, brick and plaster, which we do not furnish, these houses can be built for about $1,250.00 each, including all material and labor.

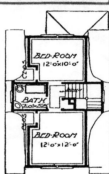

SECOND FLOOR

First Floor.
Hall contains hall seat and open stairway to second floor. Living room is connected with hall and dining room by large cased openings. Kitchen has good pantry, 4x5 feet, with pantry case. Stairway from kitchen to cellar is under the stairway to second floor. Front door and rear door are made of best quality white pine, 1⅜ inches thick, glazed with "A" quality double strength glass. Inside doors have four panels, made of best quality yellow pine, 1⅜ inches thick. Clear yellow pine trim and flooring.

Second Floor.
Two bedrooms and bathroom, each bedroom has good size clothes closet. Doors are 1⅛ inches thick, have four panels and are made of yellow pine. Clear yellow pine floors and trim.
Built on a concrete foundation. Sided with narrow clear beveled cypress siding. Cedar shingle roof. All framing timbers of No. 1 yellow pine.

Height of Ceilings.
Cellar, 7 feet from floor to joists. Second floor, 8 feet from floor to ceiling.
First floor, 8 feet 6 inches from floor to ceiling. This house can be built on a lot 25 feet wide.
Heating plant or plumbing outfit furnished for any of these houses at the following prices:

Complete Warm Air Heating Plant, for soft coal, extra.$	64.56
Complete Warm Air Heating Plant, for hard coal, extra.	67.84
Complete Steam Heating Plant, extra	144.45
Complete Hot Water Heating Plant, extra	177.81
Complete Plumbing Outfit, extra	115.97
Acetylene Lighting Plant, extra	48.70

YOUR CHOICE! $670.00 for Material to Build Any One of These Three Houses

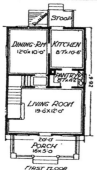

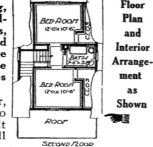

All Three Houses on This Page Have Exactly the Same Floor Plan and Interior Arrangement as Shown

MODERN HOME No. 192

For $670.00 we will furnish all the Lumber, Lath, Shingles, Mill Work, Flooring, Ceiling, Siding, Finishing Lumber, Building Paper, Pipe, Gutter, Sash Weights, Hardware and Painting Material to build the house selected. NO EXTRAS, as we guarantee enough material at the price shown to build any one of these houses according to our plans.

By allowing a fair price for labor, cement, brick and plaster, which we do not furnish, these houses can be built for about $1,250.00 each, including all material and labor.

First Floor.

Front door opens into large living room. Attractive open stairway of yellow pine across one end of living room. Small hall between living room and dining room. Stairs to basement under main stairway. Kitchen has a good size pantry in which is built a pantry case. Front and rear doors are made of best quality white pine, 1⅜ inches thick, glazed with "A" quality double strength glass. Interior doors are 1⅜ inches thick, have four panels and are made of yellow pine. Clear yellow pine trim and floors.

Second Floor.

Two bedrooms and bathroom; each bedroom has a large clothes closet. Doors are 1⅜ inches thick, made of yellow pine in four-panel design. Yellow pine floors and trim.

Built on a concrete foundation; excavated under entire house. Sided with narrow beveled cypress siding. Cedar shingle roof. Framing timbers of No. 1 yellow pine.

Height of Ceiling.

Cellar, 7 feet from floor to joists. Second floor, 8 feet 6 inches from floor to ceiling. First floor, 8 feet 6 inches from floor to ceiling.

Can be built on a lot 25 feet wide.

Heating plant or plumbing outfit furnished for either of these houses at the following prices:

Complete Warm Air Heating Plant, for soft coal, extra.$	63.47
Complete Warm Air Heating Plant, for hard coal, extra.	66.79
Complete Steam Heating Plant, extra	130.00
Complete Hot Water Heating Plant, extra	160.06
Complete Plumbing Outfit, extra	117.71
Acetylene Lighting Plant, extra	47.90

MODERN HOME No. 195

MODERN HOME No. 197

All of the houses on these two pages have the same interior arrangement. They have been built at Brighton, Ill., Godfrey, Ill., Lawrenceburg, Ind., Boston, Mass., Suttersville, Penn., Arlington, Vt., Neenah, Wis., and other cities. See suggestion for real estate operators on page 99.

SEARS, ROEBUCK AND CO.   **CHICAGO, ILLINOIS**

MODERN HOME No. 107

For $425.00 we will furnish all the Mill Work, Flooring, Ceiling, Siding, Finishing Lumber, Building Paper, Pipe, Gutter, Sash Weights, Hardware and Painting Material, Lumber, Lath and Shingles to build this Three-Room Cottage. NO EXTRAS, as we guarantee enough material at the above price to build this house according to our plans.

By allowing a fair price for labor, cement, brick and plaster, which we do not furnish, this house can be built for about $972.00, including all material and labor.

For Our Offer of Free Plans See Page 3.

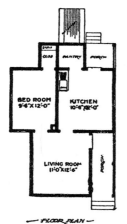

— FLOOR PLAN —

THIS cottage has three good size rooms with pantry and closet. Front porch, 13 feet by 4 feet 6 inches; rear porch, 6x5 feet. Outside cellar entrance.

Leaded Crystal front window in the living room. All other windows are glazed with "A" quality double strength glass with the exception of the pantry window which is glazed with single strength glass.

Cass front door. Inside doors are five-panel solid yellow pine. Clear yellow pine molding and trim. No. 1 yellow pine flooring, cypress siding and cedar shingles.

This is just the type of cottage that is being put up in large numbers by factory or mine owners who furnish their employes with cottages, and in that case it is sometimes built on a frame foundation instead of stone, which reduces the cost about $180.00, thereby making a very good paying investment.

Excavated basement under the entire house, 6 feet from floor to joists. Rooms on the main floor are 8 feet 6 inches from floor to ceiling.

This house can be built on a lot 23 feet 6 inches wide.

Complete Warm Air Heating Plant, for soft coal, extra.$	42.14
Complete Warm Air Heating Plant, for hard coal, extra.	45.40
Complete Steam Heating Plant, extra...................	90.25
Complete Hot Water Heating Plant, extra.............	112.73
Acetylene Lighting Plant, extra......................	45.00

SEARS, ROEBUCK AND CO.

—102—

MODERN HOME No. 142

For $298.00 we will furnish all the Mill Work, Flooring, Siding, Finishing Lumber, Building Paper, Eaves Trough, Roofing, Hardware, Painting Material, Lumber and Lath to build this Four-Room House. NO EXTRAS, as we guarantee enough material at the above price to build this house according to our plans.

By allowing a fair price for labor, brick and plaster, which we do not furnish, this house can be built for about $545.00, including all material and labor.

For Our Offer of Free Plans See Page 3.

A GOOD and well built cottage with four rooms, two closets and pantry. We furnish the same high standard quality of material for this cottage as we do for the higher priced houses shown in this book.

FIRST FLOOR PLAN

One of our high grade grained doors for the front. All windows with the exception of the pantry window glazed with "A" quality double strength glass. Clear yellow pine molding and trim. Clear yellow pine flooring.

Built on a frame foundation, frame construction and sided with narrow bevel edge cypress siding. Three and one-half-ply Best-of-all Felt Roofing. Plastered two coats inside. Painted two coats outside; your choice of color. Varnish and wood filler for two coats of interior finish.

Rooms are 8 feet 4 inches from floor to ceiling.

This house can be built on a lot 22 feet 6 inches wide.

CHICAGO, ILLINOIS

Complete Warm Air Heating Plant, for soft coal, extra.$	45.43
Complete Warm Air Heating Plant, for hard coal, extra.	48.05
Complete Steam Heating Plant, extra...................	86.00
Complete Hot Water Heating Plant, extra.............	100.21
Acetylene Lighting Plant, extra......................	45.00

MODERN HOME No. 183

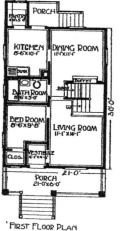

For \$859.00 we will furnish all the material to build this Five-Room Cottage, consisting of Lumber, Lath, Shingles, Mill Work, Ceiling, Siding, Flooring, Finishing Lumber, Building Paper, Pipe, Gutter, Sash Weights, Hardware and Painting Material.

By allowing a fair price for labor, cement, brick and plaster, which we do not furnish, this house can be built for about \$1,500.00, including all material and labor.

For Our Offer of Free Plans See Page 3.

A NEAT five-room cottage of conventional design, with bath. Front door is made of clear white pine, 1¾ inches thick, glazed with bevel plate glass. Colonnade between living room and dining room. Buffet in dining room. Inside doors five-cross panel, clear yellow pine, with yellow pine trim to match. Oak floor in the living room and dining room. Maple floor in the balance of the house. Bedrooms have clothes closets; windows in each closet. Kitchen has a pantry in which is built a pantry case of drawers. Large unfinished attic, could be converted into two good rooms at a slight expense.

Built on a concrete foundation, basement under the entire house. We furnish clear cypress siding and cedar shingles. Framing timbers are of the best quality yellow pine.

Basement has cement floor and is 7 feet from floor to joists. First floor 9 feet from floor to ceiling. Painted with two coats of the best paint outside. Varnish and wood filler for the interior finish.

This house can be built on a lot 25 feet wide.

Complete Warm Air Heating Plant, for soft coal, extra.$ 52.92
Complete Warm Air Heating Plant, for hard coal, extra..... 56.24
Complete Steam Heating Plant, extra................. 117.20
Complete Hot Water Heating Plant, extra............. 143.82
Complete Plumbing Outfit, extra..................... 113.93
Acetylene Lighting Plant, extra..................... 47.25

FIRST FLOOR PLAN

Built at Cicero, Ill., and Hammond, Ind.

SEARS, ROEBUCK AND CO.

MODERN HOME No. 186

For \$790.00 we will furnish all the material to build this Six-Room Cottage, consisting of Lumber, Lath, Shingles, Mill Work, Flooring, Ceiling, Siding, Finishing Lumber, Building Paper, Pipe, Gutter, Sash Weights, Hardware and Painting Material.

By allowing a fair price for labor, cement, brick and plaster, which we do not furnish, this house can be built for about \$1,375.00, including all material and labor.

For Our Offer of Free Plans See Page 3.

AN ATTRACTIVE home of six rooms and bath. Has open stairway in the living room, a large buffet in the dining room and pantry in which is built a pantry case.

First Floor.

Front door of clear white pine, 1¾ inches thick, glazed with double strength glass sand blast design. Inside doors are five-panel clear yellow pine. Clear yellow pine floor and trim. Rear door clear white pine, 1⅜ inches thick, glazed with clear glass.

Second Floor.

Stairway to second floor leads to hall. Bedrooms have good size closets. Large closet extending entire length of house for storage purposes. Doors are four-panel clear yellow pine, with yellow pine trim and floors to match.

Built on a concrete block foundation, excavated under the entire house, with cement floor in the basement. We furnish clear cypress siding and cedar shingles.

Basement, 7 feet from floor to joists. First floor, 9 feet from floor to ceiling. Second floor, 8 feet 6 inches from floor to ceiling. Painted with two coats of the best paint outside. Varnish and wood filler for interior finish.

FIRST FLOOR PLAN

SECOND FLOOR PLAN

This house can be built on a lot 25 feet wide.

Complete Warm Air Heating Plant, for soft coal, extra.$ 63.05
Complete Warm Air Heating Plant, for hard coal, extra.. 66.25
Complete Steam Heating Plant, extra................. 140.95
Complete Hot Water Heating Plant, extra............. 159.85
Complete Plumbing Outfit, extra..................... 122.59
Acetylene Lighting Plant, extra..................... 47.25

CHICAGO, ILLINOIS

MODERN HOME No. 134

$578⁰⁰

For $578.00 we will furnish all the material to build this Four-Room Cottage, consisting of Mill Work, Flooring, Ceiling, Finishing Lumber, Building Paper, Pipe, Gutter, Sash Weights, Hardware, Painting Material, Lumber, Lath and Shingles. NO EXTRAS, as we guarantee enough material at the above price to build this house according to our plans.

By allowing a fair price for labor, cement, brick and plaster, which we do not furnish, this house can be built for about $1,220.00, including all material and labor.

By using bevel siding instead of stonekote this house can be built for about $1,140.00, including all material and labor.

We will furnish cypress bevel siding for this house at $36.00 extra. We do not furnish stonekote.

For Our Offer of Free Plans See Page 3.

THIS cottage has four rooms and quite a large attic which could very easily be finished into two rooms if desired.

Monroe front and rear doors. All inside doors are five-cross panel with soft pine stiles and rails, yellow pine panels. Clear yellow pine trim. Clear yellow pine flooring for the entire house and porches.

Built on a concrete foundation, frame construction, sided with stonekote, more commonly known as cement plaster, or cypress bevel siding, and has cedar shingle roof. Varnish and wood filler for two coats of interior finish.

Excavated basement under the entire house, 6 feet 6 inches from floor to joists. Rooms on the main floor are 9 feet from floor to ceiling.

This house can be built on a lot 25 feet wide.

Complete Warm Air Heating Plant, for soft coal, extra.$	48.73
Complete Warm Air Heating Plant, for hard coal, extra.	51.35
Complete Steam Heating Plant, extra.............	107.25
Complete Hot Water Heating Plant, extra.............	126.14
Complete Plumbing Outfit, extra.................	112.86
Acetylene Lighting Plant, extra.................	46.00

SEARS, ROEBUCK AND CO.

FLOOR PLAN

MODERN HOME No. 139

$510⁰⁰

For $510.00 we will furnish all the material to build this Four-Room Cottage, consisting of Mill Work, Flooring, Ceiling, Finishing Lumber, Building Paper, Pipe, Gutter, Sash Weights, Hardware, Painting Material, Lumber, Lath and Shingles. NO EXTRAS, as we guarantee enough material at the above price to build this house according to our plans.

By allowing a fair price for labor, cement, brick and plaster, which we do not furnish, this house can be built for about $1,075.00, including all material and labor.

By using bevel siding instead of stonekote this house can be built for about $1,000.00, including all material and labor.

We will furnish cypress bevel siding for this house at $35.00 extra. We do not furnish stonekote.

For Our Offer of Free Plans See Page 3.

AN ATTRACTIVE little cottage, sided with stonekote. Bay window on the front, with colored leaded art glass front window and Queen Anne attic sash. Front porch, 6 feet by 11 feet 6 inches; rear porch, 5x4 feet. Front door opens directly into large living room which has a door leading to the kitchen and one to the side bedroom. The kitchen being large is used as combination kitchen and dining room. Good size pantry. The attic is quite high and could easily be finished off into sleeping rooms if desired.

Front door glazed with lace design glass. Rear door glazed with clear glass. Clear soft pine doors for the interior, clear yellow pine molding and trim. Clear yellow pine flooring throughout the entire house and porches.

Built on a concrete foundation, frame construction, sided with stonekote or cypress bevel siding, and has cedar shingle roof.

Rooms on the main floor are 9 feet from floor to ceiling.

This house can be built on a lot 25 feet 6 inches wide.

CHICAGO, ILLINOIS

Complete Warm Air Heating Plant, for soft coal, extra.$	50.33
Complete Warm Air Heating Plant, for hard coal, extra.	53.70
Complete Steam Heating Plant, extra...............	111.60
Complete Hot Water Heating Plant, extra.............	144.96
Acetylene Lighting Plant, extra.................	46.00

Floor Plan.

MODERN HOME No. 152

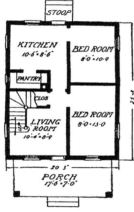

FIRST FLOOR PLAN

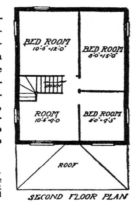

SECOND FLOOR PLAN

For $389.00 we will furnish all the Mill Work, Flooring, Ceiling, Finishing Lumber, Pipe, Gutter, Sash Weights, Roofing, Hardware and Painting Material, Lumber and Lath for this Eight-Room House. NO EXTRAS, as we guarantee enough material at the above price to build this house according to our plans.

By allowing a fair price for labor, concrete blocks, brick and plaster, which we do not furnish, this house can be built for about $770.00, including all material and labor.

For Our Offer of Free Plans See Page 3.

First Floor.

Front door of white pine, 1⅜ inches thick, opens into living room. Open stairway in living room. Well lighted pantry in kitchen. Interior doors and back door made with four panels of solid yellow pine. Clear yellow pine trim. No. 1 yellow pine floors. Plastered throughout.

Second Floor.

Stairs open on landing, from which any of the bedrooms may be entered. Solid yellow pine doors with four panels. Cement wall plastered. Beaded wood partition of No. 1 yellow pine between rooms. Queen Anne sash for two front rooms. No. 1 yellow pine floors. Roofed with Best-of-all Roofing.

Built on a concrete foundation. First floor, 9 feet from floor to ceiling. Second floor, 8 feet from floor to ceiling. Outside woodwork painted two coats. Varnish and wood filler for interior finish.

This house can be built on a lot 25 feet wide.

Complete Warm Air Heating Plant, for soft coal, extra..$	62.73
Complete Warm Air Heating Plant, for hard coal, extra..	66.53
Complete Steam Heating Plant, extra...............	147.10
Complete Hot Water Heating Plant, extra.............	184.92
Acetylene Lighting Plant, extra...................	47.90

SEARS, ROEBUCK AND CO.

MODERN HOME No. 136

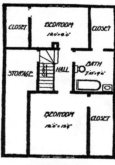

SECOND FLOOR PLAN

FIRST FLOOR PLAN

For $767.00 we will furnish all the material to build this Six-Room House, consisting of Mill Work, Siding, Flooring, Ceiling, Finishing Lumber, Building Paper, Pipe, Gutter, Sash Weights, Hardware, Painting Material, Lumber, Lath and Shingles. NO EXTRAS, as we guarantee enough material at the above price to build this house according to our plans.

By allowing a fair price for labor, cement, brick and plaster, which we do not furnish, this house can be built for about $1,435.00 including all material and labor.

For Our Offer of Free Plans See Page 3.

First Floor.

Front door is of clear white pine, 1⅜ inches thick, glazed with leaded art glass, opens into reception hall. Reception hall has yellow pine open stairway. Single sliding door between hall and parlor. Dining room has cupboard built in. Kitchen has well lighted pantry, and a closet. Interior doors, 1⅜ inches thick with clear white pine stiles and five yellow pine panels. Rear door, 1⅜ inches thick, made of clear white pine, glazed with lace design glass. Clear yellow pine trim and floors.

Second Floor.

Stairway opens into small hall. Two bedrooms, bathroom, three closets and a large storage closet. Doors have five yellow pine panels with white pine stiles. Clear yellow pine trim and floors.

Built on a concrete block foundation, frame construction, sided with narrow bevel edge cypress siding; gables and roof shingled with cedar shingles.

Excavated basement under the entire house, 6 feet 6 inches from floor to joists, with cement floor. Rooms on the first floor are 9 feet from floor to ceiling; second floor, 8 feet from floor to ceiling.

This house can be built on a lot 26 feet wide.

CHICAGO, ILLINOIS

Complete Warm Air Heating Plant, for soft coal, extra..$	76.00
Complete Warm Air Heating Plant, for hard coal, extra..	79.00
Complete Steam Heating Plant, extra...............	140.95
Complete Hot Water Heating Plant, extra.............	179.25
Complete Plumbing Outfit, extra...................	116.46
Acetylene Lighting Plant, extra...................	47.90

MODERN HOME No. 212

$566⁰⁰

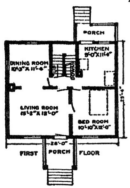

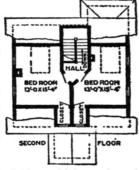

For $566.00 we will furnish all the Mill Work, Flooring, Ceiling, Finishing Lumber, Pipe, Gutter, Sash Weights, Hardware, Painting Material, Lumber, Lath and Shingles for this Six-Room House. NO EXTRAS, as we guarantee enough material at the above price to build this house according to our plans.

By allowing a fair price for labor, concrete blocks and plaster, which we do not furnish, this house can be built for about $1,400.00, including all material and labor.

For Our Offer of Free Plans See Page 3.

A CONCRETE block house with a good size living room and cased opening between the living room and dining room. Kitchen and bedroom on the first floor and two large bedrooms on the second floor with two closets. Inside cellar way to the basement under the main stairs. Front porch, 8x8 feet, with Colonial columns; rear porch, 11x5 feet.

Front door glazed with figured design glass. First floor inside doors are five-cross panel with soft pine stiles and rails and yellow pine panels. Second floor inside doors are four-panel clear soft pine. Yellow pine baseboard, casing and trim throughout the house. No. 1 yellow pine flooring for the entire house and porches.

All windows glazed with "A" quality glass. All windows throughout the house hung on sash weights.

Excavated basement under the entire house, 7 feet high. Rooms on the first floor are 8 feet 6 inches from floor to ceiling; second floor, 8 feet from floor to ceiling.

This house can be built on a lot 32 feet wide.

Complete Warm Air Heating Plant, for soft coal, extra..$ 64.75	
Complete Warm Air Heating Plant, for hard coal, extra.. 68.76	
Complete Steam Heating Plant, extra................. 131.75	**SEARS, ROEBUCK**
Complete Hot Water Heating Plant, extra............. 148.81	**AND CO.**
Acetylene Lighting Plant, extra..................... 47.25	

MODERN HOME No. 125

$764⁰⁰

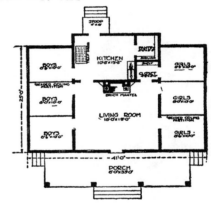

For $764.00 we will furnish Mill Work, Flooring, Ceiling, Siding, Finishing Lumber, Roofing, Building Paper, Pipe, Gutter, Sash Weights, Hardware, Painting Material and Lumber for this Eight-Room Bungalow. NO EXTRAS, as we guarantee enough material at the above price to build this house according to our plans.

By allowing a fair price for labor and brick, which we do not furnish, this house can be built for about $1,040.00, including all material and labor.

For Our Offer of Free Plans See Page 3.

A N IDEAL cottage for a summer home or water edge resort. Has a large porch across the front of the house, 33 feet by 8 feet, with Colonial columns; overhanging roof.

By referring to the floor plan you will notice the large living room, 16x19 feet, with doors leading to four of the side bedrooms and to the kitchen. The three bedrooms on each side are separated with beaded wood partition. In the living room is a brick rustic mantel and fireplace.

Front door glazed with leaded glass. Inside doors clear soft wood and clear soft wood molding and trim. No. 1 yellow pine flooring throughout the entire house and porch.

Built on a frame foundation with 8x8-inch girders. Frame construction, sided with narrow bevel edge cypress siding and has Best-of-all Roofing.

Painted two coats outside; your choice of color. Varnish and wood filler for interior finish.

Cellar, 10x18 feet, 6 feet from floor to joists. Rooms on the main floor are 10 feet from floor to ceiling.

This house can be built on a lot 46 feet wide.

Complete Warm Air Heating Plant, for soft coal, extra..$ 71.73
Complete Warm Air Heating Plant, for hard coal, extra.. 74.31
Complete Steam Heating Plant, extra................. 140.10
Complete Hot Water Heating Plant, extra............. 187.25
Acetylene Lighting Plant, extra..................... 49.50

CHICAGO, ILLINOIS

MODERN HOME No. 211

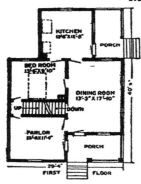

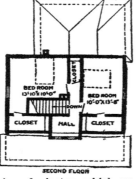

For $683.00 we will furnish all the material to build this Six-Room Concrete Block House, consisting of Mill Work, Flooring, Ceiling, Finishing Lumber, Roofing, Pipe, Gutter, Sash Weights, Hardware, Painting Material, Lumber and Lath. NO EXTRAS, as we guarantee enough material at the above price to build this house according to our plans.

By allowing a fair price for labor, concrete blocks, brick and plaster, which we do not furnish, this house can be built for about $1,710.00, including all material and labor.

For Our Offer of Free Plans See Page 3.

First Floor.

Two entrances from front porch. Parlor and dining room doors opening onto porch are clear white pine, 1¾ inches thick, glazed with sand blast design glass. Stairs to basement under main stairway. Rear door made of clear white pine, 1¾ inches thick, glazed with sand blast design glass. Interior doors have five-cross yellow pine panels with white pine stiles. Clear yellow pine trim. No. 1 yellow pine flooring. Box stairway to second floor.

Second Floor.

Two bedrooms, hall and three closets. Doors are four-panel, 1¾ inches thick, made with white pine stiles and yellow pine panels. Clear yellow pine trim. No. 1 yellow pine flooring.

Outside woodwork painted two coats. Varnish and wood filler for two coats of interior finish.

Excavated basement under the entire house, 7 feet from floor to joists, with cement floor. Rooms on the first floor are 9 feet 2 inches from floor to ceiling; rooms on the second floor, 8 feet 8 inches from floor to ceiling.

This house can be built on a lot 36 feet wide.

Complete Warm Air Heating Plant, for soft coal, extra.....$ 62.16	**SEARS, ROEBUCK**
Complete Warm Air Heating Plant, for hard coal, extra..... 65.38	
Complete Steam Heating Plant, extra.................... 176.50	**AND CO.**
Complete Hot Water Heating Plant, extra................. 209.89	
Acetylene Lighting Plant, extra........................ 47.25	

MODERN HOME No. 104

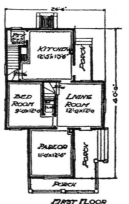

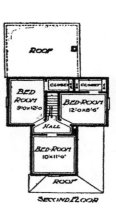

For $728.00 we will furnish all the material to build this Seven-Room House, consisting of Mill Work, Ceiling, Siding, Flooring, Finishing Lumber, Building Paper, Pipe, Gutter, Sash Weights, Hardware, Painting Material, Lumber, Lath and Shingles. NO EXTRAS, as we guarantee enough material at the above price to build this house according to our plans.

By allowing a fair price for labor, stone, brick and plaster, which we do not furnish, this house can be built for about $1,550.00, including all material and labor.

For Our Offer of Free Plans See Page 3.

First Floor.

Four rooms and pantry. Front door is made of clear white pine, 1¾ inches thick, glazed with sand blast design glass. Interior doors and rear door are five-panel, 1¾ inches thick, and made of clear yellow pine. Clear yellow pine trim. No. 1 yellow pine flooring. Box stairway from living room to second floor.

Second Floor.

Three bedrooms, two closets and hall. Doors have five panels, made of clear yellow pine and are 1¾ inches thick, with clear yellow pine trim to match. No. 1 yellow pine floors.

Painted two coats outside; your choice of color. Varnish and wood filler for interior finish.

Built on a stone foundation, frame construction, sided with narrow bevel edge cypress siding and has cedar shingle roof.

Excavated basement under the entire house, 6 feet 6 inches from floor to joists. Rooms on first floor, 8 feet 6 inches from floor to ceiling; second floor, 8 feet 4 inches from floor to ceiling.

This house measures 26 feet 6 inches wide by 40 feet long and can be built on a lot 57 feet 6 inches wide.

CHICAGO,	Complete Warm Air Heating Plant, for soft coal, extra.....$ 65.10
	Complete Warm Air Heating Plant, for hard coal, extra..... 68.31
ILLINOIS	Complete Steam Heating Plant, extra.................... 151.75
	Complete Hot Water Heating Plant, extra................. 194.71
	Acetylene Lighting Plant, extra........................ 47.90

MODERN HOME No. 100

$779⁰⁰

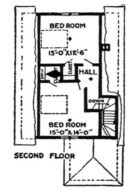

For $779.00 we will furnish all Lumber, Lath and Shingles, the Mill Work, Ceiling, Siding, Flooring, Finishing Lumber, Building Paper, Pipe, Gutter, Sash Weights, Hardware, and Painting Material for this Six-Room Cottage. NO EXTRAS, as we guarantee enough material at the above price to build this house according to our plans.

By allowing a fair price for labor, cement, brick and plaster, which we do not furnish, this house can be built for about $1,350.00, including all material and labor.

For Our Offer of Free Plans See Page 3.

A LARGE, well built cottage with all available space made good use of. A large living room with cased opening leading into the hall; also cased opening between the living room and dining room. One bedroom on the first floor; two large bedrooms on the second floor.

Front door, 1¾ inches thick, glazed with bevel plate glass. Queen Anne windows for the reception hall; twin Queen Anne windows for front bedroom on the second floor; cottage window with lace design glass for the front window in the living room. Interior trim consists of clear yellow pine casing, base and molding. Open stairway leading from reception hall.

Built on a concrete foundation, frame construction, sided with narrow bevel clear cypress siding with cedar shingle roof and gables. Porch, 8x10 feet.

Painted outside two coats; choice of color. Varnish and wood filler for two coats of interior finish.

Excavated basement, 7 feet from floor to joists. Rooms on first floor, 9 feet from floor to ceiling; rooms on second floor, 8 feet from floor to ceiling.

This house can be built on a lot 27 feet wide.

Complete Warm Air Heating Plant, for soft coal, extra.	$ 70.96
Complete Warm Air Heating Plant, for hard coal, extra.	74.24
Complete Steam Heating Plant, extra	143.10
Complete Hot Water Heating Plant, extra	187.50
Acetylene Lighting Plant, extra	49.50

SEARS, ROEBUCK AND CO.

MODERN HOME No. 106

$632⁰⁰

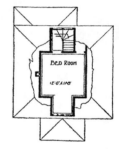

For $632.00 we will furnish all Lumber, Lath and Shingles, the Mill Work, Siding, Ceiling, Finishing Lumber, Building Paper, Pipe, Gutter, Sash Weights, Hardware, and Painting Material for this Five-Room House. NO EXTRAS, as we guarantee enough material at the above price to build this house according to our plans.

By allowing a fair price for labor, stone, brick and plaster, which we do not furnish, this house can be built for about $1,250.00, including all material and labor.

For Our Offer of Free Plans See Page 3.

A ONE-STORY COTTAGE with attic finished into one large room. Four rooms on the first floor. Cellar stairs directly under the main stairs leading from the kitchen. Outside cellar entrance. Good size pantry and closet. Marginal light attic sash. Two good size windows in each room on the first floor and four sash in the room in the attic.

Five-cross panel interior doors, soft pine stiles and rails, yellow pine panels. Clear yellow pine trim, moldings and stairs. No. 1 yellow pine flooring throughout the entire house and porches.

Built on a stone foundation, frame construction, sided with narrow bevel clear cypress siding and has cedar shingle roof. Colonial porch columns.

Painted two coats outside; your choice of color. Varnish and wood filler for interior finish.

Excavated basement under the entire house, 6 feet 10 inches from floor to joists.

Rooms on the first floor are 8 feet 6 inches from floor to ceiling; second floor, 8 feet from floor to ceiling.

This house measures 29 feet 6 inches long by 26 feet wide and can be built on a lot 30 feet wide.

Complete Warm Air Heating Plant, for soft coal, extra.	$ 53.65
Complete Warm Air Heating Plant, for hard coal, extra.	56.91
Complete Hot Water Heating Plant, extra	104.50
Complete Steam Heating Plant, extra	135.94
Acetylene Lighting Plant, extra	46.00

CHICAGO, ILLINOIS

MODERN HOME No. 216

$402⁰⁰

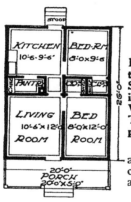

FLOOR PLAN

For $402.00 we will furnish all the material to build this Four-Room Bungalow, consisting of Lumber, Lath, Shingles, Mill Work, Ceiling, Siding, Flooring, Finishing Lumber, Building Paper, Pipe, Gutter, Sash Weights, Hardware and Painting Material. NO EXTRAS, as we guarantee enough material at the above price to build this house according to our plans.

By allowing a fair price for labor, cement, brick and plaster, which we do not furnish, this bungalow can be built for about $750.00, including all material and labor.

For Our Offer of Free Plans See Page 3.

IN BUNGALOW No. 216 we offer a house at a low price with an absolute guarantee as to the quality of the materials we furnish. Front door is of veneered oak, 1¾ inches thick, glazed with a sand blast design. All inside doors have five panels, made of yellow pine with yellow pine trim to match. All floors are of clear yellow pine. Both bedrooms have good size clothes closets. The kitchen has a large well lighted pantry.

Built on a concrete block foundation, not excavated. Frame construction and sided with narrow beveled clear cypress siding. Roofed with cedar shingles. All framing timbers are of the best quality yellow pine.

Painted two coats of best paint outside, your choice of color. Varnish and wood filler for two coats of interior finish. Rooms are 8 feet 4 inches from floor to ceiling.

This house can be built on a lot 25 feet wide.

Complete Steam Heating Plant, extra.......$ 89.50
Complete Hot Water Heating Plant, extra.. 100.21
Acetylene Lighting Plant, extra............. 45.00

SEARS, ROEBUCK AND CO.

MODERN HOME No. 205

$707⁰⁰

For $707.00 we will furnish all the material to build this Five-Room Cottage, consisting of Mill Work, Lumber, Lath, Shingles, Ceiling, Flooring, Finishing Lumber, Building Paper, Pipe, Gutter, Sash Weights, Hardware, Buffet and Painting Material. NO EXTRAS, as we guarantee enough material at the above price to build this house according to our plans.

By allowing a fair price for labor, brick, cement and plaster, which we do not furnish, this house can be built for about $1,150, including all material and labor.

For Our Offer of Free Plans See Page 3.

THIS attractive and solidly constructed cottage, sided with Oriental Gray Slate Surfaced Siding and cedar shingles and having Oriental Red Slate Surfaced Shingles for the roof, represents one of the biggest building bargains in our book.

A graceful and substantial front door, 1¾ inches thick, glazed with large beveled plate glass, leads from the porch into the living room, which is connected with the dining room by a cased opening. The dining room has a large handsome buffet. Two bedrooms are reached by doors from the living room and dining room and both have good size closets. All rooms, including the kitchen, are well lighted. Hardware in the bathroom is all nickel plated. Medicine case with plate glass mirror is provided for the bathroom. All interior doors, flooring and trim of clear yellow pine. Note the Queen Anne windows in the front.

Built on a concrete foundation. Frame construction. Painted two coats best paint outside, except shingles. Varnish and wood filler, two coats interior finish. Height from floor to ceiling, 8 feet 4 inches.

This house can be built on a lot 30 feet wide.

CHICAGO, ILLINOIS

Complete Steam Heating Plant, extra.....................$111.05
Complete Hot Water Heating Plant, extra................. 139.80
Complete Plumbing Outfit, extra........................ 115.82
Acetylene Lighting Plant, extra........................ 47.10

FLOOR PLAN

FIVE-ROOM HOUSE No. 55C17 $579.00
Size, 27x33 Feet.

We guarantee safe delivery and will replace broken glass or make good any damage, providing the customer sends us the paid expense bill with a notation signed by the freight agent, stating the condition of the shipment on its arrival at destination, so that we can use this statement of agent in making claim on the railroad company for damages.

Please remember that the prices quoted on our ready made buildings cover the entire cost of the complete structure, the prices even include screws, bolts and all other necessary hardware; in fact, we furnish everything necessary to erect these buildings with the exception of the wrench, hammer and screwdriver.

FOUR-ROOM HOUSE No. 55C38 $465.00
Size, 24x27 Feet.

READY MADE HOUSES

Simple, strong and economical. We handle a complete line of ready made buildings, garages, chicken houses, photograph galleries, real estate offices, school houses and cottages of many sizes, from one room to five rooms, all of which are attractively designed and made in such large quantities that you could hardly buy the material necessary to build one of them for the price we quote you on the complete house, ready to bolt together.

Simplex houses are portable. They can be taken apart as readily as they are put together. Ideal for lakeside or summer resorts. Anyone owning a Simplex portable building can move it from one place to another at little or no expense or store it for future use. Sections are interchangeable, making it possible to lengthen the house at any time by adding other sections.

THREE-ROOM HOUSE No. 55C22 $226.00
Size, 15x21 Feet

Strong and sturdy enough for any purpose. Many Simplex houses are being used by homesteaders in the West and Northwest for farm houses. They can easily be made warm enough for the most severe weather by lining with Peerless Wall Board, fully described in our Book of Ready Made Buildings.

Complete set of instructions furnished free, showing how the sections (sides, roof and porch) are put together.

This Catalog of Ready Made Buildings is free. Send for it today if interested.

GARAGES, OFFICES

Why our prices are so low. The cost of a ready made building depends on the cost of lumber, as half of the entire cost is in this one item alone. We manufacture our own lumber from our own logs in our big Southern mills. Our ready made building factory is operated in connection with our **big 40-acre** lumber yard in Southern Illinois. We are independent of the lumber trust and our method of "from stump to consumer" saves you the jobbers' profit, the wholesale dealers' profit and the retail dealers' profit. We make you a further saving by manufacturing our Simplex Portable Buildings in large quantities at our new modernly equipped factory.

No. 55C9 $138.00
Garage.   Size, 12x18 feet.

No. 55C7   Garage. Size, 12x15 feet. $96.50

The saving we make you on a Ready Made Building is only a secondary matter. The good quality we give you is much more important, for it insures you a building that will last for years. Shipped from factory in Southern Illinois. We carry a full stock ready for instant delivery. We can fill your order within a few days. Our houses can be built up ready to live in within a few hours. No saw or plane or other tools necessary. The only tools required are a wrench, hammer and screwdriver.

No. 55C39 $215.00
School House.   Size, 15x24 feet.

No. 55C11 $105.00
Real Estate Office.   Size, 12x12 feet.

Real estate operators opening up new subdivisions and manufacturing concerns desirous of housing their employes near their plants, will find our ready made houses offer opportunities to get quick results at small cost. We are anxious to place our Catalog of Ready Made Buildings in the hands of all interested parties and will be glad to mail it free and postpaid upon request. While our ready made houses can be made warm and comfortable in any climate by the use of our Peerless Wall Board, they are particularly suitable for the South and we invite inquiries with regard to their adaptability from our friends in the Southern states. Ready made houses are also in big demand as summer residences as they save their cost in one season's hotel bills. If you do not see the house you want on these two pages, be sure to write for our complete Catalog of Ready Made Buildings.

BARN No. 11

$440.00

For **$440.00 we will furnish all the material to build this Barn, consisting of all the Lumber, Framing Timbers Red Slate Surfaced Roofing, guaranteed for fifteen years' wear, Sash, Hardware and Paint.**

This price does not include material for stalls, mangers or inside partitions. We will furnish estimate for material according to the interior arrangement you need.

By allowing a fair price for labor, concrete blocks and concrete floors for passages, which we do not furnish, this barn may be built for about $590.00, including all material and labor.

For Our Offer of Free Plans See Page 3.

THIS barn is 26 feet wide, 46 feet long, and 16 feet to the eaves. It is built of solid timber construction, making it a very substantial building. The roof is of the gambrel type, self supporting, thus allowing free operation of the hay carrier.

The floor plan that we recommend for this barn shows four horse stalls and space enough on the other side of the building for three cows in addition to a box stall and feed room. The doorways are large enough to permit driving into with a load of hay.

The material we supply for this building is first class in every way. The framing lumber is all No. 1. The Red Slate Surfaced Roofing used on roof is guaranteed to last fifteen years and presents a better appearance than shingles.

The paint will be supplied for two coats outside work. Your choice of colors.

The barn is built on a concrete block foundation which should be put deep enough to be below the frost line.

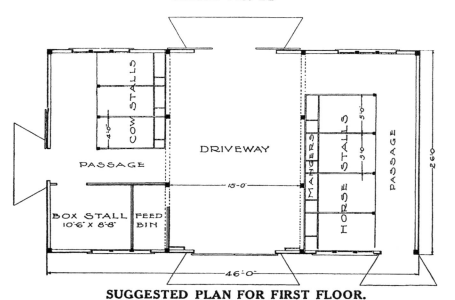

SUGGESTED PLAN FOR FIRST FLOOR.

SEARS, ROEBUCK AND CO.   **CHICAGO, ILLINOIS**

$595.00

BARN No. 12 is 36 feet wide, 46 feet long and 14 feet high to the eaves. By reference to the ground floor plan which we recommend for this barn it will be seen that provision is made for four horse stalls, one box stall, a harness room, grain room and about seven head of cattle. This leaves a space of 12 feet wide by 29 feet across one end of the barn for machinery or farm implements. The construction of this building is what is known as the Plank Frame style, that is, the timber, posts and girders are all built up out of 2-inch planks. This style of construction is coming into favor rapidly with all practical builders, as it has the advantage of cheapness and increased strength combined. The roof is of the gambrel type, self supporting, and offering no interference or obstruction to the hay carrier.

The materials we specify for this building are all first class. For the roof we furnish three-ply Red Slate Surfaced Roofing which we guarantee to wear fifteen years. It is easily put on and makes a better appearance than shingles.

We furnish sufficient paint for two-coat work for all the exterior woodwork, any color desired.

The barn is built on a concrete block foundation and all passages and driveways have cement floors.

SEARS, ROEBUCK AND CO.   **CHICAGO, ILLINOIS**

Suggested Floor Plans.

BARN No. 12

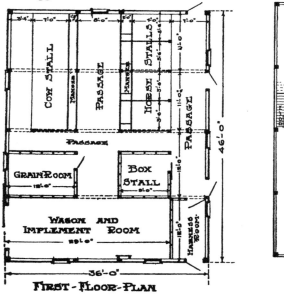

FIRST·FLOOR·PLAN

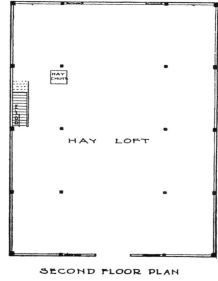

SECOND FLOOR PLAN

BARN No. 16

$571.00

For $571.00 we will furnish all the material to build this Barn, consisting of Rough Lumber, Framing Timbers, Roofing, Hardware, Sash and Paint.

This price does not include material for stalls, mangers or inside partitions. We will furnish estimate for this material according to the interior arrangement desired.

By allowing a fair price for labor, concrete blocks and concrete floors, which we do not supply, this barn may be built for about $670.00, including all material and labor.

For Our Offer of Free Plans See Page 3.

BARN No. 16 is 30 feet wide, 54 feet long and 16 feet high to the eaves. It is built of solid timber construction with gambrel roof. This roof is of the self supporting type and offers no obstruction to the free operation of the hay carrier. The suggestion for floor plans shows six horse stalls arranged across the building and two rows of cow stalls facing a feed alley running at right angles to the horse stable. This space will be found sufficient to comfortably accommodate from sixteen to eighteen head of cattle. The horse stable is entirely separate from the cattle stable, though one of the stalls may be used for a passage if desired. A stairway is provided in the feed alley leading to the second floor, and the hay chute, as well as the grain chute, are conveniently located so as to reduce the labor of feed to a minimum. The grain room is on the second floor, extending entirely across one end of the barn. This room will hold a large amount of feed and, if desired, may be subdivided into bins.

The lumber we furnish is No. 1 grade. The 3½-Ply Red Slate Surfaced Roofing is guaranteed to last fifteen years and looks better than shingles.

We furnish paint sufficient for two-coat work for the exterior woodwork. Your choice of colors.

This barn is built on a concrete block foundation and has concrete floor in all passages and feed alleys.

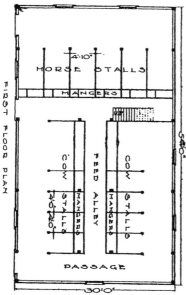

For $65.00 we will furnish all the material to build a **lean-to shed**, size 26x16 feet and 12 feet high, which can be built on one end of any barn shown in this book. Blue prints of this shed will be furnished free with the barn plans you order if requested.

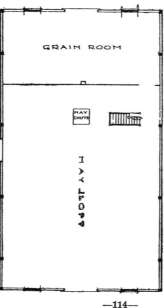

Suggested Floor Plans.

SEARS, ROEBUCK AND CO. **CHICAGO, ILLINOIS**

—114—

BARN No. 60

$868⁰⁰

For $868.00 we will furnish all the material to build this Barn, consisting of all the Lumber, Shingles, Framing Timbers, Sash, Hardware and Paint.

This price does not include material for stalls, mangers or inside partitions. We will furnish estimate for this material according to the interior arrangement desired.

By allowing a fair price for labor, concrete blocks and concrete floors for passages, which we do not furnish, this barn may be built for about $1,150.00, including all material and labor.

For Our Offer of Free Plans See Page 3.

THIS is a dairy barn of first class construction and our suggested floor plan affords economical arrangement. Stalls can be provided for twenty-eight cows with appropriate mangers, gutters and wide passageways.

There is accommodation in the large hay loft for enough hay and other feed to last throughout the entire season. Four good size ventilators insure pure air at all times, which is a very important point in a dairy barn of this size and character. Having in mind the necessity of cleanliness we would recommend that you use beaded ceiling for the entire interior of the first floor. This provision makes it possible to have the dairy barn kept as clean as a pin at all times, as the side walls and ceilings can be washed at regular intervals, doing away with all cobwebs or insects that otherwise might find a hiding place.

A glance at the floor plan will show the convenient access to this barn on all sides by means of large rolling doors. Twenty eight-light windows allow an abundance of light.

The lumber we furnish is No. 1 grade. *A* red cedar shingles for the roof. We furnish paint sufficient for two coats for the outside woodwork. Your choice of colors.

Built on a concrete foundation.

SEARS, ROEBUCK AND CO.   **CHICAGO, ILLINOIS**

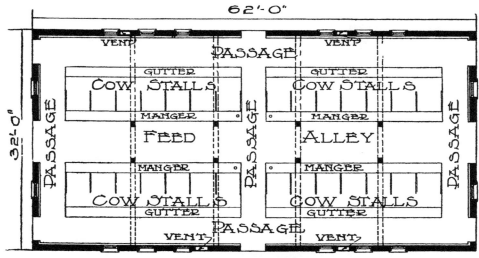

SUGGESTED FIRST FLOOR PLAN.

BARN No. 14

$875.00

For $875.00 we will furnish all the material to build this Barn, consisting of Rough Lumber, Heavy Framing Timbers, Red Slate Surfaced Roofing guaranteed for fifteen years' wear, Sash, Hardware and Paint.

This price does not include material for stalls, mangers or inside partitions. We will furnish estimate for this material according to the interior arrangement desired.

By allowing a fair price for labor and concrete blocks, which we do not furnish, this barn can be built for about $1,200.00, including all material and labor.

For Our Offer of Free Plans See Page 3.

THIS barn is 40 feet wide and 70 feet long. In our suggested floor plan 28 feet of the width and 56 feet of the length can be used for horses and cattle, providing accommodations for eight horses and seven cows; also a box stall and grain room; 14x40 feet is left in one space and may be used for a sheep shed or for young stock. In addition to this, there is a space of 12x56 feet which can be partly enclosed and will make an excellent cattle shed, or it may be utilized for the storage of farm implements.

This barn is constructed in the most substantial way and makes a practical barn at a moderate cost. Our specifications call for a heavy 3½-ply Red Slate Surfaced Roofing guaranteed to last fifteen years. Looks far better than shingles.

As will be seen from the floor plan the barn has a 12-foot driveway with doors high enough to admit a full load of hay so that the barn may be filled from the inside. A hay door is, however, also provided at one end, through which hay may be taken in with a carrier.

The barn is built on a concrete block foundation and all feed alley floors and driveway floors are made of cement.

SEARS, ROEBUCK AND CO.   CHICAGO, ILLINOIS

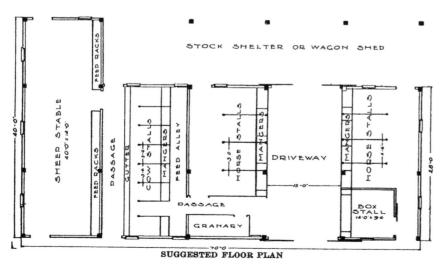

STOCK SHELTER OR WAGON SHED

SHEEP STABLE 40'0"x14'0"

FEED RACKS

PASSAGE

GUTTER

COW STALLS 3'4"x6"

MANGERS

FEED ALLEY

HORSE STALLS 3'0"

MANGERS

DRIVEWAY

MANGERS

HORSE STALLS 5'4"x9'

PASSAGE

GRANARY

BOX STALL 14'0"x9'6"

SUGGESTED FLOOR PLAN

SEARS, ROEBUCK AND CO.'S BIG SAW MILLS LOCATED IN THE HEART OF THE GREAT FORESTS IN THE SOUTH

LIGHT AND POWER PLANT — WARE HOUSES Nº 1-2-3-4 — PLANING MILLS — STEAM DRY KILNS — WARE HOUSES Nº 5 & 6 — LOG TRAIN RAMPS AND LOG POND — LOG AND LUMBER MILLS

Why pay 3 profits? Save from $100.00 to $150.00 on Enough Lumber for the Average House or Barn.

Let us prove that we can make you this big saving by shipping a carload of lumber, lath and shingles from our Southern mills or Illinois yards direct to you with but one profit (instead of the usual three profits) added to the lowest manufacturing cost. We also ship lumber in half carload lots, or smaller amounts.

STOP PAYING WHOLESALERS', JOBBERS' AND RETAILERS' PROFITS. Buy your lumber from us at **wholesale prices** and keep these big profits in your own pocket. Read what our customers say about quality and saving. We carry in stock millions of feet of lumber in every length, width and thickness. A stock larger than is carried by a hundred average size lumber yards.

WE SHIP LUMBER QUICK. On account of the enormous stock carried we are able to ship complete orders on a few days' notice from either our big mills in the South or from our big distributing yards in Illinois.

WE GUARANTEE THE QUALITY TO BE SUPERIOR to the kind retail dealers furnish. If our lumber does not prove to be better, return it at our expense and we will cheerfully return your money.

If you contemplate building according to private plans, be sure to send us your lumber bill for a free estimate. If you build one of our Modern Homes you get our estimate on the lumber in our Bill of Material which we send you with the plans.

OUR BIG LUMBER PLANT AND YARDS, LOCATED IN ILLINOIS, FROM WHICH POINT WE SHIP TO EASTERN AND NORTHERN CUSTOMERS.

SEARS, ROEBUCK AND CO.

CHICAGO, ILLINOIS

Send for Our Big Building Material and Mill Work Catalog

CONTAINING A FULL AND COMPLETE LINE OF THE FOLLOWING:

Oak and Birch Front Doors

Pine Sash Doors

Painted and Grained Doors

Panel Doors

Blinds

Windows and Sash, Glazed

French Doors and Casement Sash

Glass (Leaded and Plain)

Window and Door Frames

Moldings of Every Description

Beam Ceiling

Oak, Maple and Pine Flooring

Porch Material

Outside Trimmings

Stairwork

Colonnades and Grilles

Siding and Ceiling

Extra Heavy Steel Roofing

Asphalt Roofing

Asphalt Shingles, Red or Gray

Building Paper

Buffets

Wall Board

Extra Heavy Eaves Troughs and Pipe

Medicine Cases

Blue Plaster Board

Sheet Steel

Ornamental Metal Ceiling

Tin Shingles

Ridge Cap, Etc.

OVER 900 KINDS AND SIZES OF DOORS, 960 KINDS AND SIZES OF WINDOWS AND SASH

Just one look inside this catalog will convince you beyond a doubt that we can save you nearly one-half on everything in the building line. This beautiful Mill Work Catalog, by far the best catalog of its kind ever published, will be sent you free, postage prepaid, for the asking. It is so much more complete and is so brimful of new suggestions and ideas that anyone thinking of building; every carpenter, every contractor, in fact, anyone interested in the building trade, should have a copy of this book, because it quotes the very lowest prices, and is by far the best and most complete book of its kind in print. Handsomely illustrated in colors. Fancy doors showing the grain of wood and colors of Venetian glass, art glass windows displaying the beautiful and harmonious effects produced by art glass making and interior views are reproduced in colors. Also a full line of art glass chandeliers, electric and gas fixtures. Many new lines added in our Mill Work Catalog. This catalog shows a big line of designs of Craftsman and Mission doors, with a complete line of trim to match, and many other items that are strictly up to the minute.

Contractors, carpenters and builders, be sure to get this special Mill Work and Building Material Catalog. You cannot afford to be without it. You can rely on it for your entire supply of building material. There is no source of supply so complete for you; there is no one else that can offer you a finer quality or a larger line of more up to date designs and none that can deliver building material so promptly and in such excellent condition. Remember, it contains everything you need.

Don't delay, but write for this catalog at once. Simply say, "Mail me your Building Material and Mill Work Catalog," and it will be mailed you, postage prepaid.

Besides Our Special Catalog of Mill Work We Also Have Special Catalogs on Other Lines of Building Materials as Follows:

Catalog of Hot Water and Steam Heating Plants and Hot Air Furnaces.

Catalog of Builders' Hardware and Plumbing.

Catalog of Concrete Building Block Machinery.

Catalog of Mantels, Consoles, Brick Fire Places, Etc.

Catalog of Paints, Varnishes and Finishing Materials.

Any of these catalogs are free and postpaid on request, quoting you the lowest prices ever named on such goods, all guaranteed to satisfy you in every way or your money returned.

SEARS, ROEBUCK AND CO.

CHICAGO, ILLINOIS

"FARM AND DAIRY PROFITS"

GOOD NEWS FOR FARMERS, CATTLE RAISERS AND DAIRYMEN. WE SAVE YOU $50.00 TO $75.00 ON A SILO

We have just received from the press an up to date book showing how to increase your profits in cattle raising and dairy farming. This book must not be confused with an ordinary catalog. While it gives descriptions of our silos in different sizes and in different woods, it covers the whole field of increased profits in every branch of stock raising and dairying. We show you reproductions of photographs of champion stock exhibited at the different cattle shows, and give you the results of the elaborate experiments that have been made at the different government stations, supplemented by advice from experts in the various state universities and agricultural colleges.

It would be impossible for you without quite an outlay of money to secure the information which we can now place in your hands free. You would have to go to a book store and purchase quite a few volumes to post yourself in all matters relating to stock raising and dairying as fully as you now can do by the means of our new book entitled, "Farm and Dairy Profits." This book is printed on fine enameled paper, every page illustrated with beautiful halftones and the cover design represents

a beautiful country scene in colors, by one of the leading engraving houses in the country.

After many months of diligent investigation into the silo business and having perfected a plan for the purchase of raw materials in enormous quantities, we are now prepared to accept orders for the Columbia Silo in Oregon fir and Southern yellow pine. We can save you from $50.00 to $75.00 on a single silo.

In your own interests we invite you to write at once for a copy of our instructive silo book, which will be sent you free and postage paid on request by letter or post card. In the meantime, if you are in immediate need of a silo, we can accept your order **right now** and we will be glad to quote you a price on any size silo you require, but whether you want to buy a silo now or in the near future, we are anxious to send you our new book. We know it will be the means of saving you money. Even if you have a silo on your farm at the present time this book will show you how to get the best results from its use and how to feed the silage with the greatest prospects of profit.

This beautiful, interesting and instructive book is free. Write for it today.

THINGS YOU SHOULD KNOW

Do you know that silos in crude form were used by the Mexicans 300 to 400 years ago? We show you pictures of these interesting structures in square and circular form in our new book and we also give you the history of silage in various countries from 1786 to the present day.

Do you understand the chemistry of silage? Do you know why certain foods are calculated to produce more beef, more butter, more milk? We explain this important subject thoroughly in our book.

Do you know what crops are particularly suitable for silage? We tell you all about it.

Do you know the name of the Holstein cow that holds the world's record for greatest yearly yield of milk? Her name is Katie Gerben. She has furnished over 16,000 pounds of milk and 634 pounds of butter each year for five years. We have her picture and we will reproduce it in our book "Farm and Dairy Profits." Of course, silage is always in the ration. It is in the ration of every dairy champion in recent years.

What do you know about the value of alfalfa? Our book shows that if used with silage it will enable you to do away altogether with the use of grain feeds and mill products.

Would you like to know how silos are made and to see pictures of the forests from which we receive the raw materials? Our book contains many interesting pictures of this kind.

Do you know how to build a silo? We explain everything so fully and clearly that you cannot possibly make a mistake. Our instructions are so up to date that you can put up a silo complete without a scaffold.

There is a good deal of difference in the methods of filling a silo. We show you how to do it correctly, and even go so far as to post you fully on how to make a wagon rack for hauling fodder to the silo, thus saving you the expense of buying one.

A SILO WILL PAY FOR ITSELF AND FOR ALL THE MATERIALS FOR A HOUSE AND BARN IN THREE AND A HALF YEARS.   LET US EXPLAIN:

We propose to show you that a silo in three and a half years, by increased profits and by reducing your feeding expense, will not only pay for itself, but also for all the materials to build **a large barn and a modern dwelling house.** Please refer to page 76 of this Book of Modern Homes. where we illustrate and describe our Modern Home No. 110. The materials for this farm house, together with our Barn No. 60, illustrated on page 115, and the materials for a Columbia Silo 16x32 feet, will cost you $1,855.00. Suppose you are fattening eighteen head of cattle. for which the market value is 7 cents a pound on the hoof. The use of silage in fattening these cattle will increase their weight 150 pounds per steer more in one season than hay and grain. The total increase in weight on the eighteen cattle will be 2,700 pounds, the market value of which would be $189.00. Add to this a saving in feed of $78.00. which represents the difference between feeding with silage in the ration and ordinary feed. This makes a total profit on the eighteen head of cattle for one season of $267.00. The same half yearly profit for seven successive seasons or three and a half years would amount to $1,869.00. which leaves a balance in your favor of $13.15 after you have paid for the silo and all the materials to build the house and barn. Please bear in mind that these figures are based on actual statistics and statements from the leading agricultural authorities quoted in full in our new book "Farm and Dairy Profits," which will be sent to you free and postpaid on request.

A Brick Mantel, Wood Mantel or Console Helps to Make the Modern Home Complete

We have a complete line of red pressed brick mantels in all the modern styles and effects. Our solid oak mantels include large massive designs in full quarter sawed patterns and small cheap plain sawed bases for bedrooms, with all sizes and styles ranging between these extremes. They are finished in golden, antique and natural shades, polished and rubbed, or Mission, Weathered and Early English finishes. We also offer mantels painted white to be enameled, and any of our designs can be made in birch finished in imitation mahogany.

We also have the finest line of fireplace furnishings, including brass and iron andirons, fire tools, portable and stationary grates, gas logs and fire screens.

Our Massive Brick Mantel.

Made of Bedford red pressed brick. 10 feet high, 7 feet 5 inches wide. Fireplace opening, 3 feet 3 inches high, 3 feet 11 inches wide. Weight, 5,200 pounds. Hearth is paved with brickettes, 1 9-16x1 9-16x8 inches. Delivered on the cars at works in Pennsylvania, packed in barrels with complete blue prints and directions.

No. 61C10 Bedford Red Pressed Brick Mantel. Price $67.20

Other styles in our Mantel Book.

BE SURE to write for our Special Catalog of Mantels and Consoles before closing the contract for your modern home. It will be easier to have the mantel or console put in while the house is being finished than to order it later and put it in after the rooms are decorated. Write us a postal card or a letter today and say, "Send me your latest Mantel Catalog." We will mail it to you at once, free and postpaid.

Lowest Prices Ever Quoted on Gas Logs.

Terra cotta gas logs burned to extreme hardness and colored to represent natural oak logs. Packed with air mixer and log rest complete. Shipped from factory in Ohio.

No. 61C30 Length, 10 inches. Weight, 25 pounds. Price $2.72
No. 61C33 Length, 16 inches. Weight, 60 pounds. Price $4.14
No. 61C34 Length, 18 inches. Weight, 70 pounds. Price $4.53
No. 61C35 Length, 20 inches. Weight, 80 pounds. Price $5.09
All other standard sizes quoted in our Mantel Book.

Our Grand Parlor Console.

This console is 7 feet 6½ inches high by 5 feet wide. French plate bevel mirror, 54 inches high by 34 inches wide. Veneered columns, 5 inches in diameter. Shipping weight, 415 pounds.

Prices, delivered on the cars at the works in Ohio.

No. 61C6205 Quarter Sawed Golden Oak Console, polished, with French plate mirror............$41.00
No. 61C6206 Rich Birch, Mahogany Finish Console, complete with French plate mirror.......$41.50
Other styles in our Mantel Book.

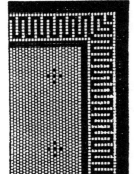

Tile for Floor and Walls for Bathroom, Kitchen and Vestibule. Don't Overlook This
Beautiful Ceramic Tile Floor Patterns in Colors, 16 Cents per Square Foot and Up.

In our Special Tile Book we show many color plates of tile floor designs. We offer a large variety of these designs suitable for any and all rooms of any size.

We maintain that a properly laid ceramic mosaic floor is the most durable material ever produced for this purpose, and we will be sustained by any high class architect, builder or contractor. Ceramic mosaics are of hard, dense, non-porous, unglazed porcelain, burned with a heat of 3,000 degrees. They are absolutely fireproof, as hard as adamant, will not absorb moisture of any kind, and make the cleanest, most sanitary aseptic flooring known. Tile floors are extremely easy to keep clean. They are simply mopped with clean water and soap. Scrubbing is rarely necessary. Sand soap should be used, and the more the floor is used and cleaned, the more beautiful it becomes.

Our line of wall tile is complete, including caps and bases. A wainscoting of wall tile is necessary in the bathroom and kitchen in these days of modern sanitation.

Don't forget that floor and wall tiles made from clay were in use 2,000 years before the inventors of substitutes were born, and they will be in use 2,000 years after the substitutes have rotted and decayed or have been thrown away as worthless.

Send us your order with a rough sketch of the floor and walls to be tiled. Our Tile Color Book shows a beautiful assortment of tile designs to help you make your selection. Write us a postal card or a letter and ask for our Special Tile Color Book. It will be sent to you immediately on receipt of your request, free and postpaid.

Warm Air Furnaces for Modern Homes

When ordering your Modern Home do not overlook the prices quoted on Warm Air Heating Plants. We can make you the same proportionate saving on a furnace, registers and fittings as we can on the material to build the house. You will find our prices quoted at the foot of each page throughout this book.

Our Special Heating Catalog gives detailed descriptions of our wonderful heaters. Learn how furnaces can be installed in old as well as new houses and read convincing letters from satisfied customers who have been enjoying the comforts of a well heated and ventilated home. Write and ask for our Special Heating Catalog, "Modern Systems of Home Heating." It will be mailed to you at once, free and postpaid.

REMEMBER, we can heat any house anywhere, whether it be a cottage, residence, flat building, schoolhouse or church, and guarantee to heat the building to 70 degrees in the coldest weather.

MODERN HEATING SYSTEMS HOT WATER, STEAM WARM AIR

SEARS, ROEBUCK and CO., CHICAGO

Write today for our Catalog of Modern Heating Systems and tell us whether you want a hot water, steam or warm air heating system.

Send us a sketch of your building, telling us whether you want a hot water, steam or warm air heating plant. Give the size of each room, the height of the ceilings of basement and first, second and other floors (if any), locate windows and outside doors and show dimensions of each. From this sketch we will figure the necessary size of radiators for each room and will make an itemized estimate showing the cost of each item of material you require to install this great modern convenience in your home.

Send us your sketch at once. Don't wait. If you have a blue print of your building, or a drawing from which the carpenter has worked, send it to us, as we will be able to figure the plant from that. When we send you the estimate we will return your blue print or architect's sketch by registered mail. We employ a force of heating engineers who have had years of experience in designing heating plants.

We make absolutely no charge for estimating on the cost of your heating plant or for designing the system when we receive your order. You will only be charged the latest catalog price of each item necessary for the complete plant, and as these prices represent the actual factory cost with but one very small profit added, you can readily see that the total cost of the heating plant will be very low.

Write for Our Free Catalog of Hot Water, Steam and Warm Air Heating Systems Today.

Hercules Hot Water and Steam Heating Plants

Lowest in cost, highest in quality. Easily installed by anyone.

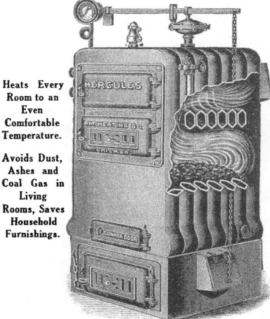

Heats Every Room to an Even Comfortable Temperature.

Avoids Dust, Ashes and Coal Gas in Living Rooms, Saves Household Furnishings.

A Great Saver of Time and Labor.

Pressure Water Supply Not Necessary.

Hot water and steam heating plants stand first among modern improvements in home comfort. They are the acknowledged ideal heating systems. We have saved you money on your other supplies, let us save you money on a guaranteed heating plant. Send us a sketch of your home as explained to the left. We will quote you figures for a hot water or steam heating plant complete, guaranteed to heat your home at a surprisingly low price as compared with what you thought such a plant would cost. Our prices are based on manufacturing cost with just one profit added, sweeping away all unnecessary expenses and profits of middlemen.

The first cost of a Hercules Heating Plant is, of course, somewhat higher than that of stoves, but the cost of fuel and maintenance is less than that of the required number of heating stoves to heat your home throughout; this and the indirect saving in home furnishings make it a much better paying investment. The Hercules system may be installed in any building, old or new, without damaging or marring the building. The boiler is placed in the basement and the piping to the different radiators is laid out to give the best possible results. This keeps the floors and walls of your house warm.

No matter where you live, whether or not you have running water, you can install a Hercules system. Water can be forced into it with a hand pump or you can fill it with a pail.

When once filled it is not necessary to add more than 5 to 8 gallons of water during a season.

MODERN PLUMBING

Our Latest Plumbing Goods Catalog Describes in Detail Our Complete Line of Modern Up to Date Plumbing Fixtures, Also Material Necessary for Installing Them.
WRITE FOR IT:

Are you interested in saving from $50.00 to $75.00 on a bathroom outfit, or $100.00 to $150.00 on the complete plumbing for your home? You can make these savings if you send us your order. It will pay you to investigate. Write for a copy of our Plumbing Goods Catalog and see for yourself whether or not the above statements are true.

We know that we can furnish you with the very best quality plumbing material at a large saving. We are able to list the highest grade material at the lowest prices, because we manufacture our own plumbing fixtures in our own factory, equipped with modern labor saving machinery.

We employ the highest skilled mechanics who are experts in making high grade plumbing goods.

Because of the care taken in manufacture we sell our plumbing fixtures under the binding guarantee that they will be absolutely satisfactory in every way, that our enamel goods, such as sinks, lavatories, etc., will not chip, flake or crack. We further guarantee that all our enamel goods are made of the best quality gray cast iron, carefully enameled with the highest quality white enamel that we can obtain. Our closet bowls, earthenware tanks, etc., are guaranteed to be best selected vitreous earthenware, heavily glazed and substantially constructed throughout.

You need not employ an expert plumber to install the bathroom outfits, kitchen sinks or other fixtures, as we can furnish all of this material threaded for iron pipe and our book of instructions and working plans make it so simple that anyone at all handy with pipe fitting tools can do the work without any trouble.

Carefully note bathroom outfit shown below and then consider whether you want to pay a fabulous price for your plumbing material elsewhere. We save you the jobbers' and retailers' profits. Our price to you is the actual cost of manufacture with but one profit added. Our Modern Plumbing Goods Catalog means unusual savings to you. Write us a postal card TODAY and ask for it.

$38⁵⁰

As an example of the enormous saving we can make you in high grade plumbing goods, we here show our Perfection Bathroom Outfit, consisting of a tub, lavatory and closet complete, with supply and waste pipes to the floor and wall, as illustrated.

The tub is made of the highest grade cast iron throughout, carefully enameled on the inside and painted on the outside. It has a large roll rim and is equipped with a No. 4½ Fuller bath cock, bath supplies, and connected waste and overflow. The bath cock, supply, waste and overflow pipes are made of brass, heavily nickel plated, and with ordinary care will last a lifetime.

The lavatory is also made of the highest grade gray cast iron and is enameled inside and outside to the bottom of the apron. It is equipped with brass supply and waste pipes, trap, and hot and cold indexed basin cocks, all of which are heavily nickel plated.

The closet is a low down closet combination. Tank and seat are of golden oak, highly polished, and the bowl is of vitreous earthenware of the siphonic washdown type, heavily glazed inside and outside.

Tub and lavatory shipped from factory in Milwaukee, Wis.; shipping weight, 380 pounds. Closet shipped from our Chicago store; shipping weight, 100 pounds.

Compare this outfit with bathroom outfits offered by other firms handling plumbing goods, who advertise in magazines and elsewhere. You will find that they cannot furnish you with an outfit of the same quality and manufacture as the one listed here at anywhere near the price we ask for it.

Ask your local plumber what he would charge for a similar outfit and note what he tells you. He will probably say that he can install the outfit in your home for $150.00. Stop and consider what this means. It means that he is making an enormous profit on the bathroom outfit he is selling you, and is also making a large profit on the material for installing it and the actual work of putting it in.

Perfection Bathroom Outfit

No. 42C9214⅓ Perfection Bathroom Outfit, complete. Price.................$38.50

For the convenience of our customers we can furnish above outfit with all fittings threaded for iron pipe connections at $1.50 extra.

Guaranteed Paints and Wall Papers for Home Decoration

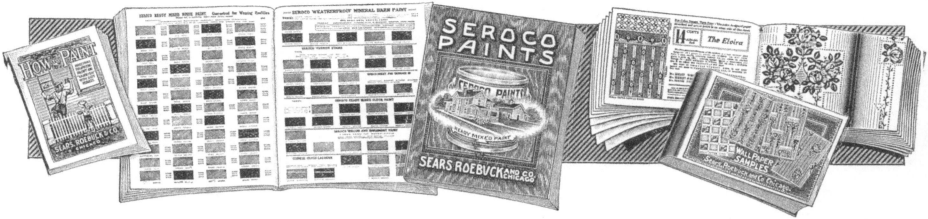

Painting Is a Profitable Investment Because It Protects Your Property

If you are going to paint now or in the near future let us save you from $5.00 to $25.00 on the job. Send for our Paint Color Sample Book and our "How to Paint" book illustrated above, compare our prices with the prices asked by any other dealer, and you will be surprised to learn how much you can save by dealing with us. In our Paint Color Sample Book we show actual color samples of our paints, together with complete instructions on how to apply them and you will find everything needed for interior and exterior finishing at prices that will save you about half compared with what you would have to pay elsewhere. Everything we sell is guaranteed to give you satisfactory service or your money will be returned. You cannot afford to miss the protection assured you by this guarantee. When you deal with us you are dealing direct with the manufacturer and are securing the best paints that modern skill can produce at a price that is possible only because we manufacture the paint ourselves and sell direct to you with but one profit added.

COMPARE OUR PRICES WITH OTHERS
Seroco Ready Mixed Guaranteed House Paint.

1-Quart Can. Price,	½-Gallon Can. Price,	1-Gallon Can. Price,	5-Gallon Kit. Per Gallon,	25-Gallon ½-Barrel. Per Gallon,	50-Gallon Barrel. Per Gallon,
33c	61c	$1.12	$1.09	$1.02	98c

Make Your Home More Attractive by Decorating With Our Artistic Wall Paper

If you dread the annual expense of hiring a paperhanger and buying paper to redecorate the walls of your home, then you should be interested in what we have to say about wall paper decoration. Send for our free Wall Paper Sample Book, and if you have ever bought paper before you will realize that the quality of our papers far excels any ever offered by any other dealer at anywhere near our price. At 3 to 50 cents a double roll of 16 full yards we are offering the latest and most up to date designs, printed on the highest quality of paper, at such exceptionally low prices that other manufacturers cannot successfully compete with us. We manufacture all our paper and deal direct with the consumer, thus eliminating all the various middlemen and letting the consumer put the middlemen's profit in his own pocket. This year our line is more complete than ever before. It includes a number of very artistic and attractive designs and a line of applique or embossed cut out borders such as have never before been included among moderate priced papers. We are sure you would appreciate having one or more of these designs to decorate the rooms of your home. Write for a copy of our free Wall Paper Sample Book. We will mail it to you postpaid the very day we receive your request.

SEARS, ROEBUCK AND CO.　　　　　　—123—　　　　　　CHICAGO, ILLINOIS

Just a Few of the Many Letters We Receive Daily

READ WHAT OUR CUSTOMERS SAY. Look at the photographic reproductions of 22 of the thousands of houses built from our plans and with our materials (see opposite page). We have satisfied the builders and saved them money. We can do the same for you. No one takes any risk when doing business with us. **WE GUARANTEE** to save you money and satisfy you in every respect.

$3,500.00 House for $2,540.00.

No. 7 is a picture of our Modern Home No. 114, built at Halifax, Penn., by Mr. N E. Noblet. He says: "All your lumber and materials are excellent. I have saved from $250.00 to $300.00 by dealing with you. Many think my home cost $3,500.00. I built it complete for $2,540.01." For floor plans and full description see page 9.

Saved 35 Per Cent.

No. 15 is a picture of our Modern Home No. 118, with some alterations, built at Terrell, Texas, by Mr. Josephus Autrey. He says: "The amount saved by buying the mill work, hardware and plumbing material of you is about 35 per cent, or at least one-third." For floor plans and full description see page 88.

Saved $225.00.

No. 17 is a picture of our Modern Home No. 147, with some alterations, built at Mandon, N. D., by Mr. Arthur Witherow. He says: "The material was fine, and I could not wish better. I saved about $225.00 after paying freight." For floor plans and full description see page 30.

One Sells Another.

No. 4 is a picture of our Modern Home No. 111, built at Ossining, N. Y., by Mr. Geo. E. Twiggar. The same house has been built at Havre de Grace, Md., by Mr. J. H. Howlett. These houses can always be put up at a big saving. The materials will be found to be far better than can be secured in the local market. For floor plans and full description see page 46.

Saved $800.00.

No. 13 is a picture of our Modern Home No. 132, built at Colorado City, Colo., by Mr. John M. Clear. He says: "I have saved on my order about $800.00, and the quality of the material far surpasses any that is being furnished here." For floor plans and full description see page 86.

Saved 50 Per Cent.

No. 19 is a picture of our Modern Home No. 114, with some alterations, built at Rochelle Park, N. J., by Mr. John C. Johnson. He says: "I could not have obtained the same material here for less than about twice the amount I paid you, which was between $800.00 and $900.00. All transactions have been attended to promptly and fairly in every respect." For floor plans and full description see page 9.

"The Talk of the Town."

No. 2 is a picture of our Modern Home No. 132, built at Paxton, Ill. The builder states that it is the "talk of the town" on account of its imposing appearance and the extra good quality of the materials with which it is constructed. None of the local concerns would compete for the job when shown our figure. For floor plans and full description see page 86.

A Double House for the Price of a Single One.

No. 11 is a picture of a house designed from private plans, built at Concord, N. H., by Mr. P. T. Gulley. He says: "I found the prices of your mill work and building hardware so reasonable that I built a large double house and made a large saving."

Saved $500.00.

No. 16 is a picture of our Bungalow No. 151, built at Greeley, Colo., by Mr. W. H. Segier. He says: "The material is the best in any house in Greeley, a town of 10,000 population. I saved $500.00." For floor plans and full description see page 18.

"A Big Saving."

No. 10 is a picture of our Modern Home No. 111, built at Havre de Grace, Md., by Mr. J. H. Howlett. He says: "I am sending you a photo of my house built from your plans and with your material at a big saving to me. Materials are far better than I could have secured in our city at a much higher price." For floor plans and full description see page 46.

Saved $500.00.

No. 6 is a picture of our Modern Home No. 123, built at Ossining, N. Y., by Mr. Samuel T. Davis. He says: "I consider that I saved about $500.00 by purchasing my materials from you. They will stand comparison with any materials I have ever seen. I take pleasure in recommending Sears, Roebuck and Co. to anyone intending to build." For floor plans and full description see page 56.

Saved $200.00.

No. 5 is a picture of our Modern Home No 167, built at Grafton, Mass., by Mr. D. S. Chase. He says: "The lumber and finishing material are much better than I could have gotten here. My contractor tells me that I have saved nearly $200.00 on the whole." For floor plans and full description see page 5.

Saved $500.00.

No. 20 is a picture of our Modern Home No. 169, built at York, Neb., by Mr. J. P. Berck. He says: "We were more than satisfied with everything received. There was not even a piece of poor material in the entire bill. We have saved fully $500.00 on this building." For floor plans and full description see page 79.

Beyond Expectations.

No. 14 is a picture of our Modern Home No. 114, built at Monongahela, Penn., by D. F. Addison. He says: "I found everything beyond my expectations and thank you for the honest way you treated me in the deal." For floor plans and full description see page 9.

Never Saw Such Good Doors.

No. 8 is a picture of our Modern Home No. 132, built at Douglas, Wyo., by Mr. G. N. Doyle. He says: "The material was satisfactory in every way, especially the inside finish. I never saw as fine oak doors." For floor plans and full description see page 86.

"Admired by All."

No. 18 is a picture of our Modern Home No. 119, built at Baltimore, Md., by Dr. S. R. Wantz. He says: "I am well pleased with the material, which is admired by all. Many thanks for the way you treated me." For floor plans and full description see page 85.

"Way Down South."

No. 3 is a picture of our Modern Home No. 119, built at Martinez, Ga., by Mr. R. T. Lyle. As can easily be seen, it is a roomy and substantial structure, and altogether a house very popular with our customers who demand something above the ordinary. For floor plans and full description see page 85.

Saved 30 Per Cent.

No. 12 is a picture of our Modern Home No. 123, built at Bay Shore, L. I., N. Y., by Mr. S. J. Smith. He says: "The red oak trim is the prettiest lot of mill work I ever saw. I saved at least 30 per cent on the material." For floor plans and full description see page 56.

Saved Nearly $400.00.

No. 1 is a picture of our Modern Home No. 146, built at New Rochelle, N. Y. The builder for good reasons of his own does not wish his name to be printed, but states that he saved between $300.00 and $400.00 on this house and got a very fine quality of lumber and mill work. For floor plans and full description see page 36.

Saved $300.00.

No. 9 is a picture of our Modern Home No. 114, built at Norwalk, Ohio, by Mr. F. D. Cronk. He says: "I have the nicest house in town for the money and saved about $300.00 by dealing with you." For floor plans and full description see page 9.

Saved $300.00.

No. 21 is a picture of two of our Modern Homes No. 133, built at Barrington, Ill., by Messrs. Halverson & Groff. They say: "The material ordered from you was better than first class if that could be possible. We saved $150.00 on each house." For floor plans and full description see page 63.

"One of the Best."

No. 22 is a picture of our Modern Home No. 118, built at Fenton, Iowa, by Mr. Philip Weisbrod. He says: "Your material cannot be praised high enough for quality. My house is one of the best in this community." For floor plans and full description see page 88.

BUILT BY OUR CUSTOMERS AT A BIG SAVING

Exact Reproductions of Photographs of Houses Built From Our Free Plans and With Our Materials. See Builders' Letters on Opposite Page.

SEARS, ROEBUCK AND CO., CHICAGO, ILLINOIS

One of the Bedrooms in Modern Home No. 187

Light and air are the two essentials in any bedroom. As will be seen by the illustration to the left, the bedroom in Modern Home No. 187 is well supplied with both.

This room and all other bedrooms have maple flooring, with yellow pine trim. Good size closets in all three rooms.

When you consider that we furnish all of the material to build this modern seven-room house for only $1,273.00 and that the house can be built complete for about $3,120.00, we think you will agree with us that we are offering you a proposition that will save you nearly $1,000.00. When built in the ordinary way, a house like our Modern Home No. 187 would cost not less than $4,000.00.

Note the beautifully colored picture of this house on the front cover page. We will furnish two coats of the best paint to give you this pleasing combination, the cost of which is included in our price for all of the material. Other concerns quote painting material extra. In addition to furnishing all the lumber, lath, shingles, mill work, ceiling, flooring, finishing lumber, building paper, pipe, gutter, sash weights, hardware and painting material for only $1,273.00, we also include a beautiful massive mantel for the living room, and a buffet for the dining room, without extra charge.

Bathroom in Modern Home No. 187

Everything in this room suggests cleanliness and sanitation. Quality is the main consideration in furnishing the necessary plumbing material. Note the cast iron white enameled bath tub with standing waste and base to floor instead of legs. The standing waste furnished with this bath tub does away with the old style rubber plug. To empty you simply pull up the top of the standing waste and the water will flow into the waste pipe. The offset supply pipes are nickel plated. The tub can be decorated any color desired with enamel paint.

We suggest that the woodwork be painted white to correspond with the white enamel plumbing and the white tile wainscoting.

This is a room that you will be proud of and you can depend upon all the material furnished to be in keeping with the high quality of everything furnished for the balance of the house. See page 4 for a complete description of Modern Home No. 187, height of ceilings and floor plans. If we have not made everything perfectly clear to you, please let us know. We will be glad to answer any questions without the least obligation on your part.

SEARS, ROEBUCK AND CO., CHICAGO, ILL.

CPSIA information can be obtained
at www.ICGtesting.com
Printed in the USA
BVHW010511011021
617863BV00006B/177